WORDS
ABOUT
THE WORD

JOHN R. KOHLENBERGER III

WORDS
ABOUT
THE WORD

A GUIDE TO CHOOSING
AND USING YOUR BIBLE

Regency
Reference Library
Zondervan Publishing House
Grand Rapids, Michigan

WORDS ABOUT THE WORD
Copyright © 1987 by John R. Kohlenberger
Grand Rapids, Michigan

Regency Reference Library
is an imprint of Zondervan Publishing House,
1415 Lake Drive, SE, Grand Rapids, Michigan 49506.

Library of Congress Cataloging in Publication Data

Kohlenberger, John R.
    Words about the Word.

    Includes indexes.
    1. Bible.   English—Versions—Handbooks, manuals, etc.
I. Title.
BS132.K64 1987   220.5'2   86-26663

ISBN 0-310-39361-2

Edited by Gerard Terpstra
Designed by Louise Bauer

Printed in the United States of America

87 88 89 90 91 92 / AF / 10 9 8 7 6 5 4 3 2 1

CONTENTS

LIST OF ABBREVIATIONS

AB	Amplified Bible
ABS	American Bible Society
ASV	American Standard Version
AV	Authorized Version
c.	approximately (used of dates)
D-E	Dynamic Equivalence translation
e.g.	for example
et al.	and others (editors or contributors)
EV	English Version
EVV	English Versions
F-E	Formal Equivalence translation
ibid.	reference to the same book
ICB	International Children's Bible
i.e.	that is (an explanation)
JB	Jerusalem Bible
JPS	Jewish Publication Society
KJV	King James Version
LB	Living Bible
LXX	Septuagint (Greek Translation of the Old Testament)
M	Majority Text (A NKJV footnote abbreviation)
MT	Masoretic Text
NAB	New American Bible
NASB	New American Standard Bible
NEB	New English Bible
NIV	New International Version
NJB	New Jerusalem Bible
NKJV	New King James Version

NOAB	New Oxford Annotated Bible
NU	Nestle/United Bible Societies Greek New Testament
NWT	New World Translation
PNT	J. B. Phillips: The New Testament in Modern English
RSV	The Revised Standard Version
RV	British Revised Version
TEV	Today's English Version
THS	The Holy Scriptures According to the Masoretic Text
TR	Textus Receptus ("Received Text")
UBS	United Bible Societies

ACKNOWLEDGMENTS

One of the great joys I have as a writer is publicly recognizing and thanking the many individuals whose names do not appear on the title page of the book, but who have shared in its production nonetheless.

I must first thank my parents, John and Doris, for beginning my biblical education in Sunday school, for although I did not stay that course in adolescence and young adulthood, it laid the foundation to which I eventually returned.

I wish to thank Multnomah School of the Bible and Western Conservative Baptist Seminary, both in Portland, Oregon, for the biblically based education they afforded me. I must single out Dr. E. W. Goodrick of Multnomah and Drs. Ronald B. Allen and Ralph Alexander of Western, who introduced me to the biblical languages and to careful research and thus greatly influenced much of the content of this book.

For the incredible privilege and eye-opening experience of being a bookseller, I must first thank David Gordon of Christian Discount Book Centers, who gave me my first job, and Meredith Bundy, the manager of their Portland store, who taught me more than he will ever realize. Again I wish to thank the Western Conservative Baptist Seminary, whose authorities allowed me to manage their bookstore. I must especially thank John van Diest and the staffs of the Christian Supply Centers of Portland, Oregon, who allowed me to develop their used-book store and put me in touch with the Christian publishing industry at large, with which I now work full time. Special thanks also to the Christian Booksellers Association and the Zondervan Corporation for providing me with an international forum for my seminars and my own learning.

Although many publishers have been generous and cooperative in assisting me in my research, I must single out two for special thanks. Oxford University Press gave me the great honor of allowing me to produce for them *All About Bibles*, and they permitted me to draw on the charts and materials of that book for the production of this one. Holman Bible Publishers commissioned me to produce their Study Bible Comparison Chart, which is reproduced in modified form in chapter 5.

I wish I could single out all the booksellers in the United States, Canada, Australia, and New Zealand with whom I have worked and who have greatly encouraged and influenced me. My gratitude, though not individualized, is no less heartfelt.

For direct input into this book and the seminars from which it developed, several names stand out. Kin Millen, as a personal friend and professional adviser, made my current occupation and this book possible by suggesting and helping develop my Bible and reference-book seminars. Larry Gadbaugh, former manager of Western's bookstore, and Galen Smith of Christian Supply Center have regularly contributed to and interacted with my research and writing. Special thanks to Rob Stone, Bible buyer for Spring Arbor Distributors, for his interaction with this book. Although I have only done seminars with Judy White, Duane Kaemmerling, Nick Conner, and Howie Van Dyke, I must acknowledge the special role of Zondervan Bible Publishers' entire sales force and staff for their tremendous encouragement, cooperation, and participation in my speaking and writing.

To my publisher, Stanley N. Gundry, and editors, Ed van der Maas and Gerard Terpstra, goes my deep gratitude for their support and incredible patience in this project. I believe I have missed every deadline since 1979 for the nine books and two study Bibles I have thus far produced for Zondervan, yet they continue to put up with me!

As always, I must thank my wife Carolyn, daughter Sarah, and son Joshua for their love and support—and for their timely distractions.

This book is about the Bible, about understanding it more clearly and using it more effectively. I consider it an honor to dedicate it to the man who I believe has done more than any other in our time for the propagation of the Bible in English and in dozens of other languages as well. For his commitment to God and His Word, his sincerity of heart, and his courage, this book is dedicated to Dr. Kenneth N. Taylor.

HELP KEEP THIS BOOK UP-TO-DATE!

Perhaps the two most frustrating flaws in any resource book are incompleteness and incorrectness. Incompleteness results from the author's (necessarily) limited research and from others' ongoing publishing. Incorrectness results from the author's carelessness or faulty resources.

I urge the reader's assistance in helping keep this resource as nearly complete as is reasonable and as nearly correct as is possible. For I am not so confident in my abilities as to believe I have covered all relevent material thoroughly or with absolute accuracy.

If you see an issue that needs to be discussed, an important *and in-print* translation or study Bible that needs to be cataloged, a publisher or distributor that needs to be listed, or an error of fact that needs to be corrected, please write to me care of Zondervan Publishing House, 1415 Lake Drive SE, Grand Rapids, MI 49506.

Thank you for your concern and participation!

PLEASE READ THIS INTRODUCTION

Words About the Word is "A Guide to Choosing and Using Your Bible." It was written for those who have not yet settled on a Bible translation as well as for those who guide others in this process. It was written for new readers of the Bible as well as for old hands who want to know more about where their Bible came from.

Some will find the content of this book overwhelming. This introduction will help them read each chapter selectively in order to cover the minimal material necessary for them to choose their Bible with care. Others may want to pick their way through the book themselves to research the background of the Bible they have already settled on and to find others for comparative study. A few may find the discussion in this book too limited. For them I have provided at the end of most chapters bibliographies that can lead them into thousands of pages of more specialized resources.

The concerns and contents of this book rose out of the various phases and responsibilities of my life that have thus far brought me into many different relationships with the Word. I am sure most readers will identify with me at a point or two.

In the 1950s, when I was a child, the Bible was a book for Sundays. I memorized enough of its verses to impress my parents and teachers and win my own award edition of the King James Version. But the Bible was no more a part of my everyday life than were the fancy clothes I wore when I carried it to church.

In the sixties, my Bible gathered dust. It was not even used on Sundays anymore, for when my parents no longer forced me to go to church, I didn't go. None of my friends did. I saw no use for Sunday school or its textbook. My award Bible had been inscribed with these words: "This Book will keep you from sin, or sin will keep you from this Book." My chosen lifestyle fulfilled the latter prediction.

But in 1972, God reached down from the heavens and lifted me from my destructive lifestyle of drugs and despair. I was a grown-up on the outside, but a child in spirit. I was back in Sunday school, but now it had become a daily school as I realized its textbook was the key to successful life. The seventies were the beginning of what I trust will be a lifetime of growing intimacy with and dependence on the Word of God.

Now that I was actually reading the Bible, I discovered its words and phrases were foreign in language as well as in content. Although I was a good reader, I could not understand my Bible. A friend informed me that I needed a more contemporary and readable translation. This was a double revelation: the Bible was not originally written in English, and there was another version besides the King James available!

My friend ushered me to a bookstore where he bought me a Living Bible. Now I could understand the text! Over the next months, during long, slow stretches at my job, I read through the Bible twice.

Then I began to go to Bible-study meetings. There I had two additional revelations: there were more than two Bible versions, and mine never seemed to come up with the same answers everyone else's did! I was told I should not be using the Living Bible for study, though I was not told why, so I switched back to my King James Version. I did better at the Bible studies, but unfortunately I cut way back on my Bible reading.

So that I would better fit in with the youth group, a girlfriend bought me my third Bible: a New American Standard. I was taught to dislike my Living Bible for its paraphrasing, to discontinue using my King James Version for its antiquity, and to revere my New American Standard Bible for its accuracy.

But as accurate as it was, our youth leader was constantly altering or expanding on its renderings, making references to the Greek. I began to feel any English version was inadequate and to believe I could never truly understand the Bible without learning Greek. My desire to know God's Word was such that I quit my job and entered Bible College with no better reason than to learn Greek.

In the Greek program at Multnomah School of the Bible I encountered E. W. Goodrick, an imposing figure who seemed to have the ability to make even a desk learn the language by the sheer force of his presence. His courses so emphasized Greek reading skills that I soon felt weaned from any dependence on the English New Testament.

At this time I also began to work in a Christian bookstore where the management was so distrustful of modern versions that we carried only the King James Version, the New American Standard Bible, and a few Revised Standard Versions. Although at that time I shared the owner's dislike of the Living Bible, I was surprised that he did not agree with my preference for the New American Standard Bible over the King James Version. Another revelation: choosing a Bible translation was not just a matter of personal preference, but of theological right and wrong!

I graduated from Bible college and the trade bookstore to seminary and my own seminary bookstore. For the next year or two I had little to do with the English Bible. Most students already had theirs or knew what they wanted; so I did not have to help anyone with choices. Even when I had opportunity to speak or teach in a church, I took my Greek or Hebrew Testament into the pulpit. I did not realize the great disservice I was doing to the congregation by implying or directly stating my disdain for the English Bible—the only Bible most of them would ever use. I am not certain if this was the reason I was rarely invited to speak anywhere twice, but I am certain it was a factor.

A combination of factors slapped me into consciousness and back into the English Bible. I was now working with Dr. Goodrick as an occasional research assistant and co-writer. He was working on an innovative Bible introduction to follow his well-received *Do-It-Yourself Hebrew and Greek*. He was very much concerned to communicate to his readers a concept I had never considered: the inspiration of the Bible-in-hand.

The King James translators had centuries ago written that "the very meanest [worst] translation of the Bible in English . . . containeth the Word of God, nay, is the Word of God," that the King's speech, no matter how badly translated into French, Dutch, Italian, or Latin is still the King's speech. Goodrick wanted to communicate to the student the awesome privilege

15

and responsibility of having the very Word of God in one's hand—in English. The man who had taught me to read the Bible in Greek was now impressing me with the importance of using the Bible in English.

This was driven home to me when I suddenly realized that when the New Testament quoted the Old, it often quoted a translation of it! And that translation was not always word-for-word; the New Testament writers felt free to cast their rendering in the form that would best express their understanding and application of the text. These new revelations, combined with my increasing sensitivity to the need to communicate more clearly in my preaching and teaching, set me on a search for an English Bible.

I was now unhappy with the New American Standard Bible for its unnatural English and its switching back to the King James language in prayers. My opinion of the King James itself and of the Living Bible had not changed. The only other real option in my circles was the New International Version, then only a New Testament. Although it took me a while to get used to its idiom, more fluid than the New American Standard Bible and my own translation style, I found myself appreciating it increasingly.

At this point, I moved out of the seminary bookstore and back into a general Christian bookstore. Once again in contact with Christians who were not professional students, I found myself daily helping people who were in the various stages of confusion and enlightenment that I had worked through during the preceding seven years. I greatly enjoyed encouraging people to have confidence in the accuracy of the Bible-in-hand and helping them choose the version that was best for them.

Then I became a Bible translator! A series of incredible circumstances (or providential encounters—depending on how Calvinistic one is) brought me into contact with Zondervan Publishing House, whose Executive Vice President, Bob DeVries, accepted my proposal to develop an interlinear translation of the Old Testament based on the New International Version.

Now in print, I became an "expert" on the Bible. Kin Millen, a close friend and at that time a book and Bible salesman for Zondervan, suggested we develop a seminar for booksellers on Bibles and biblical reference books. Kin did all the work and

I did all the talking, as we presented our "dog and pony show" up and down the West Coast. Eventually, I was invited to give an abridged edition of my lectures at the Christian Booksellers Association Convention in Anaheim in 1981. The positive response to that presentation led to a full two-hour seminar at the CBA Convention in Dallas in 1982 and to the production of an educational videotape for the CBA later that year. The videotape was supplemented with a workbook and became a correspondence course in 1984.

Words About the Word was originally intended to be just a section of *Books About the Book*, the expanded written form of the seminar. But as I have seen the questions and controversies about issues relating to the explosion of Bible translations in recent years, I found myself producing much more material than I could limit to a subsection of a larger work.

In *Words About the Word* I have attempted to deal with all the major issues relating to choosing and using a Bible version, from deciding on how inclusive its contents should be to settling on its size, shape, and color. Depending on how long a person has been reading the Bible, he or she may find *Words About the Word*—like the three bears' rocking chairs—to be too large, too small, or just right.

Those who are new Bible readers, or who want to replace or supplement the version they have been using, may want to read this book selectively. Those who are not interested in knowing why Catholic Bibles have more books than Protestant Bibles may well skip chapter 1, a discussion on the canon. However, I suggest that every reader look at the charts and read the summary on page 32 just to get a quick overview of the chief differences.

Chapter 2 on the text of the Bible may not be of immediate interest to all readers, for most people do not choose a Bible on the basis of the given text. However, sometimes a person may feel that modern versions are trying to destroy the message of the Bible by tampering with its text. For them I suggest a complete reading of chapter 2; for others I suggest a reading of the introduction and the summary on pages 37–38 and 48–49.

Chapter 3 deals with the nature of Bible translation. I think all will profit from reading this chapter through. Chapter 4 is a survey of forty-nine available Bible translations. One may wish to read through the section on the top ten versions (pp. 81–94) and then go directly to the outline on how to settle on the version or versions that will be best for each individual (pp. 110–13).

Chapter 5 deals with study Bibles, books that contain not only the biblical text, but also a collection of features to help one study and understand the text better. Chapter 6 deals with the nitty-gritty details of type size, page layout, and binding quality. I strongly suggest that one read these through before purchasing the version he or she may have decided on in chapter 4.

Finally, chapter 7 deals with a few valuable resources that will help one better read and understand the Bible. Included in the discussion is *Books About the Book*, the companion to this volume.

I believe that experienced students of the Bible will find fascinating background and firsthand resources for further study in the first three chapters. And I trust that in chapters 4 and 5 they will find as a valuable help for comparative study a version or two that they were not aware of.

Booksellers, pastors, and teachers have the incredible responsibility of guiding others on a daily basis in the choice and use of their Bibles. This book owes some of its detail and breadth of discussion to them because I kept them in mind as I researched and wrote it. I know the responsibility I have felt in helping others get into the Word and I have a high regard for the resources that have helped develop my understanding of canon, text, and translation. I hope I have provided readers with a comprehensive, self-contained manual that also points them toward years of further fruitful research and understanding.

I encountered the Bible as a child, rejected it as a rebellious adolescent, returned to it as a new believer, grew with it as a student, recommended it as a bookseller, and translated it as a writer. I know every reader can identify with me at one or more of these points. I pray that we all will continue to praise God for his amazing provision and preservation of his Word, our only light in the present darkness and our only certain source of knowledge of the God who is there and who has not been silent.

Chapter 1

WHAT IS THE BIBLE?
PART I: THE CANON

We begin our guide to choosing and using one's Bible with what must seem a stupid question: "What is the Bible?" But the answers are neither as immediate nor as obvious as one might think.

To some, the Bible is inspired; to others, it is just inspiring. To many, it is an ancient relic of an outdated religion; to millions, it is the key document of their living faith. Our job is not to catalog and survey all views of what the Bible is understood to be, but to help those who believe that it is inspired to better understand this key document of their faith.

But even among people who believe that the Bible is inspired, there are differing answers to "What is the Bible?" No one who believes the Bible to be the Word of God would argue that the Bible is not the most important book in their library. After we have agreed on that statement, however, the arguing begins. For as soon as we mention "the Bible," we raise the question, "Which Bible?"

Most of the people who read this book are probably Protestant Christians. (The book is not limited to them, nor even to Christians in general, but statistically, Protestant Christians—Evangelicals in particular—buy the most Bibles.) They will be familiar with the argument over which Bible they should choose, but to most Protestants this will mean "Which Bible translation?"

Actually, there are more fundamental options in answering "Which Bible?" than in answering those that deal with translation, because before we can translate the Bible, we must know what its contents are. And further, we must know which document or documents to translate from. The technical term for the subject that deals with the contents of the Bible is "canon," and that is the subject of this first chapter. The discipline that relates to the documents or manuscripts of the Bible is "textual criticism," which we will cover in chapter 2.

Some readers may feel that reading these chapters is an unnecessary exercise; they believe that God gave us the Bible and has preserved its essential message over the centuries. That is true. But it is also true that people who believe the Bible to be the Word of God and agree with that statement may not agree on whether the Bible has twenty-four, sixty-six, or eighty-three books! Others may say, "The Holy Spirit will tell me which books are inspired and which are not." But again, Catholics feel this as sincerely in favor of the Apocrypha as Protestants feel it against the Apocrypha.

There are no easy answers in the matters of canon and text. I will not try to convince you of any specific position, though my own convictions will be clear in the presentation. Rather, I hope to walk you through the major issues, point out the major differences, and suggest more thorough resources for deeper study.

Some readers may want to skip these first two chapters because they have chosen to accept the biblical canon and text of the church they attend. That is fine, though I believe the material is interesting and useful. I recommend that everyone read at least the summaries at the end of each chapter. However, for church leaders and teachers—and for booksellers—these chapters are required reading!

TABLES OF CONTENTS AND THE BIBLICAL CANON

A popular song in the sixties asserted, "Happiness is . . . different things to different people." "Canon," too, means different things to different people, though many are not aware that different religious bodies who use the Bible have differing contents in their Bibles. Few Bible users can name all of the books in their Bible, and fewer still can explain *why* those books are there.

Most Bible users are familiar only with translations of the Bible (in our case, English translations), so this is where we will begin. A comparison of the tables of contents of any English

Chart 1
Table of Contents of Four Major Bibles[2]

1. TANAKH	2. NIV/NOAB OT	3. NJB OT	4. NOAB APOCRYPHA[3]
Genesis	Genesis	Genesis	1 Esdras[4]
Exodus	Exodus	Exodus	2 Esdras
Leviticus	Leviticus	Leviticus	Tobit
Numbers	Numbers	Numbers	Judith
Deuteronomy	Deuteronomy	Deuteronomy	The Additions to the Book of Esther
Joshua	Joshua	Joshua	The Wisdom of Solomon
Judges	Judges	Judges	Ecclesiasticus, or the Wisdom of Jesus the Son of Sirach
	Ruth	Ruth	Baruch
1 Samuel	1 Samuel	The Books of Samuel	The Letter of Jeremiah
2 Samuel	2 Samuel		The Prayer of Azariah and the Song of the Three Young Men
1 Kings	1 Kings	The Books of Kings	Susanna
2 Kings	2 Kings		Bel and the Dragon
Isaiah	1 Chronicles	The Books of Chronicles	The Prayer of Manasseh
Jeremiah	2 Chronicles		1 Maccabees
Ezekiel	Ezra	Ezra	2 Maccabees
Hosea	Nehemiah	Nehemiah	3 Maccabees
Joel		Tobit	4 Maccabees
Amos		Judith	Psalm 151
Obadiah	Esther	Esther	
Jonah		1 Maccabees	
Micah		2 Maccabees	
Nahum	Job	Job	
Habakkuk	Psalms	Psalms	
Zephaniah	Proverbs	Proverbs	
Haggai	Ecclesiastes	Ecclesiastes /Qoheleth	
Zechariah	Song of Songs (or Song of Solomon)	Song of Songs	
Malachi		Ecclesiasticus/Ben Sira	
Psalms	Isaiah	Isaiah	
Proverbs	Jeremiah	Jeremiah	
Job	Lamentations	Lamentations	
Song of Songs		Baruch	
Ruth	Ezekiel	Ezekiel	
Lamentations	Daniel	Daniel	
Ecclesiastes	Hosea	Hosea	
Esther	Joel	Joel	
Daniel	Amos	Amos	
Ezra	Obadiah	Obadiah	
Nehemiah	Jonah	Jonah	
1 Chronicles	Micah	Micah	
2 Chronicles	Nahum	Nahum	
	Habakkuk	Habakkuk	
	Zephaniah	Zephaniah	
	Haggai	Haggai	
	Zechariah	Zechariah	
	Malachi	Malachi	

Bibles (other than a Jewish or chronological version), will indicate that all agree on the contents and arrangement of the New Testament canon. These twenty-seven books have been accepted by the majority of Christians since the fourth century A.D., so we do not need to discuss the New Testament canon here. Comparing the tables of contents for the Old Testament, however, will make clear that there is a difference in *content* between Protestant and Catholic Bibles and a difference in *arrangement* between Christian and Jewish Bibles.

Chart 1 is constructed from the tables of contents of four easily attained English Bibles. The Protestant Bible is the New International Version (North American Edition) (NIV). Two Catholic Bibles are used, the New Jerusalem Bible (NJB) and the New Oxford Annotated Bible with the Apocrypha (NOAB).[4] The Jewish Bible is the Tanakh, a New Translation of the Holy Scriptures According to the Masoretic Text.

All four of these Bibles agree on the names and order of the first seven books, Genesis through Judges. The Jewish Bible skips Ruth to go on to 1 and 2 Samuel and 1 and 2 Kings. The Protestant and Catholic versions agree until after Nehemiah, where the NJB has the books of Tobit and Judith, books not in the NIV or Tanakh and in a separate section of the NOAB. All told, there are thirty-nine books in the Tanakh and in the Old Testament of the NIV and NOAB, forty-seven in the Old Testament of the NJB (if you split Samuel, Kings, and Chronicles into two each) and eighteen in the "Apocrypha" of NOAB.

These lists summarize the (Old Testament) canons of four major groups of Bible users. The thirty-nine books of lists 1 and 2 compose the entire biblical canon of the Jew and the entire Old Testament canon of Protestants, in their respective arrangements. But these are only the "protocanonical" books of the Roman Catholic and Orthodox churches.[5] With these they include twelve to eighteen of the "deuterocanonical" or "apocryphal" books of list 4 in order to complete their Old Testament canons.

Lists 3 and 4 illustrate differing arrangements of Bibles that include the "Apocrypha." The NOAB has the "Apocrypha" in a separate section, a practice begun in the sixteenth century and still followed in "Common Bibles," Bibles intended for use by Catholics, Orthodox, and Protestants. The NJB integrates into the Old Testament the twelve books of the "Apocrypha" considered canonical by Roman Catholics. In fact, five books are so integrated as to be invisible! The Additions to Esther are in Esther; The Letter of Jeremiah is attached to Baruch; and The Prayer of Azariah and the Song of the Three Young Men, Susanna, and Bel and the Dragon are all in Daniel. This integrated organization follows the ancient versions in which these books are found.

Among the obvious questions that arise at this point are (1) Why are there different books in these lists? (2) Why are there different arrangements? (3) Who decided which books to include—and when? and (4) What do all those terms mean? The fullest answers are in books on Bible introduction (see chapter 9 of my *Books About the Book* [Zondervan, 1986] and the bibliography at the end of this chapter). But we will attempt to summarize the history of the canon and define the major terms involved in the next few pages.

THE CANON OF THE OLD TESTAMENT

There is no debate within Judaism as to which books belong in their canon. The Prologue to the Book of Ecclesiasticus, written in the late second century B.C., speaks of a threefold division of the Hebrew Scriptures. This division, "the Law, the Prophets and the other books," is mentioned three times and is the same division Jesus spoke of two hundred years later as "the Law of Moses, the Prophets and the Psalms" (Luke 24:44).

We have no listing of the exact contents of these divisions before the Babylonian Talmud (*Baba Bathra* 14b–15a), which lists all of the books that Christians know as the Old Testament, in the order of the Hebrew Bible (see chart 2). However, sources from New Testament times, Josephus (*Against Apion* 1.8), and 2 Esdras 14:44–48, number these books as twenty-two and twenty-four respectively.

Actually, Josephus's twenty-two is probably the same as Esdras's twenty-four. There are twenty-two letters in the Hebrew alphabet. Thus, a book per letter would be an excellent device for remembering the books. Probably, in order to make the twenty-four into twenty-two, Ruth was attached to Judges, and Lamentations to Jeremiah (as Ezra-Nehemiah and the twelve "Minor Prophets" form only two books in the Hebrew canon, see chart 2).

Chart 2
THE HEBREW/OLD TESTAMENT CANON

THE 22/24 BOOK HEBREW DIVISION[6]	THE 39-BOOK CHRISTIAN DIVISION
I. Torah (Law): 5 Genesis Exodus Leviticus Numbers Deuteronomy	I. The Pentateuch: 5 Genesis Exodus Leviticus Numbers Deuteronomy
II. Nebi'im (Prophets): 8	II. History: 12
A. Former Prophets Joshua Judges (with Ruth)[7] Samuel Kings	Joshua Judges Ruth 1 & 2 Samuel 1 & 2 Kings
B. Latter Prophets Isaiah Jeremiah (with Lamentations) Ezekiel	1 & 2 Chronicles Ezra Nehemiah Esther
The Twelve Hosea Joel Amos Obadiah Jonah Micah Nahum Habakkuk Zephaniah Haggai Zechariah Malachi	III. Poetry: 5 Job Psalms Proverbs Ecclesiastes Song of Songs
III. Kethubim ("Writings"): 11/9	IV. The Prophets: 17
A. Emeth ("[Books of] Truth")[8] Psalms Proverbs Job	A. The Major Prophets Isaiah Jeremiah Lamentations Ezekiel Daniel
B. Megilloth ("Scrolls") Song of Songs Ruth (or with Judges) Lamentations (or with Jeremiah) Ecclesiastes Esther	B. The Minor Prophets Hosea Joel Amos Obadiah Jonah Micah Nahum Habakkuk Zephaniah Haggai Zechariah Malachi
C. (Untitled) Daniel Ezra-Nehemiah Chronicles	

Although five of these books were disputed from time to time (Esther, Ezekiel, Proverbs, Ecclesiastes, and the Song of Songs), none was ever removed from the Hebrew canon. Thus Josephus could say near the end of the first century A.D.:

> For, although such long ages have now passed, no one has ventured either to add, or to remove, or to alter a syllable; and it is an instinct with every Jew from the day of his birth, to regard them as the decrees of God, to abide by them, and, if need be, cheerfully die for them" (*Against Apion* 1.8).

These are the books of which Jesus said, "Your word is truth" (John 17:17).

These twenty-four/twenty-two books of the so-called "Hebrew canon" became the Bible of the early church, which was born Jewish. However, the church inherited these books in a Greek translation, in a different order, and even with some additional books. The Greek translation was the "Septuagint" (LXX), a product of Jewish scholars in Alexandria around 250–150 B.C. The order was basically as it is in most non-Jewish Bibles today. The additional books were the "Apocrypha," which is listed in chart 1 (list 4) and is our next topic of discussion.

As you see, the canons are identical in content; they differ only in order and organization. The Hebrew order is roughly based on *authorship*: books by Moses, books by prophets, and books by other wise men and leaders of Israel.[9] The Greek (and English) order is based on *topic*: the books of the Law, the books of history, the books of wisdom and poetry, and the books of the prophets.

THE APOCRYPHA

The books listed in chart 2 and in lists 1 and 2 of chart 1 compose the Hebrew canon, the complete Bible of the Jews and the entire Old Testament of Protestants. But, as already mentioned, Catholics and Orthodox have a larger Old Testament canon, one derived from the Greek Old Testament, the LXX, which was the Bible of the early church. The LXX remains to this day the official Old Testament of the Orthodox church, while the Roman Catholic canon is based on another ancient translation, the Latin Vulgate. Both the LXX and the Vulgate have most of the additional books of chart 1, list 4—the "Apocrypha."

When referring to these books, we encounter a terminological nightmare. We need to understand the meaning of the words *apocrypha* and *pseudepigrapha* and see how these labels can refer to different books, depending on whether they are used by Protestants or Catholics. And we need to understand "protocanonical" and "deuterocanonical" and learn how these terms have connotations that are different for Catholics than for Orthodox.

Besides the books of the Hebrew canon, there are two sets of books, usually called the Apocrypha and Pseudepigrapha, that have been of great interest to both synagogue and church. These books are primarily Jewish in origin, with some Christian influence, and are dated between 200 B.C. and A.D. 200. Most of the books of the Apocrypha are considered canonical by Catholics and Orthodox. None of the books of the Pseudepigrapha are considered canonical by any mainline religious group.

The word *apocrypha* means "hidden things," but whether the term originally meant that the books contained hidden truths or that they should be hidden away from general use is unclear. The word *pseudepigrapha* means "false ascriptions," that is, the books claim to have been written by famous characters, but were not. Neither term clearly or satisfactorily describes the books in its group, but both are used to indicate books that are questionable as to canonicity.

Therefore, since the Roman Catholic Church canonized twelve of the eighteen books listed above, it has referred to them not as "apocryphal," but as "deuterocanonical." The thirty-nine books of the Hebrew canon are thus "protocanonical," the first books to be declared canonical, and the twelve books formerly apocryphal are "deuterocanonical," the next books declared canonical. All books outside this canon are apocryphal. Thus most of what is apocryphal and noncanonical to Protestants is deuterocanonical to Catholics. And what is apocryphal to Catholics is pseudepigraphal to Protestants, though noncanonical to both!

The Orthodox church also uses the term *deuterocanonical* to refer to canonical books outside the Hebrew canon. However, they accept all of the eighteen books listed in chart 1 (with some diversity on 2 Esdras and 4 Maccabees). The Orthodox further differ from Catholics in the connotation of deuterocanonical. To Catholics it means a canon second in sequence of canonization, but equal in authority. To the Orthodox, it means a canon secondary in authority to the Hebrew canon.

HOW THE CANONS CAME TO BE

So far, I have defined the terms and outlined the contents and arrangements of these canons, but have not yet described the process by which they came to be. Unfortunately, most of the early history of the canon is unknown and is reconstructed only by deduction and guesswork based on what little information we have. The following is a simplified summary of what is available in more detail in the books listed at the end of the chapter.

We know from reading the Old Testament that the words of God were recognized as authoritative, whether uttered from the heavens (Exod. 19:3–8; Amos 3:8), through a prophet (Deut. 18:17–19), or recorded in writing (Ps. 19:7–11). Although the word canon is not used in the text, the concept of authoritative writings is clear also from the earliest books of the Bible. The Law of Moses claimed divine authority at its writing (Deut. 32:44–47) and was recognized as authoritative in later generations (2 Kings 22:3–23:3). The writings of the prophets were quoted as the word(s) of God (Jer. 26:17–19; Dan. 9:1–3). It was inevitable that these authoritative writings would eventually be gathered into a collection to be preserved for all time.

Scholars disagree about the dates of many books of the Old Testament, about when they were written (or finished), and when they were considered canonical. However, the statements from Ecclesiasticus, Josephus, and Esdras cited above seem to indicate that the Hebrew canon was pretty well settled, though still discussed, centuries before the time of Jesus.

The books of the Apocrypha, though Jewish in origin, were never accepted as canonical by the Jewish people. Right after Josephus speaks of the twenty-two books of the Hebrew canon and just before he calls them "the decrees of God," he notes some other Jewish literature written between 400 B.C. and A.D. 100:

27

From Artaxerxes to our own time the complete history has been written, but it has not been deemed worthy of equal credit with the earlier records, because of the failure of the exact succession of the prophets (*Against Apion* I.8).

We do not know the exact books to which Josephus referred, but we know two things for certain. First, he did refer specifically in this statement to some books of the Apocrypha, because he depended on their content in his historical writings. Second, regardless of the books he had in mind *specifically*, he and the orthodox Judaism he represented considered *all* Jewish literature other than the twenty-two/twenty-four books of the Hebrew canon not to be "the decrees of God," not to be canonical. Two other important contemporary Jewish sources, Philo of Alexandria and the New Testament, refer constantly to the books of the Hebrew canon, but never formally quote any books of the Apocrypha.[10]

But as I mentioned above, various books of the Apocrypha were included in the LXX manuscripts that were the Bible of the early church. And for centuries the church wrestled with their status. Some early and influential fathers, such as Augustine, quoted them freely and considered them canonical. Others clearly considered them secondary to the Hebrew canon, notably Jerome, the translator of the Latin Vulgate. Interestingly, Catholic editions of the Bible published in Germany and France in 1527 and 1530 did not include the Apocrypha. On the other hand, the Protestant Authorized or King James Version (1611) did!

It was not until the Reformation era that the church clearly decided—and divided—on the Apocrypha. At the Council of Trent in 1546, the Roman Catholic church declared twelve books of the Apocrypha to be canonical and declared anyone who considered them otherwise to be anathema. Protestants accepted only the Hebrew canon. Luther's German Bible (1534) and early English versions, such as Coverdale (1535) and the Authorized or King James Version (1611), did have the Apocrypha, but in a separate section and usually with a statement about its secondary status. The Orthodox church had accepted the LXX as their Old Testament and formally declared all its contents canonical at the councils of Jassy (1642) and Jerusalem (1672), though those books outside of the Hebrew canon were accepted on a lower level of authority.

The church may never unite in its opinion of the apocryphal/deuterocanonical books. But Protestants should realize from the history of their use in the church that they have value at least as historical and spiritual literature. And Catholics and Orthodox should consider why Judaism, which produced them, never considered them canonical and might question—as did Jerome—any doctrine built solely on a deuterocanonical book.

THE PSEUDEPIGRAPHA AND CONTEMPORARY WRITINGS

We saw above that there was another set of books similar in date and content to the Apocrypha, usually referred to as the Pseudepigrapha. In addition to these better-known sets or *corpi*, a great deal of literature was produced by various sects and offspring of Judaism and Christianity between 300 B.C. and A.D. 300. Although the *corpi* are religious in nature, it would probably be wrong to use the word "canon" of them in the same sense as it is used above. For if these books seriously claimed inspiration and authority, they were taken seriously only by the little groups who created them.

As mentioned above, the term *apocrypha* ("hidden things") does not satisfactorily define the contents of its books. Neither does the term *pseudepigrapha*, which means "false ascriptions," that is, the books claim to have been written by famous characters, but are not. This is the case of such books as 1 Enoch and the Testaments of the Twelve Patriarchs, but not of Jubilees.

There is no fixed "canon" of the Pseudepigrapha. It seems that any Jewish or Hebrew-Christian writing between 200 B.C. and A.D. 200 is a potential member, unless it belongs to a well-defined collection, such as the Dead Sea Scrolls or the Nag Hammadi Gnostic Texts. The classic English collection of these books has been *The Apocrypha and Pseudepigrapha of the Old Testament* (Oxford, 1913) in two volumes, edited by R. H. Charles. Volume 2, on the Pseudepigrapha, listed seventeen titles, though the revised edition (*The Apocryphal Old Testament*, H. F. D. Sparks [Oxford, 1984]) lists twenty-five. The newest and most thorough collection, *The Old Testament Pseudepigrapha* (Doubleday, 1983/1985), edited in two volumes by James H. Charlesworth, contains more than fifty!

Although not considered inspired or canonical by any major religious group today, these books have great historical and theological value to biblical scholars. For they shed light on the Judaism of the Second Temple period (c. 500 B.C. to A.D. 70) and provide valuable background for understanding the New Testament and early church history. I mention them, not because we need to consider whether our Bible should include them, but because they are fascinating "collateral reading" to the "required text."

For those interested in this kind of collateral reading, there is other important Jewish literature from this era, including the writings of the philosopher and biblical scholar Philo of Alexandria, who wrote in the first half of the first century A.D., and of the historian Josephus, who wrote in the last half of the same century. The Dead Sea Scrolls, discovered as recently as 1947, are more than biblical manuscripts. They contain many writings of a separatistic Jewish sect, dated between 150 B.C. and A.D. 70, and these writings aid in understanding many books of the Apocrypha and Pseudepigrapha as well as the New Testament. The authoritative literature of contemporary Judaism, the Mishnah and the Talmud, also had their origins in this time. (See the bibliography for standard introductions and translations.)

Christianity also produced literature in addition to the canonical New Testament. Luke (1:1–4) speaks of many accounts of the life of Christ. Paul writes of forged, nonapostolic letters (2 Thess. 2:2) and even of letters he wrote that are not in the New Testament canon. First Corinthians 5:9 mentions a previous letter to Corinth, and 2 Corinthians 1:23–2:11 refers to yet another letter, which most likely was not 1 Corinthians.

These books are lost to us now, but we trust in the providence of God that they would have been preserved if they had been inspired. The earliest collection of Christian literature (which, by the way, does not claim inspiration) was written by the disciples of the disciples, usually known as the apostolic fathers. These books from the first and second centuries are very valuable for early Christian history and theology. (See the bibliography for standard introductions and translations.)

No less interesting, but of much less historical value, are the books of the so-called New Testament Apocrypha. Most of these books attempt to fill in the empty spaces in New Testament history, such as the childhood of Jesus or additional "Gospels," "Acts," "Epistles," and "Apocalypses" of the apostles. The

30

standard collection, *The New Testament Apocrypha* (Westminster, 1963), two volumes, edited by Edgar Hennecke and Wilhelm Schneemelcher, contains English translations of more than seventy such books and fragments.

Gnosticism blended Christianity with elements of Judaism and Greek, Roman, and Persian mythology and philosophy to the degree that all religious groups, especially Christianity, rejected them as heretical. For centuries, they were known only from the writings of the early church fathers who attacked them, but remnants of their own literature were unearthed in Egypt in 1945. These various Gospels, Apocalypses, and collections of sayings are known as the Nag Hammadi Gnostic Texts. The standard English collection is *The Nag Hammadi Library* (Harper, 1977), edited by James M. Robinson. It contains forty-seven texts and fragments.

An amazing amount of attention has been given to these New Testament—related noncanonical books of late, especially 1 Enoch and the apocryphal and Gnostic Gospels. These books, with such eye-catching titles as *The Lost Books of the Bible* and *The Other Bible*, often give the misleading impression that they were *removed* from the canon of the early church, whereas the early church almost from their origins judged them noncanonical. They were also suppressed by the mainstream of Christianity, because their theology was clearly at odds with that of Jesus and the apostles as contained in the New Testament books universally accepted even before the canon was settled in 397 A.D. Contemporary biblical scholars are highly skeptical of their historicity when they purport to contain the missing chapters in the life of Christ, of his family, and of the apostles.

It appears that the only people ever to take them seriously as inspired or as a part of Scripture are the individuals and groups that produced them, the sensationalistic writers who translate or edit them, and the sensationalistic publishers who continue to print and reprint them in a way that the consensus of biblical scholarship has discredited. This situation would be laughable if there were not certain people who lack the education and discernment to read beyond the publishers' blurbs and the writers' claims and make some of these documents articles of faith. The early church leaders had already weeded them out; modern scholarship agrees with their decisions, and so should we.

SUMMARY

Christians agree on the canon or the collection of books that compose the New Testament, but disagree on the canon of the Old Testament. Protestants accept only the thirty-nine books of the Hebrew canon as inspired, while Roman Catholics add to this "protocanonical" collection eleven "deuterocanonical" or "apocryphal" books from Latin and Greek sources. To these the Orthodox church adds from five to seven more.

A Jewish Bible, then, has a thirty-nine-book canon, as does the Tanakh, the most recent Jewish translation, or any separately published Old Testament of a Christian translation. A Protestant Bible has thirty-nine books in the Old Testament and twenty-seven in the New Testament. A Catholic version, such as the New American Bible or the New Jerusalem Bible, incorporates the deuterocanonical books into the other books of the Old Testament, offering a forty-seven-book Old Testament and a twenty-seven-book New Testament. A "Common Bible," designed for use by Protestants, Catholics, and Orthodox, sets the deuterocanonicals in a separate section, thus having a thirty-nine-book Old Testament, a twenty-seven-book New Testament, and a fourteen- to eighteen-book Apocrypha.

One's religious affiliation will usually determine the extent of the canon of his or her Bible. But in view of the history of the development of the canon I would again recommend that Protestants recognize the historical and devotional value of the Apocrypha and that Catholics and Orthodox carefully reconsider the validity of a doctrine developed exclusively from a deuterocanonical book.

FOR FURTHER READING ON CANON

I. Articles

Any one-volume Bible commentary, Bible dictionary, or Bible encyclopedia will have articles on canon (see *Books About the Book*, chapters 11 and 4, respectively). I recommend the following, each of which has its own bibliography. Addresses of publishers are given in Appendix B, pages 197–99.

Beare, F. W. "Canon of the New Testament." In *The Interpreter's Dictionary of the Bible*; 1:520–32. Edited by George Arthur Buttrick. Abingdon, 1962. *Academic; liberal.*

Brown, Raymond E. "Apocrypha; Dead Sea Scrolls; Other Jewish Literature." In *The Jerome Biblical Commentary*; pp. 535–60. Edited by Raymond E. Brown et al. Prentice-Hall, 1968. *This is an academic Catholic article, thus "Apocrypha" means "Pseudepigrapha." It also covers the New Testament Apocrypha.*

Freedman, David Noel. "Canon of the Old Testament." In *The Interpreter's Dictionary of the Bible: Supplementary Volume*; pp. 130–36. Edited by Keith Crim. Abingdon, 1976. *This is a unique presentation from a liberal perspective.*

Hawthorne, Gerald F. "Canon and Apocrypha." In *The International Bible Commentary* (formerly *The New Layman's Bible Commentary*), pp. 24–38. Edited by F. F. Bruce et al. Zondervan, 1986. *Conservative; Protestant.*

Payne, David F. "The Text and Canon of the New Testament." In *The International Bible Commentary* (formerly *The New Layman's Bible Commentary*), pp. 1005–11. Edited by F. F. Bruce et al. Zondervan, 1979. *Conservative; Protestant.*

Pfeiffer, Robert H. "Canon of the Old Testament." In *The Interpreter's Dictionary of the Bible*; 1:498–520. Edited by George Arthur Buttrick. Abingdon, 1962. *Academic; the classic liberal position.*

Sarna, Nahum M. "Bible: The Canon; Text; and Editions." In *Encyclopedia Judaica*; 4:816–36. Edited by Cecil Roth and Geoffrey Wigoder. Keter, 1972. *Jewish perspective.*

Sundberg, Albert C. "Canon of the New Testament." In *The Interpreter's Dictionary of the Bible: Supplementary Volume*, pp. 136–40. Edited by Keith Crim. Abingdon, 1976. *Academic; liberal.*

Turro, James C., and Raymond E. Brown, "Canonicity." In *The Jerome Biblical Commentary*; pp. 515–34. Edited by Raymond E. Brown et al. Prentice-Hall, 1968. *Academic; Catholic; deals well with Orthodox and Protestant positions.*

Ware, Timothy. *The Orthodox Church.* 3rd revised printing. Penguin, 1980 (1st ed. 1963). *Pages 203–15 summarize the Orthodox position on biblical canon and authority.*

II. Introductions

In addition to the following books devoted solely to the discussion of canon, Bible introductions and most Bible commentaries deal with the history of, or problems relating to, the canonicity of any book of the Bible (see *Books About the Book*, chapters 9 and 11, respectively).

Beckwith, Roger T. *The Old Testament Canon of the New Testament Church*. Eerdmans, 1985. *This recent title is the single most comprehensive work ever done on the Old Testament canon. It argues that the canon was closed by at least the second century B.C. and that the early church did not recognize a canon other than the twenty-four-book Hebrew canon.*

Harris, R. Laird. *Inspiration and Canonicity of the Bible*. 2nd ed. Zondervan, 1969 (1st ed. 1957). *Conservative; Protestant.*

Harrop, Clayton. *History of the New Testament in Plain Language*. Waco: Word, 1984. *This volume devotes two chapters to a concise, easily read history of the New Testament canon.*

Metzger, Bruce Manning. An Introduction to the Apocrypha. Oxford, 1957. *A well-written, informative, and anecdotal introduction to the fifteen books normally included in the Apocrypha.*

Nickelsburg, George W. E. *Jewish Literature Between the Bible and the Mishnah*. Fortress, 1981. *Academic; a historic and literary introduction to the Apocrypha, Pseudepigrapha and Dead Sea Writings.*

Rost, Leonhard. *Judaism Outside the Hebrew Canon*. Translated by David E. Green. Abingdon, 1976. *Introduction to contents and available texts of the Apocrypha and much of the Pseudepigrapha.*

Stone, Michael E., ed. *Jewish Writings of the Second Temple Period*. Fortress, 1984. *A major academic introduction the Apocrypha, Pseudepigrapha, Dead Sea Writings, Philo, and Josephus with extensive bibliography. Two volumes in preparation for this Compendia Rerum Iudaicarum ad Novum Testamentum series will deal with "Reading, Translation and Interpretation of the Hebrew Bible in Ancient Judaism and Early Christianity," and "Midrash, Mishnah, and Talmud."*

Westcott, Brooke Foss. *The Bible in the Church*. Corrected ed. Baker, reprint of the 1885 edition, 1979 (1st ed. 1864). *Subtitled "A Popular Account of the Collection and Reception of the Holy Scriptures in the Christian Churches," this classic remains an informative and readable introduction to the history of the canon in the church. Protestant; conservative.*

————. *A General Survey of the History of the Canon of the New Testament*. 6th ed. Baker, reprint of the 1889 edition, 1980 (1st ed. 1855). *This century-old classic remains a standard on the history of the New Testament canon. Academic.*

III. Select Noncanonical Texts in Translation

Each of these collections has extensive bibliography to texts and translations in other languages, modern and ancient.

Barnstone, Willis. *The Other Bible*. Harper, 1984. *This is a collection of excerpts from many noncanonical writings, which the editor feels should not have been left out of the Jewish and Christian canons.*

Beyerlin, Walter, ed. *Near Eastern Religious Texts Relating to the Old Testament*. Translated by John Bowden. Westminster, 1978. *A recent anthology of texts from Old Testament times, keyed to Old Testament texts.*

Charles, R. H. *The Apocrypha and Pseudepigrapha of the Old Testament*. 2 vols. Oxford, 1913. *The standard collection until Charlesworth (below). Recently updated by Sparks (below).*

Charlesworth, James H. *The Old Testament Pseudepigrapha*. 2 vols. Doubleday, 1983; 1985. *The most recent and largest collection, with full introductions and translations.*

Gaster, Theodor H. *The Dead Sea Scriptures*. 3rd ed. Anchor/Doubleday, 1976 (1st ed. 1956). *Translates the nonbiblical texts from Qumran.*

Hennecke, Edgar, and Wilhelm Schneemelcher, eds. *New Testament Apocrypha*. 2 vols. R. McL. Wilson, English editor. Westminster, 1963; 1965. *The standard collection.*

James, Montague Rhodes. *The Apocryphal New Testament*. Corrected ed. Oxford, 1953 (1st ed. 1924). *The standard collection until Hennecke and Schneemelcher.*

Josephus. Loeb Classical Library. 10 vols. Translated by Henry St. John Thackeray, Ralph Marcus, and Allen Wikgren. Harvard, 1926–1965. *The standard Greek text and English translation.*

Josephus. Translated by William Whiston. Foreword by William S. LaSor. Kregel, reprint, 1960 (1st ed. 1867). *The most popular English edition, available in cloth and paperback.*

Lake, Kirsopp, trans. *Apostolic Fathers*. Loeb Classical Library. 2 vols. Harvard, 1912; 1913. *A standard Greek text and English translation.*

Lightfoot, Joseph B., and J. R. Harmer, eds. and trans. *The Apostolic Fathers: Greek Texts and English Translations*. Baker reprint of the 1891 edition, 1984. *Another standard Greek and English text, with more contents than Lake.*

————. *The Apostolic Fathers*. 5 vols. 2nd ed. Baker, reprint of the 1889–1890 edition, 1981. *The standard critical Greek and English texts with full introductions.*

Metzger, Bruce Manning, ed. *The Oxford Annotated Apocrypha: Expanded Edition*. 2nd ed. Oxford, 1977 (1st ed. 1957). *This volume is also contained in The New Oxford Annotated Bible: Expanded Edition, and is the best edition of the Apocrypha for those who do not have it in their Bible.*

Neusner, Jacob. *Invitation to the Talmud.* 2nd ed. Harper, 1984 (1st ed. 1973). *An excellent brief introduction to the classic rabbinic literature: the Mishnah, Tosefta, and Talmud—with bibliographies to the standard English translations.*

Philo. Loeb Classical Library. 12 vols. Translated by F. H. Colson, G. H. Whitaker, and Ralph Marcus. Harvard, 1929–1962.

Pritchard, James, ed. *Ancient Near Eastern Texts Relating to the Old Testament.* 3rd ed. Princeton, 1969 (1st ed. 1950). *The standard collection, keyed to Old Testament texts.*

Robinson, James M., ed. *The Nag Hammadi Library.* Harper, 1977. *The standard collection of Gnostic literature in English.*

Sparks, H. F. D., ed. *The Apocryphal Old Testament.* Oxford, 1984. *An update of Charles (above) but having not nearly as many texts as Charlesworth. It includes twenty-five noncanonical texts attributed to a character or characters of the Old Testament.*

Thomas, D. Winton, ed. *Documents From Old Testament Times.* Harper, 1958. *An affordable collection of texts in English.*

Vermes, Geza. *The Dead Sea Scrolls in English.* 2nd ed. Penguin, 1975 (1st ed. 1962). *The most quoted translation of the nonbiblical Qumran texts.*

Works of Flavius Josephus, The. 4 vols. Translated by William Whiston. Foreword and appendix by Charles F. Pfeiffer. Baker, reprint, 1974 (1st ed. 1867). *The Whiston translation in larger print and 4 volumes.*

Chapter 2

WHAT IS THE BIBLE?
PART 2: THE TEXT

ON EXTRA BOOKS AND MISSING VERSES

Most Bible readers do not realize that there are differences not only in translations of the Bible, but in contents as well. Discovering these differences can be a traumatic experience.

I remember vividly an incident at a Bible study attended by both Jews and Christians. One day we were comparing the Jewish Bible and Christian Old Testament and I mentioned that their only material difference was in the addition of the Apocrypha to the Roman Catholic canon. I then pointed out that one of our participants, an evangelical, used the Jerusalem Bible, a Catholic translation with the Apocrypha, in case anyone wanted to take a look at any of these books. She actually dropped her Bible and recoiled in horror! Although she had owned and read it for years, she had no idea that her Bible contained a dozen books that evangelicals did not accept as canonical.

I was surprised that someone could be so unaware of the contents of her own Bible, but then I had memorized the books of the Bible in Sunday school at an early age. Yet, earlier, during the interview for my first bookstore job, I had been caught unaware of another category of difference. While the owner was probing my background, he asked if I was a "King James man." I replied humorously (I thought), "Well, the King James was good enough for Paul, but I use [I did then] the New American Standard Bible." He shot back rather sternly, "The NASB is an all-right translation, but I think it left too much of the text in the margin." I knew I had said something wrong, but I had no idea what!

Perhaps you, too, have noticed differences in translations that go beyond vocabulary and phrasing. If you were raised on the KJV, but have consulted or switched to a modern version, you may already know that the phrase "for thine is the kingdom and the power and the glory forever" does not end the Lord's Prayer in Matthew 6:13. Even if you do not have a KJV background, you have probably found such verses as Mark 11:26; John 5:4; and Acts 8:37 in footnotes rather than in the text. The comments relating to "important," "ancient," or "better" manuscripts have no doubt at one time meant as little to you as my former employer's comment meant to me.

It was not until my Bible-college studies brought me into contact with "textual criticism" that I began to understand what happened to those "missing" verses. And I did not have to spend much time in the bookstore before I began to encounter the strong emotional response that textual differences can evoke!

This chapter is devoted to explaining the basic principles and practices of textual criticism in order to demonstrate its value and remove some of the mysteries found in your Bible's footnotes. We will also deal with the emotional and theological debate that has been raging in this area for centuries. I hope to show that much of this debate is based on misinformation and misunderstanding, and that it has very few practical or theological ramifications.

WHAT IS TEXTUAL CRITICISM?

Whenever the word *criticism* is used in connection with the Bible, we get nervous. In everyday use, "criticism" is a negative term; it implies that something is wrong or substandard. Thus it is natural to assume that "biblical criticism" also has a negative function. But "criticism," when used in relation to scholarship, does not take on its normal judgmental or derogatory meaning. Rather, it indicates disciplined examination and discerning study, usually involving the use of the original languages.

Scholars used to speak of two categories of criticism: "higher" and "lower." Higher criticism deals with the origin and development of the Bible. Because its theories are often at odds with the Bible's self-witness and with the traditional understanding of its origin, conservative scholars usually reject its methods and conclusions. On the other hand, lower criticism deals with the transmission, or copying and translation, of the Bible and is practiced by conservative and nonconservative scholars alike. Lower criticism is another name for textual criticism.

THE NEED FOR TEXTUAL CRITICISM

As we looked at the question of canon in chapter 1 to determine which books belong in the Bible, we will look at textual criticism in this chapter to determine which document or manuscript best represents each book in its original form. I say "best represents" because we do not have any of the original writings of any of the apostles or prophets. Every ancient text of the Bible we have is a copy or a translation of a copy. And since they were all copied by hand before the invention of the printing press in the fifteenth century, no two are exactly alike. Even those carefully prepared by professional scribes contain the inevitable errors of manual copying. (Copy any book of the English Bible yourself, compare your copy with the original, and you will see what I mean!)

This may sound like bad news at first, but it isn't. The Bible is the best-preserved ancient book in the world. There are literally thousands of Old Testament and New Testament manuscripts in the original Greek, Hebrew, and Aramaic, and thousands more in ancient translations. Further, because of the many resources and the general consensus on their evaluation, scholars are certain of more than 95 percent of the exact wording of the original New Testament text. The percentage is lower for the Old Testament text, because of fewer ancient manuscripts. However, no major teaching of the Bible is lost or challenged because of the condition of the text. In other words, regardless of the manuscript, the message of the Bible is absolutely preserved!

However, because we are dealing with the Word of God, we want to have the very best copy of it available to us. And that is where textual criticism comes in.

THE HISTORY OF TEXTUAL CRITICISM

The Hebrew Text

Ever since the beginning of the recording of scriptural revelation, there was the copying and distributing of this record.

Deuteronomy 17:18–19 instructs the king "to write for himself on a scroll a copy of this law, taken from that of the priests, who are Levites. It is to be with him, and he is to read it all the days of his life."

This speaks of a controlled, professional copying of the Scriptures. But archaeologists have also turned up many examples of nonprofessional copying, done by individuals who wanted their own "family Bibles." Although subject to careless copying, eras of total disregard, wars, and exile, Israel's Scriptures were never totally destroyed. But neither were they preserved intact.

Sometime between the return from the Babylonian Exile (538 B.C.) and the time of Christ, the variant readings in the Hebrew text were standardized. The transmission of this standard text eventually became the responsibility of a guild known as the Masoretes, who passed it on until the invention of the printing press in the fifteenth century. The Hebrew text we use today is thus known as the Masoretic Text (MT).

Although there are many minor differences between manuscripts of the Masoretic tradition, few affect the meaning of the text; it is a very uniform tradition. Nonetheless, scholars were skeptical that this tradition truly represented the original form of the Old Testament, because our oldest witnesses were 1,500 years removed from the time of Ezra. However, when the Dead Sea Scrolls were discovered in the late 1940s, scholars found available to them Hebrew manuscripts and fragments dating back centuries before the time of Jesus.

The Dead Sea Scrolls do represent other manuscript traditions, but the vast majority of these texts—a thousand years older than the oldest known copy of the MT—agree exceptionally well with the MT. Because we do not have many divergent Hebrew texts of the Old Testament, most translations begin with the MT and alter it only rarely, their changes being based on alternative readings in the Dead Sea Scrolls and the ancient versions. Differences between the various translations of the Old Testament are much more often a matter of interpretation than of differences of text.

The Greek Text

Because of the more numerous and more varied resources for the Greek New Testament, more texts are in question and more controversy is evoked than for the Old Testament.

Even before the New Testament documents were considered Scripture, the apostolic correspondence was copied and circulated. In his letter to the Colossian church, Paul instructed them, "After this letter has been read to you, see that it is also read in the church of the Laodiceans and that you in turn read the letter from Laodicea" (Col. 4:16).

This nonprofessional copying had the positive result of circulating the Word of God, but it also had the negative result of introducing all sorts of errors into the text—like the ones you made if you copied a Bible book as I suggested on page 39. But besides making such accidental errors, early copyists had a tendency to update grammar and spelling, harmonize parallel passages, and even add comments and other "improvements" to the text. These expansions were preserved later by professional scribes. (See page 43 on "Principles and Practices of Textual Criticism.")

Emperor Constantine made Christianity an official religion early in the fourth century, and from 330 to 1453 his capital city of Constantinople was the center of the Greek-speaking church. The scholars of this city, earlier known as Byzantium, preserved the New Testament in Greek, while the church in the West perpetuated the New Testament in Latin.

The first English New Testament, that of Wycliffe (1384), and the first official Catholic New Testament, the Rheims translation (1582), were translated from Latin. But all other early English versions from Tyndale (1526) to the KJV (1611), were translated from the Greek, as was Luther's German New Testament (1522).

As the translation of the New Testament began, the only Greek texts readily available were those that had been preserved in Byzantium. The first printed Greek New Testament was edited from such texts by the brilliant Catholic scholar and humanist Desiderius Erasmus in 1515. In a race with another project, Erasmus worked from a mere handful of manuscripts, sometimes supplying his own Greek rendering of the Latin when his texts were missing verses! Although hastily prepared and filled with typographical errors, Erasmus' Greek New Testament was widely received and went through five editions.

The dozens of authorized and unauthorized editions and reprints issued over the next century differed from Erasmus's version only in minor details. So when the Elzevir brothers printed their own edition in 1633, they were confident enough to call it the "Textus Receptus," the received, or standard, text of the day.

The publisher's appellation stuck, and Textus Receptus (TR) is used to this day to describe the text type that Erasmus developed and which was used in the translation of most English versions until the end of the nineteenth century. Because of numerical superiority, this text type is known as the "Majority Text." Because of its association with the city of Byzantium, it is also known as the "Byzantine Text."

Although this text was widely accepted, some scholars wanted a text more thoroughly researched and critically established than the TR. But as they suggested changes in (often omissions from) the TR, their changes were perceived as destructive rather than productive. Even the continuing discovery of manuscripts more ancient than the Byzantine did not immediately lend support to their efforts. The traditionalists argued, Why should a handful of ancient texts have more value than the majority?

The majority argument was first challenged in 1725 by J. A. Bengel, who suggested that rather than the manuscripts simply being counted, they should be grouped into families of similar characteristics, and the families should be weighed against each other. Although this concept was strongly resisted for nearly two centuries, it finally won scholarly consensus when Westcott and Hort published The New Testament in the Original Greek in 1881. Because such scholars "gather out" their readings from a variety of texts, their approach is usually called "eclectic."

Although differing from Westcott and Hort in many details, all subsequent versions from the Revised Version (1881) to those of the present—except the New King James—have adopted their basic approach. For many, this break from four centuries of dominance by the TR is a positive advance in biblical scholarship, but for others it is apostacy from the faith.

Before we discuss the current debate, however, let us look at the major principles textual critics use in restoring the original text.

PRINCIPLES AND PRACTICES OF TEXTUAL CRITICISM

How do text critics arrive at the best text? When they compare variations among manuscripts, they look for the reading that best explains the others. And because textual criticism has been practiced for centuries on sacred and secular literature alike, scholars have pretty well identified all of the ways in which scribes tended to introduce errors into the text. By working through the process of elimination, these scholars find that one reading usually stands out as primary.

Identifying Errors Made in Copying

Scholars refer to scribal errors as being "intentional" or "unintentional." The latter arose from such oversights as seeing or writing a wrong letter or skipping lines or phrases—the kind of errors you made if you copied a book of the Bible as I suggested earlier (p. 39). Intentional errors arose from a scribe's desire to "correct" a text or add interpretation to it.

We can simulate these errors in English. For example, an error of seeing or writing could occur if a scribe saw the statement "They will seduce you with their gods" but wrote, "They will seduce you with their goods." Both sentences make sense, but one wrong letter changes a word and alters the meaning. Skipping lines or phrases happens when the eye jumps from one word to another of similar spelling. For example, the sentence ". . . and Paul went to Antioch and he encouraged the believers" could easily become "and he encouraged the believers" by skipping from one "and" to the other, losing a clause in the process.

Intentional errors are fewer in number and are usually easier to spot. Some scribes attempted to "improve" on or update the grammar of certain books. Others attempted to "harmonize" parallel passages, such as in the Gospels, to make parallel accounts more nearly identical. In some manuscripts, for example, the Lord's Prayer in Luke 11:2–4 is altered to match the longer reading of Matthew 6:9–13. The NIV and KJV (among others) represent those two traditions (see p. 44).

Still others added doctrinal materials to certain verses to make the text conform more closely to the theology of the scribe. An important example here is Romans 8:1. In most early

NIV	KJV
Father,	Our Father which art in heaven,
hallowed be your name,	Hallowed be thy name.
your kingdom come.	Thy kingdom come.
	Thy will be done in earth,
	as it is in heaven.
Give us each day our daily bread.	Give us this day
	our daily bread.
Forgive us our sins,	And forgive us our debts,
for we also forgive everyone	as we forgive our debtors.
who sins against us.	
And lead us not into temptation.	And lead us not into temptation,
(Luke 11:2–4)	but deliver us from evil:
	For thine is the kingdom,
	and the power,
	and the glory, for ever.
	Amen (Luke 11:2–4)

manuscripts this verse reads, "Therefore, there is now no condemnation for those who are in Christ Jesus," but later texts add the condition "who do not live according to the flesh but according to the Spirit" from verse 4.

Another characteristic of the scribes was the tendency to preserve rather than to eliminate. After all, who would want to be guilty of rejecting a portion of God's Word? Often, when a scribe was copying from more than one manuscript, he would preserve more than one reading: one in the text and one in the margin. But a later scribe, mistaking the variant for a mislocated piece of text, could add it to the verse. In this way a footnote, comment, or variant reading could become a part of the text.

One extraordinary manuscript shows the extremes to which this tendency could lead. Many late manuscripts have an additional phrase in 2 Corinthians 8:4 (here in italics), "they urgently pleaded with us for the privilege of sharing in this service to the saints *for us to receive*." One copyist noted in the margin of his manuscript, "It is found thus in many of the copies." But the scribe who used that copy incorporated the textual note, so the verse ended up like this: "They urgently pleaded with us for the privilege of sharing in this service to the saints *for us to receive is found thus in many of the copies*"![1]

Determining the Best Reading

Textual critics work with what they call internal and external evidence in evaluating readings. Internal evidence relates to the readings of the manuscripts themselves. External evidence relates to the families or groups into which these manuscripts are divided.

The use of internal evidence came first. As scholars began to compare manuscripts in the centuries following the publication of the TR, they discovered the types of differences outlined above. Noting scribal tendencies to remove grammatical and theological difficulties to make the text easier to understand, the scholars judged that the more difficult readings were original. And noting tendencies to explain, to preserve, and to harmonize, they preferred shorter readings as original. On the other hand, the longer reading was preferred when it could be shown that the scribe accidentally skipped a phrase or line.

The use of external evidence came later. As more ancient manuscripts came to light, scholars discovered similarities in their characteristics and began grouping them into families. These families were thought to correspond to the geographic centers of scholarship in the church's history. Today most scholars work with four major families—Alexandrian, Caesarean, Byzantine, and Western (Roman).

As scholars were preferring shorter and more difficult readings, they gave priority to the Alexandrian type of text. We would also expect that the older manuscripts would be closer to the originals in text, because they are closest to the original texts in time. The Alexandrian text also had preference here.

On the other hand, in spite of its history of popularity and numerical superiority, the Byzantine text settled to the bottom of most scholars' lists, because of its expansive readings and relatively late development.

THE CURRENT DEBATE

There are two basic stances in regard to textual criticism: favorable and unfavorable. Those who practice textual criticism generally argue for the superiority of the Alexandrian text but agree that the original must be established from all available texts.

Those who do not practice textual criticism maintain the superiority of the Byzantine text, the TR as its best representative, and the KJV as its best translation into English. They disagree that the history of the transmission of the text is one of scribal expansion, but argue that the shorter texts are the ones that have been deliberately mutilated. They challenge the theological integrity of modern critical texts and versions, pointing to questioned or "missing" verses and passages as evidence that textual criticism is attempting to reduce or steal the message of the Bible by its methods.

Textual "Give and Take"

It is true that in many modern versions words, phrases, verses, and even two major passages (Mark 16:9–20 and John 7:53–8:11) found in the TR and KJV are are set apart from the rest of the text in brackets or in footnotes that question whether they should be considered part of the original text. But it is wrong to characterize textual criticism as only taking words, phrases, and verses out of the text. For textual criticism does not only "take"; it also "gives back."

For example, Hebrews 1:6 quotes as Scripture the phrase "Let all God's angels worship him." This is found in Deuteronomy 32:43 of the LXX, the Greek translation of the Old Testament, but is not in any Hebrew Bibles. This, of course, creates a problem. It is fine to quote the Bible in translation. After all, the New Testament always quotes the Hebrew Old Testament in Greek. But when a translation has material not in the original text, can it considered Scripture?

This problem appears to have been solved, however, by the discovery of this phrase in Hebrew manuscripts of the Dead Sea Scrolls. Some versions now include it in the text (e.g., New English, Beck) or notes (e.g., NIV) of Deuteronomy.

But whether an omission or addition, critics of criticism are not happy with *any* change from the TR. Their arguments that God preserved the best text in the majority of manuscripts, that the TR was the first and most-used printed text, and that the KJV has had the longest history of acceptance by the church seems formidable. But as many are incorrect in assuming that textual criticism always takes away text, they are also incorrect in assuming that the TR is the same as the Majority Text and that the KJV absolutely follows the TR.

Does the Majority Rule?

If the basic argument that the "majority rules" were applied consistently, the Latin Vulgate would be our Bible! Latin manuscripts outnumber Greek about eight thousand to five thousand, and the Latin Bible has centuries more dominance in the church than all English versions combined. The Latin is the true Majority Text!

But truth is not democratic; it is not subject to "majority rule." (Remember that ten of the twelve spies did not want to enter Canaan and died for their majority opinion [Num. 13–14]!) Although it seems logical that we should simply poll the thousands of Greek manuscripts we have and accept the consensus as the correct New Testament text, *no one* would accept the results. For that text would differ dramatically from both the TR and from the modern critical texts. This was proved to me by, of all things, the New King James Version (NKJV)— something you can check for yourself in English. In its footnotes to the New Testament, the NKJV lists the variations of the KJV from the Majority Text (abbreviated M) and from the standard critical texts (abbreviated NU for the Nestle-Aland and United Bible Societies' texts).

If majority ruled, the New Testament text of the KJV and NKJV would have to be changed in more than 320 places, for neither the TR nor the KJV absolutely represent the majority. The KJV would lose such famous texts as Jesus' statement to Paul "It is hard for thee to kick against the pricks," and Paul's response "Lord, what wilt thou have me to do?" (Acts 9:5–6). It would lose whole verses, such as Luke 17:36; Acts 8:37; and 15:34. Why? Because these verses are not in most Greek manuscripts; they were imported into the KJV from the Latin Vulgate.

Perhaps most interesting, of the famous Trinitarian "proof-text," 1 John 5:7–8, the KJV would lose the portion that I have italicized:

> For there are three that bear record *in heaven, the Father, the Word, and the Holy Ghost: and these three are one. And there are three that bear witness* in earth, the spirit, and the water, and the blood: and these three agree in one."

Again, these losses would not be the result of "destructive criticism," but of following the majority of Greek texts! (By the way, the NKJV followed the choices of the KJV rather than accepting the reading of the majority.)

So in reality, the TR differs from the Majority Text in every way that the modern critical texts differ from the Majority Text, in additions as well as omissions. It just does not differ in as many texts. If KJV advocates allow the TR to differ from the Majority—and they must!—they should be willing to allow the modern texts to differ. They do not have to agree with all of the readings of the critical texts, but hundreds agree with the Majority Text against the TR! But at the very least, they should not condemn these texts wholesale as heretical mutilations of God's Word.

The Example of the New Testament Itself

The Bible itself shows us clearly that God does not honor only one text or one translation. Jesus and the apostles used different texts and versions, as is clear from the way they quote the Old Testament. In fact, when different books of the New Testament quote the same Old Testament text, they rarely quote it alike, with word-for-word exactness. Most of these differences do not show up in translation, just as most of the differences between manuscripts of the New Testament do not show up in translation. For example, Matthew 19:5; Mark 10:7–8; and Ephesians 5:31 all quote portions of Genesis 2:24 with slightly different wording. But you cannot tell the difference in your English translation because the *meaning* is not changed. More noticeable is the story of the rich young ruler in Matthew 19:18–19; Mark 10:19; and Luke 18:20, where all the Gospel writers quote from the Ten Commandments differently.

If the writers of the New Testament could live with these differences, so should we. The text or translation of the Bible one uses should never be made a basis for judging one's salvation, and it should never determine the extent of believers' fellowship.

SUMMARY

Although you probably do not practice textual criticism, you encounter its results every time you read your Bible. I hope you have seen that although there are tens of thousands of differences between the thousands of biblical manuscripts we have in our possession, no orthodox doctrine or practice of the church hangs on a questionable text. Although it may affect the interpretation of a particular verse, textual criticism will not affect your theology. Still, as in the case of the deuterocanonical books, I would strongly recommend that you do not base your beliefs or life direction on a debated reading.

There are some people who continue to challenge the theological integrity of modern texts and versions and criticize forcefully and caustically those who produced them. There is no basis for the majority of these attacks and no excuse for the mean spirit of such criticism. In fact, founders of fundamentalist theology, such as B. B. Warfield[2] and J. Gresham Machen,[3] accepted Westcott and Hort's text as closer to the original than the TR! I will conclude with this extract from the preface of the NKJV, which, though it prefers to follow the TR and the KJV, expresses a balanced perspective on the differences between texts:

> Differences among the Greek manuscripts of the New Testament such as omission or inclusion of a word or a clause, and two paragraphs in the Gospels, should not overshadow the overwhelming degree of *agreement* which exists among the ancient records. . . .

> Readers may be assured that textual debate does not affect one in a thousand words of the Greek New Testament. Furthermore, no established doctrine is called into question by any doubts about the correct reading in this or that text. The Christian can approach his New Testament with confidence. (Wide Margin Edition [Nelson, 1983], pp. iv, v.)

FOR FURTHER READING ON TEXTUAL CRITICISM

Most readers of the Bible will simply accept the text that is presented in the version they use. That is fine. But when you encounter a textual difference between versions in a personal or group Bible study, you may want to know how to resolve the problem. The books and articles in the following bibliography represent a broad cross section of approaches to textual criticism. They are labeled according to their perspective and their reading level.

I. Articles

Any Bible dictionary or Bible encyclopedia, Bible introduction or Bible commentary, will have articles or chapters on textual criticism (See *Books About the Book*, chapters 4, 9, and 11 respectively). I recommend the following, each of which has its own bibliography:

Barthelemy, Dominique. "Text, Hebrew, History of." In *The Interpreter's Dictionary of the Bible: Supplementary Volume*, pp. 878–84. Edited by Keith Crim. Abingdon, 1976. *Discussion and critique of recent major theories concerning the early transmission of the Old Testament text. Updates the article by Roberts, see below.*

Epp, Eldon Jay. "Textual Criticism, New Testament." In *The Interpreter's Dictionary of the Bible: Supplementary Volume*, pp. 891–95. Edited by Keith Crim. Abingdon, 1976. *An update to Parvis's article, see below.*

Fee, Gordon D. "The Textual Criticism of the New Testament." In *The Expositor's Bible Commentary*; 1:419–33. Edited by Frank E. Gaebelein. Zondervan, 1979. *An excellent, well-balanced overview.*

Martini, Carlo Maria. "Text, New Testament." In *The Interpreter's Dictionary of the Bible: Supplementary Volume*, pp. 884–86. Edited by Keith Crim. Abingdon, 1976. *An update to Parvis's article, see below.*

Parvis, Merrill M. "Text, New Testament." In *The Interpreter's Dictionary of the Bible*; 4:594–614. Edited by George Arthur Buttrick. Abingdon, 1962. *A thorough, critical introduction. Updated by Epp and Martini, see above.*

Roberts, Bleddyn J. "Text, Old Testament." In *The Interpreter's Dictionary of the Bible*; 4:580–94. Edited by George Arthur Buttrick. Abingdon, 1962. *A good overview with a high regard for the Masoretic Text. Updated by Barthelemy (above) and Thompson (below).*

Skehan, Patrick W., et al. "Texts and Versions." In *The Jerome Biblical Commentary*; 561–89. Edited by Raymond E. Brown et al. Prentice-Hall, 1968. *Good, detailed overview. Skehan's portion on the Old Testament text contains a good overview of the contribution of the Dead Sea Scrolls.*

Thompson, John A. "Textual Criticism, Old Testament." In *The Interpreter's Dictionary of the Bible: Supplementary Volume*, pp. 886–91. Edited by Keith Crim. Abingdon, 1976. *An update to Roberts (see above), which explains in more detail the resources and principles of Old Testament textual criticism.*

Waltke, Bruce K. "The Textual Criticism of the Old Testament." In *The Expositor's Bible Commentary*; 1:211-28. Edited by Frank E. Gaebelein. Zondervan, 1979. *An excellent overview with a high regard for the Masoretic Text.*

II. Introductions

Aland, Kurt, and Barbara Aland. *The Text of the New Testament* Eerdmans, 1986. *This recent publication by two renowned textual critics will become the student's standard introduction to New Testament textual criticism and to the critical Greek texts.*

Barr, James. *Comparative Philology and the Text of the Old Testament.* Oxford, 1968. Academic. *This is a critique of a noncritical use of ancient versions and cognate languages in Old Testament textual criticism and lexicography.*

Bible for Today, The (900 Park Avenue, Collingswood, NJ 08108). *This organization carries a large variety of new and reprint books and pamphlets that exclusively support the KJV and its textual base.*

Carson, D. A. *The King James Version Debate.* Baker, 1979. *The best introduction to the debate. The first seven chapters are written in nontechnical language to explain the different approaches to textual criticism by those who prefer the TR and by the majority of modern scholars, who prefer an eclectic text. Carson also effectively deals with the theological issues usually (and improperly!) brought into the discussion.*

Cross, Frank Moore, and Shemaryahu Talmon, eds. *Qumran and the History of the Biblical Text.* Harvard, 1975. Academic. *This is a collection of seventeen essays from the 1950s, 60s, and 70s that discuss the impact of the Dead Sea Scrolls on Old Testament textual criticism.*

Finegan, Jack. *Encountering New Testament Manuscripts.* Eerdmans, 1974. *Subtitled "A Working Introduction to Textual Criticism," this volume teaches the student the principles and practices of the textual criticism by actually working from clearly reproduced photographs of ancient manuscripts.*

Fuller, David Otis, ed. *Counterfeit or Genuine?* 2nd ed. Kregel, 1978 (1st ed. 1975). *This and the two books that follow are collections of essays, old and new, that defend the supremacy of the TR and are strongly critical, theologically and academically, of any other approach to the text of the New Testament.*

————, ed. *True or False?* Kregel, 1973.

————, ed. *Which Bible?* 5th ed. Kregel, 1975 (1st ed. 1970).

Ginsburg, Christian David. *Introduction to the Massoretico-Critical Edition of the Hebrew Bible.* 2nd ed. KTAV, reprint of the 1896 edition, 1966. *This is the classic introduction to the Hebrew text as preserved in the Masoretic tradition. The KTAV reprint has a 45-page Prolegomenon by Harry M. Orlinsky.*

Greenlee, J. Harold. *Introduction to New Testament Textual Criticism.* Eerdmans, 1964. *A standard introductory textbook.*

————. *Scribes, Scrolls, and Scripture.* Eerdmans, 1985. *This recent title is the best available primer on New Testament textual criticism for students and general readers. The author is especially sensitive to those who fear textual criticism as destructive rather than constructive.*

Harrop, Clayton. *History of the New Testament in Plain Language.* Word, 1984. *The first five chapters of this book present for general readers the eclectic approach to textual criticism.*

Klein, Ralph W. *Textual Criticism of the Old Testament.* Fortress, 1974. *This primer emphasizes the role of the Septuagint in Old Testament textual criticism.*

Metzger, Bruce Manning. *The Text of the New Testament.* 2nd ed. Oxford, 1968 (1st ed. 1964). *This book, presenting the standard text, is well written and thoroughly documented.*

Pickering, Wilbur N. *The Identity of the New Testament Text.* 2nd ed. Nelson, 1980 (1st ed. 1977). *This work is the most thorough modern defense of the supremacy of the Byzantine or Majority text.*

Sturz, Harry A. *The Byzantine Text-Type & New Testament Textual Criticism.* Nelson, 1984. *The author argues that the Byzantine or Majority text-type should be given more regard as a valid, ancient text-type than most scholars have given it for the past century.*

Weingreen, Jacob. *Introduction to the Critical Study of the Text of the Hebrew Bible.* Oxford, 1982. *This is a well-written student's introduction to the practice of Old Testament textual criticism.*

Wurthwein, Ernst. *The Text of the Old Testament.* 2nd ed. Translated by Erroll F. Rhodes. Eerdmans, 1979 (1st ed. 1957). *This basic introduction to Old Testament textual criticism is also a specific introduction to the standard critical Hebrew text, the Biblia Hebraica Stuttgartensia.*

III. Special Guides to Specific Textual Problems

In addition to the following, "critical" commentaries (see *Books About the Book,* chapter 11) usually deal with major textual difficulties on a verse-by-verse basis.

Barthelemy, Dominique, et al. *Preliminary and Interim Report on the Hebrew Old Testament Text Project.* 5 vols. United Bible Societies, 1973–80. *A verse-by-verse treatment of the major textual and translational difficulties of the Hebrew text. It is very valuable for translation and exegesis.*

Metzger, Bruce Manning. *A Textual Commentary on the Greek New Testament.* United Bible Societies, 1971. *This is a verse-by-verse treatment of the major textual difficulties of the New Testament, based on the 3rd edition (1975) of the United Bible Societies' Greek text, for which Metzger was one of five editors.*

IV. Four Greek Testaments

For those who read Greek or are studying to read it, the following are Greek Testaments they will want to consult:

The Greek New Testament of the United Bible Societies (3rd ed., 1975) and Nestle-Aland's *Novum Testamentum Graece* of the Deutsche Bibelstiftung Stuttgart (26th ed., 1979). *These are the standard critical Greek Testaments, practically identical in text but with very different listings of textual variants. These texts, or texts similar to them, underlie most modern translations of the New Testament.*

Greek New Testament (Textus Receptus). This is a reprint of the second edition of the Elzevir text of 1633, which coined the term Textus Receptus. It is available from the Trinitarian Bible Society, 217 Kingston Road, London, SW19 3NN, England or 39 Caldwell Crescent, Brampton, Ontario, Canada, L6W 1A2.

Hodges, Zane C., and Arthur L. Farstad. *The Greek New Testament According to the Majority Text.* 2nd ed. Nelson, 1985 (1st ed. 1982). *This is the first attempt to create a one-volume critical Majority Text. Two lists of variants show differences from the TR and from the critical texts listed above. It is not actually a collation of Byzantine texts themselves, but of other critical texts.*

Chapter 3

WHAT MAKES A TRANSLATION GOOD? FACTS AND FALLACIES ABOUT THE NATURE OF BIBLE TRANSLATION

In the previous chapters on canon and text, I said that for most readers the question "Which Bible?" meant "Which Bible *translation*?" In the next two chapters we will begin to tackle that question.

A century ago—even *half* a century ago—these chapters would not have been necessary. The Authorized or King James Version (KJV) had reigned supreme for three centuries and was the only real choice for Protestants. The standard Catholic version was the Douay-Rheims translation of the Latin Vulgate. For Jewish readers there was the Holy Scriptures According to the Masoretic Text. True, there were other English versions at this time, many of which are still in print, but nothing seriously threatened these standards until the appearance of the Revised Standard Version (RSV) New Testament in 1946. With the publication of the RSV Old Testament in 1952, the question "Which Bible?" was truly born. And with each passing year the number of possible answers has increased.

It is not simply because of numbers, however, that the answer to "Which Bible?" is complex. It is complex because different Bibles were produced for different readers and for different purposes and many factors must be considered when choosing among them. But it is also *made* complex by individuals who favor one Bible over another for theological reasons and by publishers who promote one version over another at least partly for economic reasons.

The realm of Bible translation is filled with "experts," loaded with opinion, choked with rhetoric, confused by misused terminology and short on objective information. For every translation available, there is someone somewhere who will tell you it is the best of all possible versions! Those with a theological investment in a given translation can make the choice a matter of faith and fellowship. And those with an economic investment in a given translation can help muddy the waters with half-truths and overstatement.

Most of the realities of this complex tangle of confusion fall under three major headings: (1) So Many Versions, (2) So Much Opinion, and (3) So Many Shapes and Sizes. We can discuss the many versions and shapes and sizes of the Bible rather objectively. However, opinion is opinion. I may be able to list opinions objectively, but of course my own opinion will become clear as I discuss them more fully. Unless you simply want to accept someone else's opinion secondhand, you must do a bit of research and evaluation in order to come to your own conclusions about Bible translations.

We will look at the many versions—and the much opinion about them—in two phases. This chapter will discuss translation theory, asking and answering the question "What makes a translation good?" The next will describe in brief the top ten translations of the Bible and survey about forty others, some of which are only New or only Old Testaments. We will conclude chapter 4 with an outline of the process by which you can decide which good Bible is the best for you.

The discussion on the many shapes and sizes of the Bible will be reserved for chapters 5 and 6. There I will define and discuss the many features that can be found in study Bibles and the many sizes and styles of bindings in which they are available. These chapters will also conclude with outlines of how to select the exact Bible product that is best suited for each person's own purpose and desires.

WHICH BIBLE IS BEST?

No translation is perfect. Neither is any absolutely imperfect. Most are good. The problem is deciding which is best.

But the question "Which Bible is best?" must be answered initially with another question, "Best for whom?" This is because most modern versions were created with a specific purpose and a specific audience in mind. Contrary to some opinion, most new translations are not created to push a specific

55

theological system or simply to make a buck. Rather, new translations are necessary to update translation language to contemporary idiom, to make use of the results of continuing biblical scholarship, and to reach to a specific age, special interest, or special needs group.

The Need for New Translations

New translations are necessary because language is always changing. In the first printed English New Testament, William Tyndale's translation of 1526, John 6:63 reads:

> It is the sprete that quyckeneth, the flesshe proffeteth nothinge. The wordes that I speake unto you, are spret and lyfe.

The KJV of 1611 needed only to update the spelling:

> It is the Spirit that quickeneth, the flesh profiteth nothing: the wordes that I speake vnto you, they are Spirit, and they are life.

By 1881 the Revised Version had to redefine "quickeneth":

> It is the spirit that giveth life; the flesh profiteth nothing: the words that I have spoken unto you are spirit, and are life.

But it took the RSV of 1946 to update the verbal inflections and create a translation that still speaks clearly to the contemporary reader:

> It is the spirit that gives life, the flesh is of no avail; the words that I have spoken to you are spirit and life.

Translations must change as language changes. This means that one aspect of the answer to "Which Bible is best?" is that it must be written in the language of its user. It also means that no translation of the Bible can serve the church indefinitely, regardless of its quality. After all, only the Greek Orthodox continue to use the LXX as their Old Testament, though it was the Bible of the early church!

New translations are also necessary because of *biblical languages.* Although the biblical languages do not change, our understanding of them does. We have already seen (in chapter 2) how our knowledge of ancient texts and versions has grown immensely with the hundreds of discoveries and continuing scholarship of the preceding four centuries. The same is true of "lexicography," the study of the meaning of words.

More than 1,530 of the 5,436 different words in the Greek New Testament occur only once. You can imagine how difficult it is to come up with an exact definition for these, many of which are also unknown in Greek classical literature! The Old Testament has a larger vocabulary, more rare words, and fewer ancient resources with which to compare. Any major discovery rates a journal article; several such discoveries can demand a revised translation.

Take, for example, the Hebrew word רְאֵם, nine times rendered "unicorn" in the KJV. The KJV translators simply followed the definitions of the Greek LXX (μονοκερως, "one-horned") and the Latin Vulgate (unicornis, "one-horned") in identifying this animal. Whether or not the translators actually believed in this mythical beast, because of their limited lexical resources they have made (for some) a belief in the existence of the unicorn an issue in the matter of biblical inerrancy! Later discoveries have turned up in the Akkadian and Ugaritic languages related words that clearly mean "wild ox," as all modern versions—including the NKJV—have it.

The first translators of the English Bible simply wanted to get the Hebrew and Greek (or Latin) into common English. William Tyndale, in a debate with a "learned man" over the necessity for both clergy and laity to have access to the Bible in the vernacular, said, "If God spare my life, ere many years I will cause that a boy that driveth the plough shall know more of the Scripture than thou dost."[1] In the religious turbulence of the sixteenth and seventeenth centuries, getting any translation of the Bible into print—and staying alive in the process—was a major undertaking.

Contemporary translators, on the other hand, have the time and opportunity to prepare versions not only for common use, but also for children and others of limited vocabulary, for those who demand a word-for-word rendering, and for those who appreciate the elegance of a very literary translation. So a third aspect of the need for new translations involves the specific needs and/or desires of the reader.

Many people, if not most, look at the incredible contemporary proliferation of Bible versions and exclaim with Richard

Bancroft, "If every man's humour were followed, there would be no end of translating."[2] Fortunately for the English-speaking church, his statement was ignored. For Bancroft was attempting to dissuade James I of England from hearing a proposal to give royal sanction to a new translation of the Bible that would serve the church better than the dozen or so that had appeared in the previous century. If King James had listened to Bancroft, the Geneva Bible would have remained the Authorized Version. However, he did listen to the Puritan proposal, and the rest is history.

It is true that many of the hundreds of English translations that have appeared throughout the past five centuries have merely represented a certain individual's "humour." But these idiosyncratic versions have usually perished as quickly as they sprang up. The translators were not wrong, however, to offer them to the church. The fact that there are many versions currently in print after twenty, thirty, forty, or even a hundred years demonstrates that translations done since the KJV have met a concrete need and have been acceptable to a large segment of the church. This, combined with the noticeable annual decline in sales of the KJV (see chart 5), shows that readers are looking elsewhere for their English Bible.

Whether or not there will ever be another "Authorized Version" is unclear. (Actually, the KJV was only one of several licensed and authorized versions; interestingly, there is no documentary evidence for *its* authorization!)[3] What is clear, however, is that readers and students of the Bible need to know how to evaluate the current options in order to choose the version—or versions—best suited to their needs and desires. That is our next topic of discussion.

What Makes a Translation Good?

For a translation to be "good" it must meet at least two criteria. First, it must be *accurate*, because it is purporting to represent the Word of God. Second, it must be *readable*, because it must be understood.

I doubt if anyone would argue my first criterion. But many—pastors, teachers, and laypeople alike—hedge when it comes to the second. Because English versions from Wycliffe to the present day have often reflected the word order and idiom of

Hebrew and Greek, a lot of people expect their Bible to read with an accent. For them, a version that reads in normal English cannot be a Bible, any more than one can address God by the pronoun "you" instead of "Thee" in prayer. They consider readability a concession and consider that idiomatic renderings are too interpretive and affect a translation's accuracy.

I strongly disagree with this evaluation. In the first place, it is impossible to make an intelligible word-for-word translation from Greek or Hebrew into English in every case. Just read any page of an interlinear translation and you will see what I mean! So even the most "literal" translations make "concessions" to English idiom. Second, the less a translation reads like normal English, the greater potential it has for misunderstanding and misinterpretation. In other words, the English may seem an accurate representation of the Greek or Hebrew to some, but the English is not an accurate representation of English to most people!

There is a place for a word-for-word translation. But it is not for the tens of millions who just want to read and understand the Bible, nor for the hundreds of millions who have never read the Bible and who probably won't if it is not in a readily understandable idiom. On the other hand, the desire for readable translations is clear from the amazing success of the Living Bible and Today's English Version, easy-reading versions that have sold tens of millions of copies internationally.

READABILITY

Readability is, of course, subject to the reader. Many factors can determine the reader's needs. One that springs to mind immediately is *age*. Formerly a "Children's Bible" was a KJV with color pictures on and between the covers. But now there are true children's versions available, versions that use a limited vocabulary and larger print. Another facet of the age factor is that older Bible readers, raised on and familiar with the Elizabethan English of the KJV, may prefer to stick with the KJV or a newer version that uses a more traditional ecclesiastical vocabulary and style.

Education, or lack of it, also figures prominently in readability. Education usually gives one a larger vocabulary and the ability to handle longer and more complex sentences. And those whose education has included a study of the biblical languages often appreciate word-for-word translations because they have an appreciation for the syntax of Greek and Hebrew.

Another aspect of education is the degree of *literacy* a person may achieve. Those more educated often have a greater appreciation of literature and prefer a more elegant literary translation. The Bible is, after all, a collection of books, each with some uniqueness in vocabulary, style, and literary form.

Another factor related to readability is the *purpose* for which the version is used. Many people use a "literal" translation for detailed study and analysis but prefer to read through books and chapters in an idiomatic rendering. Those who choose a Bible for public reading, must consider the needs of the congregation. Here, conformity is the key, though a young pastor of an established church may wish to introduce the congregation gradually to the modern version he prefers for study.

Readability, as I said earlier, is subject to the reader. However, two recent studies attempted to analyze readability objectively. In the 1970s, Dwight Chappell prepared a battery of language comprehension tests for the purpose of determining which of the versions most popular among evangelicals communicated best to school children in the middle grades. The New International Version (NIV) proved consistently and dramatically more readable than the New American Standard Bible (NASB) and the updated KJV of the New Scofield Reference Bible. The findings were confirmed when the same tests were given to high school students.[4]

The second study was undertaken in 1978 by Drs. Linda H. Parrish and Donna Norton of the Education Department at Texas A & M University. At the request of the World Bible Translation Center in Arlington, Texas, these researchers applied the Fog Readability Index to thirty-six passages of the most popular translations of the New Testament then available, in order to determine the reading grade level of the text. The results were as shown in chart 3, on the following page.

The Fog Index deals with sentence structure and multisyllabic words. Had it also dealt with archaic verbal inflection and vocabulary, the more readable versions would have been even further separated from the less readable.

Although not an absolute indicator, this study does place most popular modern versions in useful relative positions. No one should be surprised that the ICB was the most readable; that was its specific design. However, many are surprised that the NIV is so close to the TEV and that the LB is *less* readable than both. Actually, the major stylistic difference between the NIV and the TEV is in vocabulary. The TEV eliminates most "ecclesiastical" words, substituting, for example, "boat" for "ark" in Genesis 6–8. In sentence structure and syntax, the NIV and TEV are often very similar.

Chart 3
READABILITY LEVELS OF MAJOR VERSIONS OF THE NT[5]

VERSION	GRADE LEVEL
International Children's Bible (ICB)	3.9
Today's English Version (TEV)	7.3
New International Version (NIV)	7.8
Living Bible (LB)	8.3
New English Bible (NEB)	8.5
New King James Version (NKJV)	9.1
Phillips (PNT)	9.6
Jerusalem Bible (JB)	10.1
Revised Standard Version (RSV)	10.4
New American Standard Version (NAS)	11.3
American Standard Version (ASV)	11.6
King James Version (KJV)	14.0

The LB is clearly the best selling and most popular of the easy-reading versions. But most people find it easy to read, not because of its English, as indicated above, but because of its explanations. A paraphrase, the LB rephrases the ASV into more understandable English. But in the process of restatement, a great deal of commentary enters the text. This commentary all but eliminates difficult passages and obscure idioms. Because its concepts are therefore easier to understand, the LB gives the impression that it is easier reading than the versions that actually use a simpler English style and vocabulary. Publishers promote their Bibles, but the reader is the final judge of the readability of a version.

ACCURACY

Most readers are at the mercy of the "experts," however, when it comes to the accuracy of a given translation, for being an expert on translation assumes a knowledge of the original languages and of English, of linguistics and translation theory, and of textual criticism. Few Bible readers can claim such expertise. Also, unfortunately, few of the so-called experts can do so.

Most Bible colleges and seminaries offer only two or three years of courses on biblical languages. Their curricula usually cover basic grammar and limit translation to a few books or portions of each Testament. Most teach only reading, rather than composition. Few teach linguistics. Even seminary graduates who have concentrated on biblical languages have not taken as many courses or translated as much literature as would be required for a bachelor's degree in any liberal arts college. And no one in educational or academic circles would consider a bachelor's degree an indication of expertise.

As a result, most of the pastors, teachers, and other Christian leaders who speak or write to commend or to criticize modern versions do so more from a theological perspective than a linguistic one. There is nothing wrong with this, as far as it goes. But few qualify their criticisms with such statements as "I disagree with the theological implications of that word choice," or "This rendering could imply . . . ." We more commonly hear of "mistakes" and "errors," of "bad," "misleading," and "deliberately deceptive" translations as opposed to the "literal meaning" of the word or text.

Even those who know no other language than English can understand a few of the linguistic issues involved in translation. Although this is a superficial survey, I believe we will still see some important things about language, specifically word order and word meanings, that will help us see through some of the popular misconceptions and miscommunication about modern versions of the Bible. My purpose is not to eliminate any versions from consideration but to make people aware of the value of more versions than they may have considered valuable in the past.

LITERAL VERSUS PARAPHRASE

So far in this chapter I have used the word *literal* three times, and each time have enclosed it in quotation marks. That is because I dislike the way it is normally used in discussing translations and its implications in the discussion. "Literal" is usually used to describe "word-for-word" translations and usually implies accuracy. On the other hand, "paraphrase" is used to describe a "free" or "idiomatic" translation and often implies that the accuracy of the rendering is suspect.

Technically, neither word is used correctly. The word *paraphrase* technically means a restatement in the same language, a saying of the same thing in other words. Of all the major versions on the market, the LB is the only paraphrase and is so labeled. The problem with the word *literal* is not so much its definition as its implications. It implies exactness and correctness; it is the opposite of figurative or speculative. But labeling a translation "literal" simply because it follows the word order of the original is implying too much about its accuracy. A "literal" translation style does not guarantee a literal meaning.

Think about the concept of the "literal meaning" of a word. What, for example, is the literal meaning of the word *trunk*. Depending on whether the subject is an elephant or a car, the "literal" meaning will be radically different. For "trunk' can literally be the front end of an elephant, the back end of a car, the bottom of a tree, the middle of a person, or the entirety of a large suitcase! And "trunks" can be more than one of the above, or what you wear to cover your trunk when you go jogging. Biblical words are no different; they have no "literal" meaning apart from a specific context.

It is the same with word order. Anyone who speaks more than one language knows that to communicate in a second language one needs to know not only a different vocabulary, but a different syntax as well. A simple German sentence like *"Ich liebe dich"* translates well into English as "I love you." But the sentence *"Ich habe dich gern"* translated "literally" as "I have you willingly" misses the literal meaning "I like you." Again, a "literal" translation style does not guarantee a literal *meaning.*

A linguist prefers the term "formal equivalence" (F-E) to "literal" to describe the style of translation that mimics the form of the original language. And a linguist uses the term "dynamic equivalence" (D-E) instead of "paraphrase" to describe a free or idiomatic translation. (As used by linguists, "dynamic" means that the form of the receptor language—the language one is translating into—is flexible, dynamic. It does not mimic the form of the original.)

Regardless of the terminology, the big issue remains: Does *form* determine *accuracy*? Or in other words, can an idiomatic (D-E) translation be accurate or does accuracy (and a conservative view of inspiration) demand a word-for-word rendering (F-E)?

FORMAL EQUIVALENCE VERSUS DYNAMIC EQUIVALENCE: WORD CHOICE AND INTERPRETATION

Sometimes the form of the language does not create a problem in translation. John 1:17, for example, can be translated word-for-word (though not in the same word order) as it was in the 1611 edition of the KJV:

> For the Law was giuen by Moses, but grace and trueth came
> by Iesus Christ.

Four centuries later, the NIV is almost identical:

> For the law was given through Moses; grace and truth came
> through Jesus Christ.

Notice that I said *almost* identical. Although these are basically word-for-word translations, the KJV adds a single word that imposes a specific interpretation on the text. By inserting "but" between the clauses, where there is no conjunction in the Greek, it forces the reader to think of the verse as making a contrast between "Law" and "grace and trueth." The NIV more closely follows the Greek by using a semicolon instead of a conjunction and lets the reader decide if the verse speaks of a contrast or a continuity. In this case, the NIV is even more "literal" than the KJV![6]

Interpretation is more clearly seen when the form of the English differs greatly between two versions, thus implying that at least one of them differs from the form of the original. The TEV reads:

> God gave the Law through Moses, but grace and truth came
> through Jesus Christ.

The TEV presents two overt interpretations. The first, "but," follows the KJV. The second provides a subject, "*God* gave the Law" for the passive "the law *was* given" (italics mine). Although this reading is interpretive, I doubt if anyone would argue with the subject the TEV provides! Of course, it is only when we disagree with an interpretation that we complain about interpretation.

But even defining words is interpretation, so a word-for-word translation is not "beyond suspicion" or "untouched by human hands." The NASB has:

> For the Law was given through Moses; grace and truth were realized through Jesus Christ.

The NASB renders "came" as "were realized," which is a real puzzler. Were "grace and truth" not reality until Jesus came, or did no one realize what they were? I have no idea what the translators were getting at. In its previous occurrences in John 1 (vv. 3 [three times], 6, 10, 12, 14, 15), they translated the same Greek word as "came/come into being," "came/comes," "was made," and "become/became." This is the only place in the New Testament where they used the translation "realized." This variety of English terms, not all synonyms, within three paragraphs demonstrates that even a "literal" version like the NASB must use interpretation in its word choice.

But interpretation is necessary in word choice, because words have no meaning apart from contexts. As we saw above, the word *trunk* has no meaning until you know if it is used in relation to an elephant, a car, a tree, a person, or a suitcase. Bible words are no different. A dictionary or lexicon can list the *potential* meanings of the Greek, Hebrew. and Aramaic words of the Bible, but only when the word is used in a sentence is it possible to determine its *literal* meaning in that sentence. Therefore, it seems to me, "literal" should be used to describe the *meaning* of a translation, and not the *form* of a translation.

TRANSLATION LOSS AND TRANSLATION DISTORTION

Translators have to face also the problem of translation loss and translation distortion. As they wrestle with finding just the right words to render the biblical languages into English, they face a special struggle with words of deep theological significance or cultural nuances and with word forms that cannot be easily reproduced in English. Two major problems arise: translation loss and translation distortion. Both occur because no two languages use words in precisely the same way.

"Translation loss" occurs when a good deal of meaning must be left behind when words are matched with words.

Expanded translations, such as the Amplified Bible (AB) and Wuest's New Testament: An Expanded Translation, demonstrate attempts to recover this loss, but they make these attempts at the expense of readability. The AB renders John 1:17 in this way:

> For while the Law was given through Moses, grace—unearned, undeserved favor and spiritual blessing—and truth came through Jesus Christ.

Wuest reads:

> Because the law through the intermediate agency of Moses was given, the aforementioned grace and the truth came through Jesus Christ.

The AB amplifies the word "grace." Wuest amplifies "through," uses "the aforementioned" to explain the use of the Greek article, and more closely follows the word order of the original. But in attempting to deal with the loss of word meanings, the versions lose the simple style of the original. The dashes, parentheses, brackets, and synonym lists of the AB interrupt the flow of the text as does the verbose and unnatural language of Wuest. Translation loss is a regrettable reality that should probably be dealt with in commentaries and notes rather than in the text itself.[7]

"Translation distortion" occurs when too much meaning or improper connotations are imported into a word by the term chosen to translate it. For example, the word *dog* has a primarily positive connotation in our culture (unless one happens to be a jogger) as man's best friend, faithful companion, and guardian of the home. Some may read, "Outside are the dogs" (Rev. 22:15) and think, "Someone should let them in for some puppy chow!" But in the Bible, the dog is undesirable, unclean, and dangerous; the connotations of the word are always negative (e.g., Phil. 3:2). Although not of the same biological species, a canine like the jackal, hyena, or dingo might be a better choice to communicate this negative nuance in translation.

Again, even defining words involves interpretation. I mentioned a problem that I had with the NASB in John 1:17 (p. 65), to show that even a word-for-word rendering could be questioned. But because additional words and explanatory renderings are easier to spot, they are the ones more commonly singled out for criticism. And because the LB has the highest profile of such versions, it is the most readily available target for this negative criticism. In John 1:17, the LB reads:

> For Moses gave us only the Law with its rigid demands and merciless justice, while Jesus Christ brought us loving forgiveness as well.

We could be picky and criticize the appropriateness of using "while" as a conjunction, of combining "grace and truth" into "loving forgiveness," and of using "as well," which seems to imply that Jesus added "loving forgiveness" to the Law. But what really catches our attention is the astonishing modification of "the Law" by the phrase "with its rigid demands and merciless justice"! This phrase is not in the original, nor is it justified as restoring "translation loss," because it has nothing to do with the definition or connotations of the Greek or Hebrew words for law. It is a theological comment that comes from the background of the author and, in my judgment, would do much better in the notes than in the text.

In other words, although all translation involves interpretation, when that interpretation goes beyond the immediate meaning of the text, it becomes a commentary rather than simply a translation. No version is free from such commentary. However, the LB is characterized by its explanations. And, because it is labeled a paraphrase, "paraphrase" has unfortunately become synonymous with "commentary." And other idiomatic versions, improperly labeled paraphrases, have wrongly shared in its criticisms.

I must insert a comment at this point about the author of the LB, Kenneth N. Taylor. In criticizing some elements of the LB, I by no means want to criticize Dr. Taylor, his intentions, his ministry, or his work that has benefitted millions. I know of no Bible translator or Christian writer who has done more for the propagation of the Bible throughout the world than has Ken Taylor. Yet he has refused the wealth and celebrity status the success of the LB could have brought him. I have nothing but respect and admiration for Dr. Taylor and deplore the unfair personal attacks he has endured from those who dislike the LB. I feel I must criticize aspects of his version but will not tolerate criticisms of the man.

FORMAL EQUIVALENCE VERSUS DYNAMIC EQUIVALENCE: THE PROBLEM OF SYNTAX

No, "syntax" is not something new the government is planning to assess its citizens for! It has to do with word order, word forms, and sentence structure. F-E translation not only desires a one-to-one word correspondence, it also seeks to match word forms—participle to participle, adjective to adjective— and word order. As no two languages use words with exactly the same meanings and connotations, so no two languages structure their sentences in exactly the same way. (Remember the example in German on page 63?)

The problem, even the impossibility, of an absolutely F-E translation can be seen on almost any page of an interlinear translation. If we translated 2 Corinthians 10:13 into English with absolute formal equivalence, hyphenating words that require English helper words to indicate inflection, we would get this reading:

> We but not to to-the to-immeasurables we-will-boast but
> according-to to-the to-measure of-the of-rule which he-
> divided to-us the God in-measure to-reach as-far-as even to-
> you.

Even Marshall's well-known interlinear translation does not render this so pedantically! The above effort is good Greek, but poor English.

One of the major raps against the ASV is its slavish adherence to F-E style:

> But we will not glory beyond our measure, but according to
> the measure of the province which God apportioned to us as
> a measure, to reach even unto you.

Not much of an improvement on our interlinear! But despite such criticisms of the original ASV, the NASB followed its lead with the following translation:

> But we will not boast beyond our measure, but within the
> measure of the sphere which God apportioned to us as a
> measure, to reach even as far as you.

A few words have been changed, but neither version communicates clearly what the "measure of the province" or "sphere" is. (Of course, I have taken this sentence out of its context, but in my judgment this emphasizes the need for more understandable words and sentence structure.)

The italicized "our" points out another weakness of the strictly F-E translation. Ever since the Geneva Bible (1560), F-E versions have indicated with italics, words supplied for clarity that are not in the wording or word forms of the original. But every other piece of English literature uses italics for *emphasis*. Thus the vast majority of readers, churched and unchurched, will read, "We will not boast beyond *our* measure" as emphasizing the word "our," which is exactly the opposite of what the translators intended!

But as Ronald Knox, the renowned Catholic translator, expressed it, "The business of a translator is not to ask, 'How do I make this foreigner talk English?' but 'What would an Englishman have said to express this?' "[8] This is the essential difference between formal translation and dynamic-equivalent translation.

D-E translations such as the NIV and TEV can alter the syntax, omit redundant words and phrases unnecessary in English, and even repeat words for clarity, and all without italics. The result is a verse intelligible even in isolation from the context:

> We, however, will not boast beyond proper limits, but will confine our boasting to the field God has assigned to us, a field that reaches even to you (NIV).

> As for us, however, our boasting will not go beyond certain limits; it will stay within the limits of the work which God has set for us, and this includes our work among you (TEV).

By choosing to speak of the "limits of a field" or "work" instead of "measure of a province" or "sphere," these versions begin to communicate that Paul was defending his boasting about his ministry, but was limiting his boasting to the people in the territory that God had specifically given to him. So by word choice and sentence structure, these fluid renditions of the Greek not only read more easily, but also communicate more clearly.

FORMAL EQUIVALENCE VERSUS DYNAMIC EQUIVALENCE: THE PROBLEM OF IDIOMS

Idioms are those delightful, colorful, and unique expressions that add charm to regional dialects and can express the perceptions and values, the heart and soul of a people. All languages have in common the use of idioms, but no two languages share their idioms consistently. Idioms translated word-for-word usually will not communicate.

For example, someone could paraphrase "He was bent on seeing her" as "The sight of her doubled him over." But understanding "bent" idiomatically as "inclination" or "desire" would give a rather different picture. Ronald Knox is worth quoting here at length. In discussing a Portuguese-English phrase-book entitled *English as She Is Spoke*, he observes:

> You do not need much critical insight to detect the fact that this well-meaning gentleman knew no English at all. He knew French; so he translated his sentences into French and then did them into English with a dictionary. Consequently, when he wanted to render a Portuguese idiom which meant, 'to wait about, to kick one's heels', he could do all right for the first part of his process; he knew that the corresponding idiom in French was 'croquer le marmot'—I have no notion why. The English, therefore, for kicking one's heels was 'to crunch the marmoset'. It is an extremely entertaining book; but, if you come to think of it, practically every translation of the Bible you have ever read makes errors which are quite as ludicrous—only we are accustomed to them.[9]

The "ludicrous errors" to which Knox refers are not the use of a too-idiomatic English. This is one of the flaws of the New English Bible, which presents the first line of Proverbs 19:19 as "There is a rod in pickle for the arrogant." It is not until you get to the parallel line "and blows ready for the stupid man's back" that you can understand what "in pickle" means. Rather, Knox refers to the word-for-word rendering of Hebrew and Greek idioms into English.

Think for a moment about the "horn of salvation." What is it? Is it something you blow on when you come forward to repent? More realistically, is it related to the horns of the altar, where propitiatory sacrifice was offered? Or does it picture the horns of a powerful beast as a symbol of strength?

We so often hear such idioms, that by now they have lost the strangeness they had when we first encountered them. But that does not mean that we understand their meaning. Try explaining what it means to "call upon the name of the Lord." And if you think you can, then explain how the Lord can call upon the name of the Lord in Exodus 34:5!

The examples I have cited demonstrate a vagueness or loss of communication when Hebrew or Greek idioms are slavishly rendered into English. However, sometimes these idioms can actually miscommunicate. Such an example, which also illustrates the earthiness of Hebrew idiom, is the KJV's rendition of 1 Kings 21:21:

> Behold, I will bring evil upon thee, and will take away thy posterity, and will cut off from Ahab *him that pisseth against the wall,* and him that is shut up and left in Israel (italics mine).

Although the italicized phrase is a good word-for-word translation of a common Hebrew idiom for "male," it is certainly not a common English idiom and is not even suitable for public reading! And if we did use this phrase to describe someone, it would probably conjure up the picture of a specific kind of male, a vagrant or drunkard, hardly the image of princes and kings that this passage has in mind.

CONCLUSION: ACCURACY DOES NOT DEPEND ON FORM

By looking at a few examples of translation related to word meaning, word order, and idioms, we have seen that a "literal" translation style does not guarantee a literal meaning. In other words, *accuracy does not depend on form.* Those who have been raised on an F-E translation or who have had a smattering of biblical language training might feel uncomfortable with a D-E version. But consider this: if interpretative skills are necessary to find good English words to translate the originals, why not apply the same skills to cast those words into good English sentences!

I especially hope that pastors, teachers, and other leaders will take the time to think through the implications of using the words "literal" and "paraphrase" to describe the translation style of an English version. Instead of calling a word-for-word translation "literal" or even "formal equivalent," simply say it more closely follows the Hebrew or Greek word order. And I hope you will recognize that a "literal" translation is much more helpful to someone who knows a bit about the original languages than to the other 99 percent of the church! And instead of calling a dynamic equivalent version a "paraphrase," call its translation style "idiomatic," "free," or "fluid." Obviously, you can still criticize or commend the accuracy of a version, but do it by explanation rather than by implication.

I also hope you will agree that in principle the TEV has every bit as much potential to be accurate as does the ASV. Eugene Nida, translations secretary of the American Bible Society and a leading authority on linguistics and Bible translation, would go further than that:

> In practice, F-E translations tend to distort the message more than D-E translations, since those persons who produce D-E translations are in general more adept in translating, and in order to produce D-E renderings they must perceive more fully and satisfactorily the meaning of the original text. For the most part a translator who produces D-E renderings is quite aware of the degree of distortion, and because of greater conscious control of his work is able to judge more satisfactorily whether or not the results seem to be legitimate. On the other hand, a translator who produces strictly F-E renderings is usually not conscious of the extent to which his seemingly "faithful" translations actually involve serious distortions.[10]

Translation and Theology

Some object to translating the Bible with the same principles that linguists use for contemporary languages and secular literature. They argue that if indeed God inspired the Bible, then each word is as he wants it and we should not presume to dabble with those words. I feel this argument, well intentioned as it is, is faulty on two points.

First, this understanding of verbal inspiration assumes that words have meanings in and of themselves. As we saw in the case of *trunk* (p. 63), this is not so. A quick survey of any page of the Greek-English or Hebrew-English indexes to Strong's or Young's well-known concordances will show that even the KJV uses a wealth of English terms to translate most words.

Many know that the famous Greek word ἀγάπη (agapē) is translated not only as "love" but also as "charity" in 1 Corinthians 13. The KJV also renders it "feast of charity" and "dear." Many words are translated more than a dozen different ways; ποιέω is translated thirty-nine ways by itself and another eighteen in combination with other words. Does this imply the KJV denies verbal inspiration? Of course not!

Second, in concentrating on the words God inspired, this view misses the significance of the *meaning* those words convey. As in the case of the text (see p. 48), the way the New Testament writers quote the Old Testament shows that they were concerned with communicating the message of the Old Testament and not simply reproducing its words.

Matthew 27:46 quotes Jesus' words on the cross (from Ps. 22:1) in Hebrew while Mark 15:34 quotes them in Aramaic, and their Greek translations are not identical in word or form. Paul quotes Psalm 8:6 in 1 Corinthians 15:27, but changes the subject from "you" to "he." Paul drastically alters 2 Samuel 7:14 in 2 Corinthians 6:18, even adding the phrase "and daughters" to include his female readers in his application! But in all of these cases, and dozens of others that we could cite, though words and forms are altered, the meaning is preserved—or even made more clear than a word-for-word rendering could be.

I believe in verbal inspiration, but I do not believe a word-for-word translation best honors that view of Scripture. Where the form of the originals is similar to the form of English, as in John 1:17 (see p. 64), an F-E translation is fine. But where the form differs, as in 2 Corinthians 10:13 (see p. 68), an F-E translation can bring the words over but hold the message back.

Arguments about form aside, many people criticize modern versions for what they perceive to be unorthodox theological tendencies. Some go so far as to say that *all* versions other than the KJV are the work of the devil.

No version has caught more theological flak than the RSV. And the text its critics most often turn to to prove its "fiendish and perverse" tendencies is Isaiah 7:14:

> Therefore the Lord himself will give you a sign. Behold, a young woman shall conceive and bear a son, and shall call his name Immanuel.

The obvious objection is to the phrase "young woman," for which the KJV has "virgin." Many are convinced that this rendering is specifically intended to deny the virgin birth and deity of Christ. But if we wanted to be absolutely certain that the RSV translators wanted to deny this crucial doctrine, we should check to see how they handled the Gospels. Matthew 1:23 reads:

"Behold, a virgin shall conceive and bear a son,
and his name shall be called Emmanuel"
(which means, God with us).

Why did they translate "young woman" in Isaiah 7:14?
Because they *could*—there is another Hebrew word more often
used for "virgin." Why did they translate "virgin" in Matthew
1:23? Because they *had to*—that is the only meaning of that
Greek word in New Testament times. The RSV translators chose
what they thought to be the best rendering in each context. And
many conservative scholars agree with their choices. It is clear
from Matthew 1:23 (and 1:18, 20, 25 and Luke 1:27, 34–35) that
the RSV does not obscure the virgin birth of Christ.

If we really *want* to, we can find texts in the KJV that "deny"
the deity of Christ. Compare Titus 2:13 in the KJV and RSV:

Looking for that blessed hope, and the glorious appearing of
the great God and our Saviour Jesus Christ (KJV).

Awaiting our blessed hope, the appearing of the glory of our
great God and Savior Jesus Christ (RSV).

The RSV calls Jesus "our great God and Savior," whereas the KJV
calls him only "our Saviour" and makes him distinct from "the
great God." Does this mean the KJV teaches Jesus is a lesser God
or no God at all? Of course it doesn't! But if the renderings were
reversed, I am certain someone would accuse the RSV of
intending to teach that very error!

Most modern versions render Titus 2:13 as does the RSV
because of the increase in understanding of Greek syntax in the
centuries since the translation of the KJV. In fact, if we compared
all the verses of the New Testament that can be translated in
such a way that they directly call Jesus "God," we would find
that the KJV missed half of them!

As you can see from chart 4 on the following page, the ten
most popular modern translations of the Bible *all* have more
verses that call Jesus "God" than the KJV has. Only the NWT
consistently refuses to do so.[11] And that *is* a clear case of a
version denying the deity of Christ, because the NWT is the New
World Translation of the Jehovah's Witnesses!

Translations do evidence the theological convictions of
their translators. Once in a while, we notice an occasional word
or phrase that catches our eye. The NEB, for example, begins

Genesis 11:1 with "Once upon a time . . . ," which can only mean the translators intended to convey that this story is a fairy tale! No version is free of theological bias, the KJV included.[12]

Chart 4
VERSIONS THAT IDENTIFY JESUS AS "GOD"[13]
(NO* = The margin offers an alternate translation that = YES)

	John 1:1	John 1:18	John 20:28	Romans 9:5	2 Thes. 1:12	Titus 2:13	Hebrews 1:8	2 Peter 1:1
KJV	YES	NO	YES	YES	NO	NO	YES	NO
ASV	YES	NO*	YES	YES	NO	NO*	YES	NO*
AB	YES	YES	YES	YES	NO	YES	YES	YES
JB/NJB	YES	NO*	YES	YES	NO	YES	YES	YES
LB	YES	NO	YES	NO	NO	YES	YES	YES
NAB	YES	YES	YES	NO	NO	NO	YES	YES
NAS	YES	YES	YES	YES	NO	YES	YES	YES
NEB	YES	NO*	YES	NO*	NO	YES	YES	YES
NIV	YES	YES	YES	YES	NO*	YES	YES	YES
NKJV	YES	NO	YES	YES	NO	YES	YES	YES
RSV	YES	NO*	YES	NO*	NO	YES	YES	YES
TEV	YES	YES	YES	NO	NO*	YES	YES	YES
NWT	NO	NO	YES	NO	NO	NO	NO	NO

But, with the exception of the NWT, no major modern translations were created specifically to promote a particular system of theology. All were intended to serve the whole church.

On the KJV as the Model Translation

Throughout this chapter and the one preceding, the KJV has been considered the point of departure in the discussion, the standard against which all modern versions of the Bible are compared. This was obvious and necessary because the KJV has been appreciated by the English-speaking church as the best version of the Bible ever produced. But because of four centuries of change in the English language and biblical scholarship, its time has run out.

Although a monument to the scholarship of its day, the KJV is out of date academically. We noted in chapter 2 that most scholars feel the text that underlies the KJV New Testament is inferior to that which has been assembled from the hundreds of ancient manuscripts discovered since 1611. We saw on page 57 that continuing scholarship has shown many of the word choices of the KJV to be incorrect.

Although it is a model of elegance and rhythm of Elizabethan English, the KJV is out of date idiomatically. As we saw in the chart on page 61, the KJV is measurably less readable than any other version on the market. Its pronouns and verbal inflections are no longer used. Hundreds of its words have dropped out of use. Many have dramatically changed their meanings. Take, for example, 1 Thessalonians 4:15 and 2 Thessalonians 2:7:

> For this we say unto you by the word of the Lord, that we which are alive *and* remain unto the coming of the Lord shall not prevent them which are asleep.

> For the mystery of iniquity doth already work: only he who now letteth *will let,* until he be taken out of the way.

"Prevent" in contemporary English means to stop, but in the KJV it meant to go before or precede. Similarly, "let" now means to allow, but in the KJV meant *not* to allow—that is, to hold back. Most people, even those raised on the KJV, would get exactly the opposite meaning from these verses that the original languages—and the translators of the KJV—intended.

Still, many defend the KJV as inspired, as God-given, and as the only accurate translation of the Bible available. Remarkable as it may seem, the translators of the KJV would not agree with this estimation of their work! The original preface to the KJV, "The Translators to the Reader," is no longer printed with the Bible. However, Nelson recently issued a facsimile of the 1611 printing of the KJV which has this valuable essay. Listen to what the translators say about Bible translation in general and about the KJV in particular:

> Wee doe not deny, nay wee affirme and auow, that the very meanest translation of the Bible in English . . . containeth the word of God, nay, is the word of God.

How do you think the translators would respond to the contention that the KJV alone is the Word of God in English?

Concerning alternate translations of difficult words and phrases, which they placed in the margin, they wrote:

> Now in such a case, doth not a margine do well to admonish the Reader to seeke further, and not to conclude or dogmatize vpon this or that peremptorily? For as it is a fault of incredulitie, to doubt of those things that are euident: so to determine of such things as the Spirit of God hath left (euen

in the iudgment of the iudicious) questionable, can be no lesse then presumption. Therfore as *S. Augustine* saith, that varietie of Translations is profitable for finding out the sense of the Scriptures.

The translators admit the limits of their scholarship and the value of other resources, especially other translations, to aid the reader in understanding the Scriptures. They would never have condoned the use of just one version, theirs included, and would have welcomed the results of continuing biblical scholarship.

Concerning translation style, they noted:

Wee haue not tyed our selues to an vniformitie of phrasing, or to an identitie of words, as some peraduenture would wish that we had done, because they obserue, that some learned men some where, haue beene as exact as they could that way. . . . Thus to minse the matter, wee thought to sauour more of curiositie then wisedome, and that rather it would breed scorne in the Athiest, then bring profite to the godly Reader. For is the kingdome of God become words or syllables?

Here the translators explain what we already noted, that they were not tied to a "literal" translation for each word, a concept they felt would breed scorn in the atheist rather than bring profit to the godly reader. In so many words, the KJV translators say they produced a D-E translation using many texts and versions as guides and appreciated the use of other versions for study!

Of all the versions on the market, the one that best incorporates the translators' description of the style and resources of the KJV is the NIV. And, although no one is calling it the new Authorized Version, sales in the United States would indicate that as the KJV declines in popularity, the NIV is making the greatest gains (see chart 5, p. 81). The NIV, though not perfect, is the most widely accepted modern version in the United States and internationally. Although I do not like such renderings as "sinful nature" and "sinful man" in Romans 8:3 and "he made himself nothing" in Philippians 2:7, I know of no better all-around version.

No one version satisfies everyone; that is why new versions keep coming out. That is also why we will continue in the next chapter with a survey of the top ten modern translations and several special interest versions and with an outline of how to choose the version—or versions—that will best meet your needs.

SUMMARY

In order for a translation to be good, it must be both accurate and readable. Readability is subject to the reader and is not a matter of debate. But from the very beginning of English Bible translation, there has been a major difference in the understanding of what makes a version accurate.

Some feel that only a word-for-word translation honors the doctrine of inspiration and produces an accurate rendering. Others feel that translation must be by thoughts, by phrases and sentences, or it will not communicate concepts accurately. Because of the problems of rendering word-for-word—problems of vocabulary, syntax, and idioms—our survey concluded that accuracy does not depend on form. A free and idiomatic translation has equal or better potential to be accurate in comparison to an exacting word-for-word translation.

No version is perfectly readable, nor is any perfectly accurate; all are open for criticism and acceptance. You can determine readability and accuracy only by use and study. The next chapter surveys the top eleven versions, and an additional thirty-eight, and outlines the procedures by which you can decide the version—or versions—that will best suit your needs for reading and research.

FOR FURTHER READING ON TRANSLATION THEORY

Barr, James. *Comparative Philology and the Text of the Old Testament.* Oxford, 1968. *Academic. Mentioned in chapter 2 in relation to textual criticism, it also discusses problems of word definition and translation.*

Bruggen, Jakob van. *The Future of the Bible.* Nelson, 1978. *Argues from the perspective of a theologian and linguist for F-E translation and for the text underlying the* KJV.

Glassman, Eugene H. *The Translation Debate.* InterVarsity, 1981. *Argues from the perspective of a linguist and missionary translator for D-E translation.*

Louw, J. P. *Semantics of New Testament Greek*. Fortress, 1982. Written for students of the New Testament Greek, this book is an excellent introduction to "semantics," which deals with the meaning of verbal communication. It demonstrates the problems of transferring meaning accurately between languages when faced with the reality of their different use of words and syntax.

Nida, Eugene A. *Toward a Science of Translating*. Brill/UBS, 1964.

————. *God's Word in Man's Language*. Carey, 1952. This is an anecdotal look at the history of missionary translation, which secondarily shows the linguistic and cultural necessity of D-E translation.

Nida, Eugene A., and C. R. Taber. *The Theory and Practice of Translation*. Brill/UBS, 1969. This work and the following are classic technical works on linguistics and Bible translation, promoting D-E translation.

Silva, Moises. *Biblical Words and Their Meaning*. Zondervan, 1983. Subtitled "An Introduction to Lexical Semantics," this volume is an extremely important introduction to the problems of understanding the meaning and significance of biblical words, especially when those words are used in interpretation and theology. This is must reading for all pastors and teachers who do any kind of word studies in their communication. It is also a valuable introduction to James Barr's important book *The Semantics of Biblical Language*. Oxford, 1961.

Wonderly, William L. *Bible Translations for Popular Use*. UBS, 1968. Intended as a guide for translators, it introduces the principles necessary to create common or simple language translation. It is more basic than Nida's works [above].

Chapter 4

SO MANY VERSIONS?
A SURVEY OF THE BACKGROUND
AND CHARACTERISTICS OF
AVAILABLE ENGLISH VERSIONS

In chapter 3, we saw that most Bible translations were produced to update or simplify languages because of changes in English, advances in biblical scholarship, and a desire to meet special needs. Very few versions have been produced to promote a theological system or are so bad that we can reject them out of hand.

My express goal in the preceding chapter was to show that there are more trustworthy and useful versions than many people had thought. In the present chapter I want to give some background and principles that may help one make selections from the more than fifty versions of the English Bible that are currently in print. We will begin by looking at the KJV and the top ten other best sellers, for their wide acceptance demands our primary consideration (see chart 5 on the following page). But we will also survey in brief another three dozen works of varying quality and usefulness for those who really want to make a thorough investigation of the various versions that are available today.

This chapter concludes with a step-by-step program for evaluating and choosing the versions that one wishes to use for reading (such as for personal or family devotions), those that are intended to be used for research, and those that are more useful for comparative study.

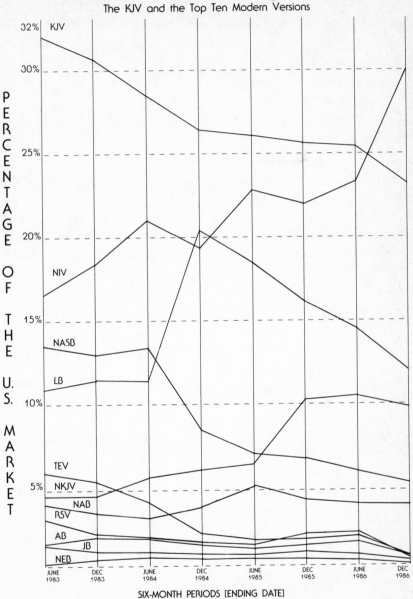

Chart 5
THE BEST-SELLING ENGLISH BIBLES IN THE UNITED STATES[1]
The KJV and the Top Ten Modern Versions

PERCENTAGE OF THE U.S. MARKET

32% KJV
30%
25%
20%
NIV
15%
NASB
LB
10%
TEV
5% NKJV
NAB
RSV
AB
JB
NEB

JUNE 1983 — DEC 1983 — JUNE 1984 — DEC 1984 — JUNE 1985 — DEC 1985 — JUNE 1986 — DEC 1986

SIX-MONTH PERIODS [ENDING DATE]
Source: Spring Arbor Distributors; Rob Stone, Bible Buyer
Copyright © 1986 — John R. Kohlenberger III

[1] This chart is based on the sales statistics from Spring Arbor Distributors, the largest wholesaler of Christian books and Bibles in the United States. Their report is the best single gauge of Bible sales in the country.

THE BEST-SELLING MODERN VERSIONS OF THE BIBLE

The following survey summarizes the background, history, and features of best-selling and special-interest English Bibles. It is arranged chronologically. Chart 7 (pp. 120–21) presents the essential facts in a tabular form for quick reference and comparison. For more thorough discussions, reviews, and critiques, consult the bibliography at the end of the chapter.

The Revised Standard Version

The RV of 1881/1885 and ASV of 1901 were the first major versions to break from the tradition of using the standard Greek text of the sixteenth century, the so-called Textus Receptus (TR), and to incorporate the results of three centuries of continuing biblical scholarship. However, their slavish F-E style did not win them much of a popular audience, though they continue to appeal to students of biblical languages who want to analyze the form of the originals in English.

In 1928 the International Council of Religious Education, now the Department of Christian Education of the National Council of Churches of Christ, appointed a committee of fifteen scholars to consider another revised version. Interrupted by the Depression, the work to create a revision of the KJV began in 1937; this revision was to use modern knowledge of the Greek and Hebrew languages and texts and modern English idiom. Thirty-two translators, including one Jewish scholar, undertook the revision, which was then reviewed by a committee of fifty denominational representatives.

The New Testament appeared in 1946, the complete (Protestant) Bible in 1952, and the Apocrypha in 1956. The first printing of the complete Bible numbered one million, at that time the largest print-run ever made for a Bible. The New Testament was subsequently revised in 1971. The Apocrypha was expanded to include three additional books in 1977.

The RSV followed the lead of the RV/ASV and formatted the text into paragraphs. The RV/ASV had also noted the major feature of Hebrew poetry, "parallelism" (where two or three successive lines make identical, similar, or opposite statements), by starting each parallel on its own line. It limited this practice, however, to the Psalms and Proverbs. The RSV indicates poetry wherever it occurs.

Although the RSV did use a more contemporary English than the KJV, RV, and ASV, it reverted to archaic pronouns and verbal inflections when addressing God in prayer and praise, such as in the Psalms. This practice has been followed by several other versions, such as the NEB and NASB, though not by the NIV, TEV, and LB. As to form, the RSV is a mixture of predominantly F-E translation, with D-E used when necessary for English style.

The RSV followed the RV/ASV in preferring a modern, eclectic Greek text to the traditional TR and also applied much new scholarship, including studies on the recently discovered Dead Sea Scrolls, to its Old Testament text and translation. Most variations from the traditional Masoretic Text [MT] are noted in footnotes.

The furious opposition with which some conservatives met its publication all but died away as the RSV truly became the standard version among scholars, mainline denominations, and some evangelical and Catholic circles. However, the RSV currently accounts for less than 5 percent of Bible sales and is losing ground. That, combined with the controversies surrounding its forthcoming revision, give the RSV an uncertain future.

The Amplified Bible

The AB first appeared as a New Testament in 1958, jointly issued by the Lockman Foundation and Zondervan Publishing House. The Old Testament appeared in two parts in 1962 and 1964. The work was headed by "Research Secretary" Frances E. Siewert, who worked with about a dozen other translators.

The basic text is a simple F-E translation, but key words are "amplified," that is, supplied with synonyms and explanations to bring out shades of meaning and nuances that are not possible in a word-for-word rendering. Parentheses and dashes signify these amplifications, brackets contain words inserted for clarification that are not in the originals, and italics point out certain familiar passages now recognized as not adequately supported by the original manuscripts (the AB New Testament was based on the Westcott and Hort Greek New Testament). Brackets also enclose cross references, and italics also indicate supplied conjunctions. The AB follows the Geneva Bible tradition in indenting each verse as a separate paragraph.

In the New Testament, many of the amplifications were

noted to indicate their sources, mostly word studies and lexicons by Cremer, Souter, Thayer, and Vincent. In the Old Testament, the amplifications are much fewer and the footnotes are apologetic and explanatory. The translators were apparently not aware of the richness of the Hebrew vocabulary, possibly because of the lack of popular-level resource books, which are so numerous for New Testament Greek.

The AB has sold well in recent years, probably because its built-in word studies (at least in the New Testament) are useful in personal and group Bible studies. But because of its extensive amplification, involving much commentary and multiple-choice approach to word meanings, I do not recommend the AB for reading or as one's only Bible. As a study tool for the New Testament, if it is discerningly used, it can be helpful.

The New English Bible

In 1946, long before the RSV was completed in the United States, the General Assembly of the Church of Scotland proposed a new British translation of the Bible. Scholars from the various Protestant denominations of Great Britain, the Bible Societies of Britain and Scotland, representatives of Oxford and Cambridge University Presses, and a panel of Roman Catholic observers began the work in 1947.

Forty-seven participants were divided into panels appointed to work on the Old Testament, the New Testament, and the Apocrypha; an additional panel was appointed to deal with English style. Individual scholars prepared the first drafts of each book, which were reviewed by a panel of translators and by the English stylists and then rechecked by the translators before being approved by the final committee. The New Testament was published in 1961 and sold seven million copies before the complete Bible—Old Testament and Apocrypha and a revised edition of the New Testament—appeared in 1970.

The format of the NEB is similar to that of the RSV, with its paragraphing and poetic indentations. However, the chapter and verse numbers are printed in the margin rather than in the text. As to text, the NEB generated its own eclectic New Testament text, similar to the standard critical texts, but chose to depart from the traditional MT more than any other English version had done before. For this, it has received its share of academic as well as popular criticism.

But the most criticized aspect of the NEB has been its language. Although it aimed at a nontechnical, even "timeless" English, its literary and often British idiom was not the language of the people in Britain or elsewhere in the English-speaking world. The NEB was also the first "official" English version to use D-E translation style throughout, rather than only in those instances where the originals could not be rendered formally. But, although it is a free D-E translation, the NEB retained the RSV practice of using archaic pronouns and verb forms when addressing God directly.

In the United States, the NEB is at the bottom of the top-ten list, and even in Great Britain it is outsold by the NIV and the TEV. An elegant literary translation, one of the best English renderings of the Apocrypha in print, the idiosyncracies of its language and occasionally of its scholarship demands a thorough revision, which is forthcoming.

The Jerusalem Bible and the New Jerusalem Bible

The first official Catholic translation of the Bible into English was the Douay-Rheims version. It was primarily the work of one scholar, Gregory Martin, who translated from the Latin Vulgate. The New Testament, though finished last, was published first in Rheims in 1582, and the Old Testament, including the Apocrypha, was published in Douay (or Douai) in 1609–10. The Douay-Rheims Bible currently in print is not the 1582/1610 edition, however. It is the thoroughly revised edition of Bishop Richard Challoner, first published in 1749 and available in an excellent reprint edition from TAN Books.

The last official translation of the Vulgate was produced by Ronald Knox. The New Testament was published in 1945. The Old Testament appeared in two volumes in 1949, but was not authorized until the slightly revised edition of the whole Bible in 1955. This elegant, literary, D-E version is no longer in print.

The first Catholic version based on the Greek New Testament, though unofficial, was released in parts between 1913 and 1935 under the editorship of Cuthbert Lattey and J. Keating. Known as the Westminster Version of the Sacred Scriptures, its Old Testament was left incomplete when Lattey died in 1954.

The release of the JB in 1966 marked the first official Roman Catholic Bible translated into English from the original languages. Although a direct translation of the originals, the JB was influenced by the French *La Bible de Jérusalem*, produced by the Ecole Biblique in Jerusalem and published in Paris in 1956. The notes of the JB were taken directly from the French version of 1961.

Twenty-seven principle translators worked under the general editor, Alexander Jones, the best known of whom was the father of the Hobbits, J. R. R. Tolkien. The first edition of 1966, with its extensive annotations, was over three inches thick and five pounds in weight. The Reader's Edition, with abbreviated notes, came out two years later.

Besides being the first official Catholic translation from the originals, the JB is known for its excellent literary D-E renderings, its extensive annotations and cross references, and its use of the divine name "Yahweh," where most modern versions have LORD.[2] Like the RSV and NEB, the text is formatted into paragraphs and poetic indentation. However, this indentation extends into the New Testament, notably used in most of Jesus' discourses in the Gospel of John. Also, as in the NEB, chapter and verse numbers are in the margin, though "bullets" (•) in the text mark the verse divisions.

The JB has been criticized for the liberal scholarship of its annotations, for its excesses in deviating from the standard critical texts of the Old Testament and New Testament, and for the freedom of its D-E translation style. But in 1985, many of these criticisms were countered by the release of the New Jerusalem Bible (NJB).

The NJB was undertaken in response to a new edition of *La Bible de Jérusalem*, published in 1973. Its introduction names Henry Wansbrough as the general editor and Alan Neame as the principle Old Testament translator. The notes of the NJB are drawn from the French, though the translation proper is less dependent on it than was the original JB.

In format and appearance, the NJB is identical to the original JB. However, its notes are more up-to-date and less exclusively Catholic in orientation. Its translation is less free, though no less readable, and more consistent in vocabulary and style. Its textual base is more conservative, though still leaning to conjectural emendation of difficult passages (e.g., Job 24).

The NJB is a good revision of an already well-received version. This new edition is a useful study Bible that should prove acceptable to a broad segment of the church.

The New American Bible

In 1941, before the JB had gotten underway, a revision of the Rheims-Challoner New Testament was produced from the Vulgate by members of the Catholic Biblical Association of America. Sponsored by the Confraternity of Christian Doctrine, it became known as the Confraternity Version. But in 1943, an encyclical by Pope Pius XII opened the door for a new Catholic translation from the original languages. From 1952 to 1969 the Old Testament appeared in four separate publications. With a revised New Testament, translated this time from the Greek, the completed New American Bible was issued in 1970—the same year as the New English Bible.

The NAB has the distinction of being the first Catholic version translated in America from the original languages. But it was not produced solely by Catholics; five of the fifty translators were Protestant scholars.

The NAB has a paragraph format, with the verse numbers imbedded in the text, and uses poetic indentation in both testaments. The translation is D-E, but stays closer to the originals than the JB or NEB. As to text, it is the most idiosyncratic of all English versions. In 1 Samuel alone, the text departs from the traditional MT in 251 places. The Psalms follow a different Hebrew text altogether and follow the versification of the Hebrew. The text is often rearranged, as in Job 28, where verse 4 is not translated, verses 7–8 follow verse 21, and verses 3 and 9–11 follow verse 24. Three different endings are supplied to the Gospel of Mark.

But despite these criticisms, many reviewers feel that the NAB is the best English translation of the Bible approved by the Roman Catholic church. In the United States, it is currently the best-selling Catholic version and is growing in popularity.

The New American Standard Bible

Although similar in name and initials, the Protestant NASB bears little resemblance to the Catholic NAB. The NASB was consciously titled and patterned after the ASV and, like the AB, was sponsored by the Lockman Foundation of La Habra, California. The translation was done by fifty-eight anonymous translators, all conservative Protestants. The New Testament was released in 1963, and the Old Testament in 1971, though the text is covered by nine copyrights from 1960 to 1977.

The NASB followed the ASV in adopting readings from modern critical Greek and Hebrew texts and in attempting a basically F-E translation, but it reverted to earlier English versions in matters of format. The ASV used paragraphing and poetic indentation, but the NASB indents each verse as a separate unit. The ASV translated the proper name of God as "Jehovah," the NASB as "LORD." The ASV consistently used archaic pronouns and verbal inflections, the NASB uses archaic language only when directly addressing God. Both use italics to note words supplied in translation that are not in the original text, though the NASB uses them more often than the ASV.

The NASB was welcomed in evangelical circles, especially by those who wanted a more up-to-date and more readable version than the KJV but had rejected the RSV. It was not well received, however, outside the United States or in academic circles outside of evangelicalism. Since the appearance of the NIV in 1978, the popularity of the NASB has been declining. But the NASB will remain in use among those who prefer its F-E style to the readability of the other modern versions.

The Living Bible

The LB has received more attention and more criticism than any other modern version. But with thirty million copies in circulation, it has also been the most widely accepted of the modern versions.

The LB is primarily the work of one man, Kenneth N. Taylor, who in 1954 began paraphrasing the ASV for family devotions. He self-published the New Testament epistles as The Living Letters in 1962 to a mild reception. But following an endorsement by Billy Graham in 1963, interest skyrocketed, and Taylor became a full-time paraphraser. Following Living Prophecies (1964) and The Living Gospels (1966), the complete New Testament was published in 1967. Four more separate publications preceded the whole Bible in 1971. A Catholic edition was made possible in 1973 with the inclusion of the Apocrypha as paraphrased by Albert J. Nevins.

No one denies that the LB communicates. Many, however, are concerned with *what* it communicates. In fact, after noting that "the question of good or bad translations is no longer a linguistic question, but a Doctrinal one," the writer of the introduction to the Catholic Edition of 1976 comments:

> Perhaps more than other translations, this translation cannot be used as a basis for Doctrinal or traditional disputes. . . . People from various Doctrinal traditions may rejoice or be chagrined at the particular translations found within this volume, depending on whether or not the translation supports their particular Doctrinal bias.

Thus, despite the fact that the LB was "born out of a sincere desire to have the Word of God reach as many people as possible," its own Catholic edition can commend it only for private reading, not for doctrinal study or discussion. Kenneth Taylor himself states, "For study purposes a paraphrase should be checked against a rigid translation."

The LB was the first Bible I read through after I became a Christian, but I soon found it an inadequate version for research when I started using it in Bible studies. Although I admire and respect Dr. Kenneth Taylor more than any other author I know, I cannot recommend his LB as anyone's primary reading or study Bible. With the appearance of several more readable and less idiosyncratic versions since 1971, the LB no longer fills the void it once did. Despite the shortcomings of the LB, Dr. Taylor should be honored for his sincere, loving, and even courageous efforts in making the Word of God more accessible to all English readers.

Today's English Version

In 1966, the year before the appearance of the New Testament of the LB, another easy-reading New Testament came off the press under the title of Good News for Modern Man. As with the LB, the New Testament of this version was primarily one man's work, that of Robert G. Bratcher, Research Associate of the Translations Department of the American Bible Society (ABS). Unlike the LB, it is an exacting translation of the Greek, though cast in very idiomatic English.

Bratcher, who holds a doctorate in New Testament studies and had served in Brazil as a missionary translator, undertook the project in 1964 at the request of the American Bible Society.

His work was reviewed by translation consultants to both the American Bible Society and the British and Foreign Bible Society. The monumental success of the New Testament prompted the formation of a committee to translate the Old Testament. Bratcher was the chairman of the committee and worked with six other scholars, all with doctorates and all but one with missionary translation experience. After translation and intercommittee review, each book was reviewed by eight Bible specialists representing seven religious groups, by English stylists, and by the Translations Committee of the ABS. In other words, the TEV reads easily, but it was not translated casually!

The whole Bible of the TEV was released in 1976. By then the New Testament was in its fourth edition and had sold 52 million copies. Three members of the Old Testament committee then translated the Apocrypha, completing their work in 1979.

In format, the TEV followed the lead of most of the other translations of the sixties and seventies. The text is paragraphed with verse numbers imbedded. Poetry is indented, as are lists (Num. 1–2) and letters (Ezra 4–6). Also like most other modern versions, the TEV follows the modern critical Greek and Hebrew texts, with most major departures discussed in footnotes.

Unique to the TEV are its vocabulary, helps, and illustrations. The TEV has often been criticized for its common-language vocabulary, but that is the major point of its appeal to the tens of millions who read it. A common criticism is the substitution of the "death" of Christ for the "blood" of Christ in such passages as Romans 5:9. Such conceptual renderings are the result of the communicative goals of D-E translations. If the TEV had wanted to deny blood atonement, it would not have translated 1 John 5:6–8 so clearly. A list of nearly two hundred Bible words defines terms such as "amen," "Messiah," and "tithe," which were retained in translation. More than six hundred simple, charming illustrations by Mlle. Annie Vallotton accompany the text and help capture the message and spirit of many passages.

Chart 5 on page 81 shows that sales of the TEV have been declining in recent years. Whether this is a temporary trend or not, the TEV has made a significant contribution to the history of the English Bible. For it brought to light the enormous need the English-speaking world had for an easy-reading version of the Bible, and it demonstrated to many that the D-E style of translation could communicate effectively and accurately. Be-

GOOD NEWS BIBLE

cause of the linguistic expertise involved in its translation and because of its broad base of prepublication review, I feel the TEV to be as trustworthy a translation as any for reading. It has special value for the new Bible reader, for children, for those with limited vocabulary or learning disabilities, and for those for whom English is a second language.

The New International Version

The background and history of the NIV appears in the preface to each of its editions. A transdenominational project from the beginning, the NIV received its impetus from committees from the Christian Reformed Church and the National Association of Evangelicals. Their studies into the need for a new translation of the Bible in contemporary English were discussed by a group of biblical scholars at Palos Heights, Illinois, in 1965 (when the RSV was the only complete modern-language version). The project was endorsed by a large number of leaders from many denominations who met in Chicago in 1966.

A group of fifteen scholars organized as the Committee on Bible Translation to take responsibility for the new version. In 1967 the New York Bible Society (now known as the International Bible Society) undertook its financial sponsorship, and the committee was able to secure the services of over 110 scholars from the United States, Canada, Great Britain, Ireland, Australia, and New Zealand. Besides the geographic diversity, the translators represented a wide denominational diversity, yet all were committed to the authority and infallibility of the Bible.

After each book was translated by a designated panel, it went through three levels of committees for evaluation, revision, and uniformity of language. The New Testament appeared in 1973. When in 1978 the complete Bible was published, 1,200,000 copies had been ordered, resulting in the largest first printing of a Bible in history.

The NIV follows the paragraph format and poetic indentations of most other modern versions, but also uses double-spacing and special indentations to mark off other forms and features of the biblical literature. See, for example, the indentations that mark off the days of creation in Genesis 1, the Ten Commandments in Exodus 20, the offerings in Numbers 7, the lists in Ezra 1–2, and the letters in Ezra 4–6.

Although traditional in much of its vocabulary, the NIV broke the pattern of the RSV, NEB, and NASB and abandoned archaic pronouns and verbal inflections in recorded prayers, as there is no difference in the style of the Greek and Hebrew between ordinary narrative and prayers. This, combined with its more fluid D-E style and more contemporary vocabulary, weakens the criticism that the NIV is simply an "evangelical's RSV."

The Old Testament is based on the traditional MT. All major departures are mentioned in footnotes. The New Testament is based on an eclectic Greek text, close to the standard United Bible Societies and Nestle-Aland texts. All phrases and verses of the KJV that are omitted from the text of the NIV appear in the footnotes.

The NIV has been evaluated as reading at a seventh-grade level, the average reading level of the American adult. Its readability, combined with its traditional sound and innovative format, have made it the current best-selling modern translation in the English-speaking world.

The New King James Version

The latest modern-language version of the complete Bible was the first to be initiated and underwritten by a publishing house, Thomas Nelson Publishers. Nelson invited leading clergymen and lay leaders to meetings in Chicago and Nashville in 1975 and in London in 1976 to discuss the need for a revision of the KJV that would update this classic English version as much as possible but change it as little as possible.

In 1976, over 130 scholars from all over the English-speaking world were invited to participate in this new translation. Theologically, they shared the same conservative commitment as the translators of the NIV. Various books of the Bible were assigned to various scholars who independently proposed changes to the text of the KJV. After the executive editors reviewed the recommendations, they submitted them to an English editor. Advisory overview committees from North America and Great Britain interacted with this editorial process. Final approval came from Old Testament and New Testament executive review committees. The New Testament was published in 1979, the Old Testament in 1982.

In most of its vocabulary and verbal inflections, the NKJV

improves on the KJV. Although extravagant claims are made about its "retaining the cadence and rhythm of the KJV," there is no similarity to the cadence or rhythm or sound between "certain men clave unto him" and "some men joined him" (Acts 17:34), to cite but one example. Vocabulary aside, it is impossible to retain cadence and rhythm when syllables are lost as archaic verbal inflections like "believeth" are changed to "believe."

Although the NKJV makes advances in readability and comprehension over the KJV, it makes no move to change its format or text. The text is set in two-column format, with each verse starting on a new line. Each parallel line of poetry within a verse also starts a new line and indentations are used to set off letters—for example, the Acts 15 letter to the Gentile believers. Italics indicate words supplied in translation that are not in the originals.

In the New Testament, the translators of the NKJV decided to retain the underlying text of the KJV. Its introduction and supporting literature argue for the superiority of this text against the modern critical texts. Differences between the KJV/NKJV text and the Byzantine or Majority Text are indicated with an "M" in the notes, while differences from the Nestle-Aland and United Bible Societies texts are indicated by "NU." These notes mark more than 320 places were the KJV/NKJV differ from the Majority Text and about 840 differences from the Nestle/UBS texts. In about 240 places, "M" and "NU" agree with each other against the KJV/NKJV. And these agreements cover all types of differences from the KJV/NKJV text—omissions, additions, and alterations alike.

I have taken the time to point this out because the major difference between the NKJV and other basically F-E translations, such as the NASB or even the NIV, is the New Testament text. Much of the literature that supports the NKJV characterizes modern versions as tending to leave out words and verses that were in the KJV, but does not go on to say that the Majority Text also has many such omissions. It often equates some scholarly reevaluation of the past two centuries' severe criticism of the Byzantine tradition as a return to the so-called Textus Receptus. More honest is the current preface to the NKJV that states that "most textual variants have no practical effect on translation." I hope that in the future this attitude becomes the thrust of materials that promote the NKJV.

Simply stated, the NKJV was intended as one in a chain of revisions of the KJV. Certainly the most far-reaching in terms of linguistic changes, the NKJV incorporated no changes from the text of the KJV; it relegated all comments to the notes. The NKJV has been well received in conservative circles and is often seen as a bridge between the KJV and the contemporary reader in churches where the KJV is used for reading and proclamation. It will not become the new Authorized Version, but the NKJV will help preserve the life of the KJV.

SOME OTHER MAJOR VERSIONS

The following is a brief survey of some other versions of the English Bible in the order of their original publication. Some are immensely valuable for reading and study, others are relics, a few are simply curiosities. I have limited my descriptions to just a few salient characteristics.

Other Nineteenth- and Twentieth-Century Translations of the Whole Bible

Outside the "top ten" translations, many of the other versions of the Bible and portions of the Bible still in print are the work of individuals whose unique contribution have merited keeping their work available.

Such is the case of Young's Literal Translation of the Bible (1862) and Darby's New Translation From the Original Languages (1890). Robert Young is best known for his *Analytical Concordance*, which identifies the Greek and Hebrew terms underlying the English of the KJV. His own translation is about as nearly word-for-word as a translation can be and thus is of more use to those who are studying biblical languages than for those who know only English. Young's Literal Translation has been reprinted by Baker.

John Nelson Darby is best known as a leader of the Plymouth Brethren and an early advocate of dispensationalism (see pp. 148–49). But he was also an energetic translator, producing a German and a French Bible and an Italian New Testament before he turned to English. The Bible currently reprinted by Holman incorporates the second edition of his New Testament (1871) and the Old Testament that was completed by translating from his German and French versions (1890). The text is paragraphed, the New Testament was one of the first to incorporate the results of modern textual criticism and was consulted by the translators of the RV. He also anticipated the ASV in translating the proper name of God as "Jehovah" throughout the Old Testament.

The RV of 1881/1885 and the ASV of 1901 were mentioned throughout this chapter as the first major versions to break from the textual tradition of the KJV and its predecessors, and as among the most F-E translations in print. The RV is still available from Oxford; the ASV from Nelson.

Another important F-E translation, more readable in vocabulary and format than the RV/ASV, is the Emphasized Bible. Remarkably progressive for its era, the Emphasized Bible was the work of one scholar, Joseph Bryant Rotherham; used the text of Westcott and Hort for the New Testament; and noted textual differences in the Old Testament between the Hebrew and ancient versions. It was paragraphed and also used indentation for poetry, lists, discourses, and letters. Special symbols mark emphasis in the original languages. And it was the first major English version to translate the proper name of God as "Yahweh." Kregel has reprinted the 1902 edition; it is still a useful translation for study.

James Moffatt was a brilliant New Testament scholar whose translation of the Bible was one of the first modern-language versions, though very Scottish in idiom. His New Testament appeared in 1913 and was revised in 1917. The Old Testament was published in 1924–25 and the "revised and final edition" came out in 1935. This is the edition Harper & Row reprints. Moffatt's is a very lively D-E translation, in paragraphed and poetic format; it takes quite a bit of liberty with the order and arrangement of the text but remains exciting reading.

While Moffatt was translating in English, the American Edgar J. Goodspeed was producing another modern-speech version—The New Testament: An American Translation, published in 1923. The Old Testament was completed in 1927 by four Hebrew scholars under editor J. M. Powis Smith, and the combined Bible was revised in 1935. Goodspeed then translated the Apocrypha in 1935 to create The Complete Bible: An American Translation. It is similar in appearance to the ASV but is much more readable and literary. The University of Chicago Press is its original and current publisher.

One of the first simple-English translations was The Bible in Basic English. The New Testament was released in 1940, the whole Bible in 1949, published by Cambridge University Press. Basic English is a vocabulary of the 850 words most essential to communication. The translation committee, under the editorship of S. H. Hooke, added to these 850 another 50 "Bible words," like "cubit," and 100 words important in reading English verse, making a total of only 1000 English terms. The Bible in Basic English is useful for those learning English as a second language and for those with learning or reading disabilities.

All that needs to be said about the New World Translation is that it was produced by the Jehovah's Witnesses in order to have an English Bible that conformed to their doctrines. This is especially clear in John 1:1, which ends "and the Word was a god," and in the use of "Jehovah" for the proper name of God throughout the Old Testament *and* the New Testament. The New Testament appeared in 1950 and the Old Testament in portions from 1953 to 1960. A revised edition of the whole Bible was published in 1961.

What is now known as the Modern Language Bible began as the Berkeley New Testament in 1945. This New Testament was translated by Gerrit Verkuyl, who aimed at an idiomatic and free, but noninterpretive translation. Verkuyl worked with nineteen other translators in preparing the Old Testament, first published in 1959. Published before the translations explosion of the 1960s and 70s, the Berkeley Version was well received. Zondervan secured the rights to the version in 1958 and had the New Testament revised in 1969. The text is paragraphed with some poetic indentation and is accompanied by many explanatory notes.

The Holy Bible in the Language of Today: An American Translation is the product of Lutheran scholar William F. Beck. The New Testament was completed in 1963. Beck completed the Old Testament in 1966, but died shortly thereafter. His translation was worked over by Elmer Smick and Erich Kiehl and was finally published in 1976 by Holman. The text is in paragraphed and poetic format, and the very readable translation makes use of the latest manuscript discoveries.

The Reader's Digest Bible (1982) is not a new translation, but a "condensed" edition of the RSV under the general editorship of Bruce M. Metzger. The introduction notes that condensation is not abridgement. Abridgement eliminates whole blocks of text and even whole books. Condensation reduces the text by eliminating repetition and some detail (in this case about 40 percent of the words of the Bible) without eliminating essential content. While many have denounced this version, it introduces itself as a Bible *reader* that is intended to supplement—not replace—the full text of a complete Bible. Certainly not a study Bible, it is a valuable first reader for those who have never tried to read or never succeeded in reading the Bible through, and it is a useful overview of basic Bible content for any reader.

The International Children's Bible (ICB) was developed by Sweet Publishing Company from a "base text," which also produced The New Testament: English Version for the Deaf and the New Testament of The Word/New Century Bible. (Although these versions are similar, they are not identical.) The New Testament was published in 1983; the Old Testament in 1986. Twenty-one evangelical and interdenominational translators—most of whom had worked on the RSV, NAS, NIV, or NKJV—were involved in its production.

The ICB is perhaps the first translation produced specifically for children. As indicated in chart 3 (p. 61), the text reads at a high third-grade level, based on its simple sentence structure and limited vocabulary. The text, in paragraph style and with special indentation, is also accompanied by many explanatory footnotes. Words defined and explained in these notes are also treated alphabetically in a concise dictionary.

A well-done and easy-to-read translation, the ICB is excellent for children and will appeal especially to those who want an alternative to the TEV and LB.

Two new New Testaments were released in the early 1980s as the first installment of announced whole Bibles. As of the completion of this book, neither was yet complete.

The Simple English Bible was produced by the International Bible Publishing Company. The international edition came out in 1980, the American edition in 1981. The New Testament is in large, readable print and uses paragraphing and other indentations. It has a vocabulary of about three thousand words, uses italics to indicate words supplied in translation, and uses bold print to indicate emphasis. The Old Testament is scheduled for release in 1987.

The Word/New Century Bible was developed by Sweet Publishing Company from the same "base text" as their ICB (see above). The Word has fewer footnotes than the ICB, a slightly larger vocabulary, and a somewhat longer sentence structure, but it still reads at a level lower than the TEV. Both versions use paragraphing and other indentation and have a brief dictionary to key words and concepts. The Old Testament of The Word is slated for 1987.

All three of these versions are translations, less free in idiom and more traditional in vocabulary (though less energetic in style) than the TEV. Because of this, they will probably appeal to those churches and individuals who appreciate the concept of a simple-English version but do not appreciate the vocabulary or idiom of the TEV and the LB.

Other Nineteenth- and Twentieth-Century Translations of Portions of the Bible

John Wesley's *Explanatory Notes Upon the New Testament* (1768) is not only a commentary but also a revision of the KJV designed to bring it "nearer to the original" in both translation and text. Wesley's *Notes* are reprinted by Baker, Beacon Hill, and Hendrickson. Zondervan has published a one-volume edition of *Notes* (without KJV text), based on the entire Bible.

One of the first modern-language translations was Richard Francis Weymouth's New Testament in Modern Speech. The first edition came out in 1903, a year after Weymouth's death. Kregel currently reprints the third edition (1909) by Ernest Hampden-Cook. The text is paragraphed with verse references in the margin and many brief explanatory notes at the bottom of the page.

Two other New Testament translations from this decade have recently been reprinted—W. B. Godbey's Translation of the New Testament (1902?) by Schmul Publishing and The Worrell New Testament (1904) by Gospel Publishing House. Both of these are idiosyncratic in purpose and style. Godbey's Gospels are laid out as a four-column harmony; the rest of the text, in paragraph form. He felt constrained by the requests of the church to produce his translation, which he "candidly" believed to be "the most literal, lucid, and perspicuous translation" available. Worrell attempted to reproduce the Greek tenses "literally" and was especially concerned to translate the Greek *baptizō* as "immerse" and *ecclēsia* as "assembly," because of his understanding of the mode of baptism and the importance of local, "primitive" church assemblies. Both editions are annotated, Worrell's extensively.

Helen Barrett Montgomery was president of the American Baptist Convention from 1921 to 1922 and translated The New Testament in Modern English in 1924. This New Testament is still published by Judson Press. It is a basically F-E translation, in simple (though dated) English, set in paragraphs with many subject headings.

The Concordant Literal New Testament was "compiled" by A. E. Knoch and first printed in 1926. Its sixth edition appeared in 1976. The concordant method of translation involves, as much as is possible, not only a word-for-word rendering, but also the exclusive coupling of English and Greek words so that only one English word is used to translate any given Greek word wherever it appears in the New Testament. A complex set of symbols and abbreviations give further representation of Greek syntax and inflections. The translation of the Old Testament began with Genesis in 1957 and continued with Isaiah (1962), Daniel (1968), Ezekiel (1977), the Minor Prophets (1979), Exodus (1982), Leviticus and Numbers (1983), and Deuteronomy (1984).

Charles B. Williams translated the New Testament into "the language of the people" in 1937. A fiftieth-anniversary reprint was issued by Holman in 1986. Williams attempted to translate the tense of Greek verbs exactingly while retaining readability. In syntax and vocabulary, however, his translation is often not "the language of the people." (Charles B. Williams should not be confused with Charles Kingsley Williams, whose New Testament in Plain English appeared in 1952 and is no longer in print.)

A unique translation of the New Testament was produced in 1955 by a Jewish scholar, Hugh J. Schonfield. Originally entitled The Authentic New Testament, a revised edition, The Original New Testament, was issued in 1985 by Harper & Row. By his translation and annotations Schonfield attempts to bring out the Jewish character of the background and content of the New Testament. But his translation and textual base also demonstrate that he feels all references to the deity of Jesus are not part of the original New Testament (e.g., John 1:1; Phil. 2). The books are arranged in Schonfield's chronological order, including the division of 1 and 2 Corinthians into four letters. The text is in paragraph style, with chapter and verse divisions in the margin.

Certainly the most respected and arguably the best individual translation of the New Testament is J. B. Phillips' New Testament in Modern English. Phillips's intimacy with Greek and his excellence in English produced an outstanding and exciting D-E translation that captures the spirit as well as the substance of the original. This translation began with *Letters to Young Churches* in 1947 and, at the urging of C. S. Lewis and others, continued with *The Gospels in Modern English* (1952), *The Young Church in Action* (Acts, 1955), and *The Book of Revelation* (1957). The first edition of his one-volume New Testament appeared in 1958. The second edition, based on the first edition of the UBS text and with fewer expansions on the Greek text, was published in 1973. His only attempt at Old Testament translation, Four Prophets (Amos, Hosea, Isaiah 1–35, Micah), came out in 1963. Still a best-seller, Phillips is published by Macmillan. Phillips' autobiography, *The Price of Success*, and personal testimony to the historicity and reliability of the New Testament, *The Ring of Truth*, are published by Harold Shaw.

Kenneth S. Wuest taught Greek at the Moody Bible Institute and devoted much of his time outside the classroom to making insights from the Greek New Testament available to English readers in his Word Studies series and his Expanded Translation of the New Testament, both of which are published by Eerdmans. His translation came out in three volumes—the Gospels in 1956, Acts through Ephesians in 1958, and Philippians through Revelation in 1959. The one-volume New Testament was first printed in 1961. Wuest's translation follows the Greek word order and is "expanded" to bring out word meanings and nuances of the Greek inflections, especially the verb. It is set in paragraph form, without marking individual verses, to show the context in which verses should be read.

William Barclay is best known for his New Testament commentary, the *Daily Study Bible*, but he also produced his own New Testament translation. The Gospels and Acts were released in 1968, the Epistles and Revelation in 1969. Westminster currently publishes the one-volume edition. Barclay sought to make a translation for the common reader that "did not need a commentary to explain it." The result is a readable translation with many explanatory additions relating to word meanings and customs.

The New Life New Testament is another simple-English version, translated by Gleason H. Ledyard and published in 1974 by Christian Literature International. "The reason for this translation of the New Testament is to take difficult words that are found in most translations of the Bible and put them into words or phrases that are easy to understand." Only about 850 words are used in this version.

The New Testament: English Version for the Deaf and The New Testament: A New Easy-to-Read Version are the same translation, published with different introductions and titles by Baker in 1978. As I said above (pp. 97–98), this version was developed by the World Bible Translation Center and formed the base text from which the International Children's Version and The Word were developed. Unique to this edition are many brief explanations and synonyms of key words, which are included in the text in parentheses and italicized.

Author Jay E. Adams felt there was no accurate New Testament translation in modern everyday English and so produced his own in 1979. It is a straightforward translation, set in verse format (verses beginning paragraphs are indented), with few notes and no section headings. The New Testament in Everyday English is published by Baker.

The most recent private translation of the New Testament is A New Accurate Translation of the Greek New Testament into Simple Everyday American English. It was produced and published by Julian G. Anderson in 1984. Anderson felt that no one had yet produced a satisfactorily accurate and readable translation. He arranged the books in the order he believed them to have been written and sometimes he has rearranged the text. His translation is keyed to 160 pages of notes at the end of the book.

Jewish Translations of the Hebrew Scriptures

Three major Jewish translations of the Hebrew Scriptures, the Protestant Old Testament, are currently available. The

Jewish Publication Society (JPS) began preparations for a new translation of the Hebrew Bible into English in 1892. This cooperative effort of more than two dozen rabbis and scholars from Britain and America was issued in 1917 as The Holy Scriptures According to the Masoretic Text. Similar in appearance to the ASV, the text is in paragraphs and poetic indentation. The books are in the order of the Hebrew Bible. The style and verbal inflections are similar to those of the KJV, though the vocabulary is more up-to-date.

In 1962 a beautiful edition of the Hebrew Bible was produced in Jerusalem by Koren Publishing, the first Hebrew text edited, typeset, and printed in Israel. In 1977 a volume containing the Koren text and an English translation on facing pages was published as The Jerusalem Bible, not to be confused with the Roman Catholic version of the same title. The English text was a modernized and revised version of the English translation of Michael Friedlander, first published in Britain in 1881. Harold Fisch was the English editor. It is an F-E translation that follows the paragraphing of the Hebrew text and is characterized by its transliteration of Hebrew names (e.g., "Iyyov" for "Job" and "Yirmeyahu" for "Jeremiah"). This volume is distributed in the United States by Philipp Feldheim, Inc.

The translation destined to become the new standard appeared in three volumes over three decades. The Torah was begun in 1955, published in 1962, and revised in 1982. The Prophets appeared in 1978, and The Writings in 1982. Fourteen translators and editors were involved. The JPS released the one-volume edition in 1985. It is entitled The Tanakh, a word composed of the first letters of the three divisions of the Hebrew Bible (Torah, Nevi'im, and Kethuvim).

The text of the Tanakh is in paragraph and poetic format. Footnotes list alternate renderings and explanations and point out the version's infrequent departures from the traditional Hebrew text. The translation is basically F-E, but is not wooden. Notes on the New Translation of the Torah (JPS, 1969), by its primary translator Harry M. Orlinsky, provides insights into the procedures and practices of the committee that produced the Torah.

The Tanakh is not only a monument to Jewish scholarship but also a superb translation of the Hebrew text. It should be consulted by Christian students of the Old Testament. One will not find the overt messianic renderings of most Christian versions, such as the capitalization of the nouns "anointed" and "son" throughout the Psalms, and one may wonder at the interpretation of such passages as Genesis 3:15 and Isaiah 9:5; but this honest and useful translation of the traditional Hebrew text is without doubt valuable for reading and for study.

Translations Based on Texts Other Than the Originals

The versions we surveyed thus far, with the exception of the paraphrased LB, all claimed to have been translated from the original Greek, Hebrew, and Aramaic texts. Three major English translations of ancient versions are also still in print.

The first Catholic translation of the Bible, made from the Latin Vulgate, was the Douay-Rheims Bible (see p. 85). The revised edition of Bishop Richard Challoner (1749) is currently published by TAN Publications.

The Hebrew Scriptures were translated into Greek in the third and second centuries before the birth of Jesus. The form of the Greek Old Testament we have today is known as the Septuagint (LXX), named for the legend that credits seventy-two translators with its production (though the Roman number LXX is actually 70!). In 1851 Sir Lancelot C. L. Brenton translated the LXX of Codex Vaticanus, in comparison with Codex Alexandrinus, the two oldest known complete LXX texts available. This text and translation of the thirty-nine books of the Hebrew/Protestant Old Testament canons and fifteen apocryphal books is reprinted by Zondervan as *The Septuagint With Apocrypha: Greek and English*.

The Syriac version, the Peshitta, is a translation of the Greek New Testament and the LXX. However, in his book *The Holy Bible From Ancient Eastern Manuscripts*, George M. Lamsa presents the Peshitta as representing the apostles' original writings, from which the Greek was derived! Thus he feels his translation to be the only accurate rendering of the Bible because it is the only English rendering of the Peshitta.

Although most scholars would agree with Lamsa that Aramaic, closely related to Syriac, was the mother tongue of Jesus and his disciples, few—if any—would agree with him that the New (or Old) Testament was originally written in

Aramaic or Syriac. Lamsa's version is valuable as a translation of the Syriac Peshitta. But this is of more value to scholars than to students and general readers. Where it departs from translations of the Hebrew or Greek, it should not be preferred to those translations (e.g., Matt. 27:46, "My God, my God, for this I was spared!" instead of "My God, my God, why have you forsaken me!"). Lamsa's version was released in portions beginning in 1933. Harper & Row currently reprints the final edition of 1957.

Parallel Bibles

When more than one version of the Bible is set on the same page or on facing pages, the result is a "parallel" Bible. In the days before the English Bible, Greek and Latin parallel Bibles were common. As texts and translations multiplied, so did "polyglots," as these multilanguage Bibles were known ("diglot" means "two languages"; "triglot" means "three languages," etc.). Parallel Bibles remain the most space-efficient— and economical—way to collect and compare different versions of the Bible. There are four noteworthy parallel Bibles:

The New Layman's Parallel Bible contains three major translations—the KJV, NIV, and RSV—and the paraphrased LB. It was first published by Zondervan in 1981. These four versions are printed in readable type, two versions per page, so all four appear across a two-page spread.

Zondervan's Comparative Study Bible came out in 1984 and also contained the KJV and NIV. But in the place of the LB was the AB and in place of the RSV was the NASB, thus making this parallel Bible an instant hit in evangelical circles. Again, the texts are printed in clear, readable type, two versions per page.

A classic English parallel, The New Testament Octapla, combined eight historic English versions in one volume. Published in the 1960s by Thomas Nelson & Sons, it is now unfortunately out of print. Tyndale House has created a modern octapla in their Eight-Translation New Testament. Set four versions per page are the KJV, LB, TEV, NIV, PNT, RSV, JB, and NEB—the New Testaments of eight of the twelve best-selling versions of the Bible.

AMG and Mathis Publishers released the three-volume 26 Translations of the Holy Bible in 1985. (Zondervan had previously published The New Testament From 26 Translations and

The Old Testament Books of Poetry From 26 Translations.) This parallel does not contain the full text of twenty-six versions, but lists several illuminating and differing renderings for each verse of the KJV, which it does print in full. Although it does not draw from the NIV, NASB, or NKJV, this set is very valuable for comparative study.

Interlinear Translations

An "interlinear" translation is a book in two languages, with each line of the original interlined with a basically word-for-word translation. A New Testament interlinear (for English readers) is, of course, in Greek and English, and an Old Testament in Hebrew and English.

Some people think they are getting a more "literal," even a more accurate translation by getting an interlinear. That is not true. They are simply getting the ultimate F-E version.

I remember talking with a young man in a bookstore where I was employed several years ago. I noticed he had spent half an hour in the language section, and I thought I might be of some assistance. He showed me the interlinear he was examining and asked, "Isn't this here the Greek?" to which I replied, "Yes, it is." He continued, "Isn't this here what those Greek words mean?" to which I responded "Yes, that is a translation of those Greek words." He concluded, "Then why don't they take these words and publish them in a New Testament so we wouldn't argue about what the Greek meant!"

As do so many people—pastors and teachers included—he confused a word-for-word translation with an accurate translation. And he felt that the Greek, printed on the same page, imparted some special sanctity to the English rendering. But as we discussed above, no Greek or Hebrew word can be consistently translated by any one English word, nor does Greek and Hebrew word order communicate to those who know only English word order.

Interlinear translations are best used by those who are studying (or reviewing) biblical languages. They give others no more help in understanding vocabulary than a concordance gives, and they actually give less help in understanding sentences than a comparative study of English versions gives. Therefore, I do not recommend them to anyone other than language students, even though I invested four years of my life producing the four-volume *NIV Interlinear Hebrew-English Old Testament* (Zondervan, 1979–85).

There are basically two different New Testament interlinears, though they are available from a variety of publishers accompanied by a variety of modern versions for comparison. George Ricker Berry's translation of the so-called Textus Receptus, originally published in 1897, is paralleled by the KJV and uses its vocabulary. It is reprinted by Zondervan, Baker, and a number of reprint houses. Jay Green's interlinear (Baker) differs little from Berry's. Alfred Marshall's more up-to-date and readable translation of the twenty-first edition of Nestle's *Novum Testamentum Graece* was first published by Bagster in 1958. It has been reprinted by Zondervan and is available in a choice of parallel versions: KJV, RSV, NIV, or NASB.

For the Old Testament, besides my four-volume *NIV Interlinear Hebrew-English Old Testament*, there is a three-volume interlinear by Jay Green as well as a one-volume *Interlinear Bible*, both published by Baker, the latter work containing both Old Testament and New Testament interlinears in a small and often barely legible print.

For a discussion of the use of interlinears, see chapter 13 of *Books About the Book* and E. W. Goodrick's *Do-It-Yourself Hebrew and Greek* (Multnomah/Zondervan, 1976).

Bible Translations in Modern Languages Other Than English

The forty-seven versions we have just considered represent only one of the more than 1,800 languages into which the Bible and portions of the Bible have been translated. Those reading this book can obviously read English, but for some people English may not be the primary language. In fact, Spanish Bibles currently outsell the NEB and PNT in the United States.

We cannot take the time (nor do I have the expertise) to survey the best versions in the twenty or thirty best-represented languages. However, there are resources available to booksellers and the general public that list these versions and their sources.

The American Bible Society is the primary source in the United States for ancient- and foreign-language Bibles, though the International Bible Society has some unique versions, such as the Spanish NIV. These Bible societies sell to the general public as well as to bookstores. Catalogs and price lists are available on request. (Appendix B lists the addresses and telephone numbers of all the publishers and distributors mentioned in this book.) Booksellers can also order Bibles in as many as thirty-five languages from distributors in Spring Arbor and Riverside.

Michael Adeney of Logos Bookstore in Seattle developed a pair of catalogs, one for booksellers and one for the general public; these catalogs list sources for Bibles in three hundred languages. They also describe the eighty-three top translations in twenty-two major languages. Entitled "God Speaks Many Languages: A Multi-Language Bible Catalog for North America," these catalogs are available through bookstores from Spring Arbor and Riverside. (Those who do not have access to a local bookstore can order a catalog from the Logos Bookstore, 4510 University Way N.E., Seattle, WA 98105.)

HOW TO CHOOSE A TRANSLATION FOR YOUR PERSONAL USE

Selecting a translation of the Bible is like shopping for groceries: there are so many choices, but some translations are better for a person than others are. Those who are even moderately conscientious about their diets will cater not only to their tastes—loading up on munchies and desserts!—but will select tasty but varied foodstuffs for preparing balanced meals. Certainly there is a place for snacks and treats, but these should be in addition to, rather than in place of, the staples of the major food groups. So too with Bible translations. One needs a good, widely respected version for a basic diet. And then, to supplement this standard with a variety of resources, add some staples and some treats for their value in illuminating and critiquing the standard text.

As an example of such illumination, compare the well-known KJV translation of Romans 12:2 to the brilliant and trenchant rendering of Phillips:

> And be not conformed to this world: but be ye transformed
> by the renewing of your mind, that ye may prove what is that
> good, and acceptable, and perfect will of God. [KJV]

> Don't let the world around you squeeze you into its own
> mould, but let God re-make you so that your whole attitude
> of mind is changed. Thus you will prove in practice that the
> will of God is good, acceptable to him and perfect. [PNT]

Not only does Phillips' version communicate more clearly the
very same message the KJV intends, but also the outstanding
metaphor makes its rendering as memorable as the more
rhythmic prose of the KJV.

When other versions agree with the interpretation of the
standard text one has chosen, one often ends up with a deeper,
more exciting, and more meaningful insight into a given
Scripture passage. However, when the interpretations disagree,
such as in the renderings "young woman" of the RSV versus
"virgin" of the KJV in Isaiah 7:14 (see pp. 73–74), one can feel
frustrated, insecure, and defensive. But, rather, this most basic
type of disagreement should become an invitation to deeper
study!

In regard to the alternate renderings in the margin of the KJV,
the translators wrote:

> Now in such a case, doth not a margine do well to admonish
> the Reader to seeke further, and not to conclude or dogmatize
> vpon this or that peremptorily?

Thus differences in interpretations admonish one to study, to
"seeke further," and to take care before he applies a given
passage to doctrine or daily life, "not to conclude or dogmatize
peremptorily." The rest of this chapter is devoted to helping the
reader select standard and supplemental versions of the Bible
for his or her personal use.

Books About the Book, the companion to this volume, is a
guide to building one's own biblical reference library for
studying such problems. It also outlines how to best use
reference books for efficient and discerning study.

Selecting a Bible: Determine the Contents

As we saw in chapter 1, "the Bible" means different things
to different people. One's religious affiliation will determine the
canon of the Bible used in corporate worship. However, a Bible
student may want supplementary versions with more or fewer
books, both for the quality of the translation and for the insights

of the additional (though noncanonical) contents. The options are as follows:

A 66-BOOK CANON

The 66-book canon, 39 Old Testament books and 27 New Testament books, is the standard contents of the English Bible and is preferred by Protestants.

THE 73- OR 81-BOOK CANON

A canon larger than 66 books includes the Apocryphal or Deuterocanonical books and is intended for Catholics and Orthodox as well as for common use. The 73-book canon integrates the Deuterocanonicals into the Old Testament, resulting in 46 Old Testament books and 27 New Testament books. The 81-book canon separates the Deuterocanonicals into a separate section of 15 (or 18, as in the New Oxford Annotated Bible) alongside the 39 Old Testament and 27 New Testament books of the 66-book canon.

THE 24- OR 39-BOOK CANON

This represents the Hebrew canon, the Protestant Old Testament, and is found in Jewish versions or in the separately published Old Testaments of Christian translations. The difference between the 24- and 39-book grouping is in arrangement, not in contents (see chart 2, p. 24). This canon is preferred by Jewish readers.

THE 27-BOOK "CANON"

I have "canon" in quotes because this grouping represents only the New Testament. Although many pride themselves in being "New Testament Christians" and limit their Bible reading to the New Testament or the thirteen Epistles of Paul, no major denomination considers the New Testament alone as the complete biblical canon. I list it, however, because of the dozens of versions that cover only the New Testament and for those who limit their reading or research to the New Testament.

Selecting a Bible: Determine the Translation

Here is the tough part. The easiest way to decide on a translation is to let someone else make the decision. Although this method may be acceptable for a child or for a new reader or a beginning student of the Bible, eventually the mature person may want to supplement or change his or her standard translation. The only way one can do this is by personal evaluation—evaluation of one's needs and desires and evaluation of the options.

One can also use the following outlines when purchasing a Bible for a child, spouse, relative, or friend.

Selecting a Bible: Determine the Needs
(Reading Level and Purpose)

This first outline lists the factors one should consider before actually beginning to look at the Bibles themselves.

A. Reading level (see chart 3, p. 61)
   1. Age
     Generally the younger the reader, the simpler the translation should be. Also for younger readers a D-E translation is preferable to F-E.
   2. Education: secular and ecclesiastical
     Generally, the more educated you are, the better your vocabulary and appreciation for language, and the fewer the restrictions on the version you can consider for your major use.
   3. Literacy or literary appreciation
     As in education, the more literate and literary you are, the greater your appreciation of the elegant D-E translations and the classic literary versions will be.
   4. Familiarity with ecclesiastical vocabulary
     The more time you have spent in religious circles, whether or not you have been formally educated, the more familiar you are with ecclesiastical vocabulary, and the less will be your need for a simple-English version.

B. Purpose
   1. Reading
     a. General study
       For general reading, you may want to use an accurate D-E translation. The more normal the vocabulary and syntax, the easier your reading and the greater your comprehension will be.
     b. Devotional reading
       For devotional reading, you may receive additional insights from the additions of an expansive translation or paraphrase, or a heightened sense of worship from the traditional, ecclesiastical vocabulary of an older version. But it is important to remember in both of these cases that you may also get a *wrong*

impression because of the interpretive bias of the expansion or the unclear meanings of the antiquated English.

   c. Public reading

Those who are regularly involved in the public reading of Scripture will want to conform to the advice of their leaders. However, as in the case of private reading, it is often beneficial to read publicly in a different version from that which the majority of the listeners use; but to do this properly and beneficially, you should first secure the permission of the church leaders and be convinced that the selected version gives illumination in those passages where it differs from the version of the majority!

2. Detailed analysis: word study and diagramming

Analysis is the one clear purpose for which F-E translations are always preferable to D-E. One drawback is that one must be at least familiar with Greek and Hebrew lexicography and syntax in order to derive maximum benefit and interpretive accuracy from word and sentence analysis in English. (This is the substance of chapter 13 of *Books About the Book*.)

3. Comparison: in general or within body

When choosing Bibles for comparison, you should begin with widely accepted versions that are different in translation style and in methodological or interpretive approach from those of your standard version. This will provide the person with the most cases of illumination and potential differences. Parallel Bibles offer the most space-efficient and economic way to collect comparative versions.

4. Communication

Whether you are preaching, teaching, or writing, you need to consider the needs of those you address. Those who read the originals still need to communicate in English—in a translation that sounds like English. A lot of preachers I have heard in person and on the radio spend as much time explaining the words of the KJV as they spend expositing the meaning of the text. The end result of such word studies is often the rendering of a modern version, which they should have used in the first place.

Selecting a Bible: Determine the Options

When you have determined the canon you believe is correct and the desired reading level and the purpose for which you version will be used, you have eliminated most of the options! The following outline lists (in order of *my* preference) the versions I consider to be the best choices for each category, though I have not included all forty-seven versions discussed above.

A. For children (through junior high) who read (rather than simply looking at pictures):
   1. International Children's Bible
   2. Today's English Version

3. New Life Testament
4. Children's editions of the NIV, RSV, LB, NKJV, and KJV
   Note that "children's editions" of standard versions include some helps and colorful pictures, but the text reads at the same level as those of the standard editions. (See chart 3, p. 61.)

B. **For people with limited reading ability and little or no church background:**
   1. New Century Version/New Testament: A New Easy-to-Read Version
   2. Today's English Version
   3. Simple English Bible
   4. Bible in Basic English
   5. New Life Testament

C. **For youth and adults with no reading difficulty but little or no church background:**
   1. New International Version
   2. New Century Version
   3. Today's English Version
   4. Simple English Bible
   5. New King James Version

D. **For youth and adults from a conservative church background:**
   1. New International Version
   2. New American Standard Bible
   3. New Century Version
   4. Simple English Bible
   5. New King James Version
   6. Living Bible

E. **For youth and adults from a mainline or a liberal church background:**
   1. Revised Standard Version
   2. New International Version
   3. New Jerusalem Bible
   4. New American Bible
   5. New English Bible

F. **For youth and adults from a Catholic background:**
   1. New Jerusalem Bible
   2. New American Bible
   3. Revised Standard Version: Common Edition
   4. New International Version, supplemented with the RSV *Annotated Apocrypha*
   5. New English Bible: Common Edition
   6. Today's English Version: Catholic Edition

G. **For youth and adults from a Jewish background:**
   1. Tanakh (New Jewish Version)
   2. The (Koren) Jerusalem Bible
   3. The Holy Scriptures According to the Masoretic Text

H. **For those with an appreciation of literature and literary English:**
   1. King James Version
   2. New English Bible
   3. New Jerusalem Bible
   4. Moffatt: A New Translation

I. For those who want to do word and sentence analysis:
  1. The Emphasized Bible
  2. American Standard Version/(English) Revised Version
  3. Wuest: The New Testament: An Expanded Translation
  4. The (Koren) Jerusalem Bible or The Tanakh
  5. New American Standard Bible

Two Omitted Criteria

In these outlines for selecting a version of the Bible, two important criteria were missing. The first was *accuracy*. I mentioned on page 58 that accuracy and readability were the most important criteria in determining whether a version was good or bad. The outlines dealt with readability and purpose, but not with accuracy. The reason that I left accuracy out is that one person's accurate version is another's tendentious or biased rendering. You can see a bit of my impressions about the accuracy of the versions outlined above by the order in which I recommend them—but accuracy is not the only key to understanding that order! In my judgment, the only way you can determine the accuracy of a version to your own satisfaction is to read that version in comparison with others.

The other missing criterion relates to the *form* of the Bible: study features, bindings, size, etc. These considerations are secondary to choosing the translation proper, but they are by no means unimportant. In fact, chapters 5 and 6 are devoted to those very considerations. Choosing a reliable and readable translation for a lifetime of reading and study is your first priority. Choosing the features that accompany the translation and the form it comes in are your last.

Selecting a Bible: Making the Choice

Once you have evaluated your needs, desires, and purposes, you have limited your choices to about half a dozen versions. All of these are good; perhaps more than one could be "best." In order for you to determine which is best for you, you must evaluate all of the possibilities together. This will take time, but it will be time well spent.

During the process of evaluation, especially if you do not want to make a hasty decision to purchase a well-bound, lifetime Bible, you could purchase an inexpensive paperback edition of the version most recommended by others or borrow a copy from a friend or library. You can also consult local church and public libraries for the versions you may wish to compare. These versions most likely can also be found in the local Christian bookstore. I doubt if any booksellers mind if you use their store to evaluate the Bibles you will eventually purchase from them.

Because the Bible is made up of different kinds of literature, it is best to sample sections and whole books that represent the various kinds of literature of the Bible. I recommend a look at narrative, at poetry, at wisdom, at prophecy, at discourse, and at epistle. For narrative, I recommend Ruth; for poetry, Psalms 1–8 and 23; for wisdom, Proverbs 1–3 and 12; for prophecy, Habakkuk; for discourse, Matthew 5–7; for epistle, 2 Timothy. If you are evaluating a New Testament only, substitute Mark 1–3 for Ruth, Revelation 4–5 and 18–19 for Psalms, James for Proverbs, and Matthew 23–25 for Habakkuk.

Each of the books that I suggest takes only ten to twenty minutes to read aloud. Thus in an hour or two, you can compare an entire book in six versions. In six days, comparing a book a day, you can work through all six recommended types of literature. Thus in a comparatively short time one can complete the kind of study that will give confidence in selecting a basic or favorite Bible.

Making copies or photocopies of chart 6 (on pp. 118–19) will help record the process of evaluation. Six copies will be needed, one for each book and passage being compared. When the comparisons are completed, you will have a written record of observations and impressions from which to make your own choice and to help others in making theirs. Please note that all of the charts in this book are protected by copyright, and the special use of this chart is intended for personal use only.

A recommendation for booksellers, teachers, and other leaders: because of the responsibility you have in helping others to choose between the many available versions, read the six suggested passages in as many Bibles and New Testaments as you have available to you. If you set aside an hour a day for a month, you could evaluate as many as thirty different whole Bible and New Testament translations. Then your own recommendations would be based on firsthand encounters and not simply on hearsay.

PUBLISHER/DISTRIBUTOR LIST OF 49 ENGLISH BIBLES AND TESTAMENTS DISCUSSED IN THIS CHAPTER

Adams: The New Testament in Everyday English
  Baker
American Standard Version
  Nelson
An American Translation
  University of Chicago
Amplified Bible
  Zondervan
Authentic New Testament, The: *see* Original New Testament
Barclay: The New Testament
  Westminster
Beck: The Holy Bible in the Language of Today: An American Translation
  Holman
(New) Berkeley Version: *see* Modern Language Bible
Bible in Basic English, The
  Cambridge
Book, The: *see* Living Bible
Brenton: The Septuagint and Apocrypha in Greek and English
  Zondervan
Concordant Literal New Testament (and Old Testament Portions)
  Concordant Publishing Concern
Darby: A New Translation from the Original Languages
  Holman
Douay-Rheims Version
  TAN Books
Emphasized Bible (Rotherham)
  Kregel
English Version for the Deaf (New Testament)
  Baker
Godbey: The New Testament
  Schmul
Good News Bible: *see* Today's English Version
Holy Scriptures According to the Masoretic Text, The
  Jewish Publication Society
International Children's Bible
  Sweet
Jerusalem Bible (Roman Catholic translation)
  Doubleday
  (*See also* New Jerusalem Bible)
Jerusalem Bible (Koren—Jewish translation)
  Phillip Feldheim, Inc.
King James Version
  Available from dozens of publishers
Lamsa: The Holy Bible From Ancient Eastern Manuscripts
  Harper & Row
Living Bible
  Here's Life
  Our Sunday Visitor
  Tyndale
Modern Language Bible (New Berkeley Version)
  Zondervan

Moffatt: The Bible: A New Translation
     Harper & Row
Montgomery: The New Testament in Modern English
     Judson
A New Accurate Translation of the Greek New Testament into Simple Everyday
American English
     Self-published by Julian G. Anderson
New American Bible
     Catholic Book Publishers
     Nelson
     Our Sunday Visitor
     World
New American Standard Bible
     Cambridge
     Foundation Press
     Here's Life
     Holman
     Moody
     Nelson
     World
     Zondervan
New Century Version (The Word)
     Sweet
New English Bible
     Cambridge
     Oxford
New International Version
     International Bible Society
     Kirkbride
     Oxford
     Zondervan
New Jerusalem Bible
     Doubleday
New Jewish Version: *see* Tanakh
New King James Version
     Moody
     Nelson
New Life Testament
     Christian Literature International
New Testament: A New Easy-to-Read Version
     Baker
New World Translation
     Watchtower Bible and Tract Society
Original New Testament (Schonfield)
     Harper & Row
Phillips: New Testament in Modern English
     Macmillan
Reader's Digest Bible
     Reader's Digest
     Random House
Revised Standard Version
     American Bible Society
     Cambridge
     Christian Board of Publications
     Holman
     Nelson

Oxford
World
Zondervan
(English) Revised Version
Oxford
Rotherman: *see* Emphasized Bible
Simple English Bible
International Bible Publishing
Tanakh (New Jewish Version)
Jewish Publication Society
Today's English Version (Good News Bible)
American Bible Society
Nelson
Our Sunday Visitor
World
Wesley: Explanatory Notes Upon the New Testament
Baker
Beacon Hill
Hendrickson
Weymouth: New Testament in Modern Speech
Kregel
Williams, C. B.: The New Testament in the Language of the People
Holman
Word, The: *see* New Century Bible
Worrell New Testament
Gospel Publishing House
Wuest: The New Testament: An Expanded Translation
Eerdmans
Young's Literal Translation
Baker

Major Parallel Editions

Comparative Study Bible (NIV, NAS, AB, KJV)
Zondervan
Eight Translation New Testament (KJV, PNT, RSV, JB, LB, NIV, TEV, NEB)
Tyndale
Layman's Parallel Bible (KJV, RSV, LB, NIV)
Zondervan
26 Translations of the Holy Bible: 3 volumes
AMG Publishers
Mathis Publishers

Interlinear Translations

Interlinear Bible, Jay Green
Baker
Hendrickson
Interlinear Greek-English New Testament (KJV parallel), George R. Berry
Baker
Zondervan
Interlinear Greek-English New Testament (available with KJV, NASB, NIV, RSV; also KJV with NIV, and NASB with NIV parallels), Alfred Marshall
Zondervan
NIV Interlinear Hebrew-English Old Testament (4 volumes), John R. Kohlenberger III
Zondervan

Chart 6
COMPARATIVE READING AND EVALUATION OF BIBLE VERSIONS

BOOK or PASSAGE: TYPE of LITERATURE:

VERSION 1:

    Difficult or odd renderings:

    Great renderings:

    Major differences from other versions:

    General impressions:

        Readability:

        Accuracy:

VERSION 2:

    Difficult or odd renderings:

    Great renderings:

    Major differences from other versions:

    General impressions:

        Readability:

        Accuracy:

VERSION 3:

    Difficult or odd renderings:

    Great renderings:

    Major differences from other versions:

    General impressions:

        Readability:

        Accuracy:

VERSION 4:

    Difficult or odd renderings:

    Great renderings:

    Major differences from other versions:

    General impressions:

        Readability:

        Accuracy:

VERSION 5:

    Difficult or odd renderings:

    Great renderings:

    Major differences from other versions:

    General impressions:

        Readability:

        Accuracy:

VERSION 6:

    Difficult or odd renderings:

    Great renderings:

    Major differences from other versions:

    General impressions:

        Readability:

        Accuracy:

Chart 7

COMPARATIVE CHART OF THE BEST-SELLING VERSIONS OF THE BIBLE

(Arranged in Chronological Order of Publication)

Version	Year Published NT/OT [Apoc]	Number of Translators	Theological Orientation	Publishers	Comments [EV = English Version, FE = Formal Equivalence, DE = Dynamic Equivalence]
KING JAMES "Authorized Version"	1611 [1611]	54 (or 47)	Church of England	Many	Historically and currently the best-selling EV, though dated in textual base and vocabulary. Basically FE, but with much free and poetic rendering. Verse format.
REVISED STANDARD	1946/1952 [1957]	32 [10]	Protestant, Catholic, (1 Jewish)	ABS, Holman, Nelson, Oxford, World, Zondervan	The text of the OT revised more than previous EVV, more DE than previous EVV, but retained archaic language in prayers. Broadly based in relation to translators. Paragraphed. Sponsored by National Council of Churches.
AMPLIFIED BIBLE	1958/1964 [No Apoc]	Francis E. Siewert + 12 others	Conservative Protestant	Zondervan	FE translation with many bracketed expansions, explanations and footnotes to word study resources. Verse format. Sponsored by the Lockman Foundation.
NEW ENGLISH BIBLE	1961/1970 [1970]	47	Protestant (Catholic observers)	Cambridge, Oxford	Strove for literary excellence, primarily DE and very British in idiom. Emended the OT more than previous RSV. Paragraph format.
JERUSALEM BIBLE (See also New Jerusalem Bible below).	1966 [1966]	27	Roman Catholic	Doubleday	Poetic DE translation, quite a bit of textual emendation in both Testaments, the first major EV to use "Yahweh" as the proper name of God. First official Catholic version translated from Greek and Hebrew. Paragraph format.
NEW AMERICAN	1970 [1970]	55	50 Catholic 5 Protestant	Nelson, Our Sunday Visitor, World	DE translation from Greek and Hebrew, much textual emendation and rearrangement in OT. Paragraph style. Sponsored by the Confraternity of Church Doctrine

Version	Date	Translator / No.	Tradition / Publishers	Publisher	Notes
NEW AMERICAN STANDARD	1963/1971 [No Apoc]	58	Conservative Protestant Here's Life, Holman, Moody, Nelson, Riverside, World, Zondervan	Cambridge, Foundation	FE translation based on ASV (though using "LORD" instead of "Jehovah"), employs archaic English in prayers, American in idiom. Verse format (though some editions paragraphed). Sponsored by the Lockman Foundation.
LIVING BIBLE	1967/1971 [1973]	Kenneth N. Taylor [Albert J. Nevins]	Conservative Protestant [Catholic]	Tyndale, Here's Life, Our Sunday Visitor	Paraphrase of the ASV (with consultation of Greek and Hebrew) with much expansive commentary. Has been translated into more than 40 languages. Paragraph format.
TODAY'S ENGLISH VERSION (GOOD NEWS BIBLE)	1966/1976 [1979]	NT: Robert G. Bratcher OT: RGB + 6 APOC. 3	Protestant	American Bible Soc., Nelson, World	DE translation with limited vocabulary and simple syntax, avoids ecclesiastical terms. Illustrated with line drawings. Paragraphed. Sponsored by the American Bible Society.
NEW INTERNATIONAL VERSION	1973/1978 [No Apoc]	115	Conservative Protestant	International Bible Soc., Kirkbride, Oxford, Zondervan	Primarily DE with some FE characteristics, uses internationally based English idiom, retains ecclesiastical terms and traditional tone. Paragraph format. Sponsored by the (New York) International Bible Society.
NEW KING JAMES VERSION	1979/1982 [No Apoc]	119	Conservative Protestant	Moody, Nelson	FE revision of the KJV, retains KJV textual base while changing archaic inflections and obsolete words. Verse format.
NEW JERUSALEM BIBLE	1985 [1985]	Henry Wansbrough General Editor	Roman Catholic	Doubleday	Revision of JB, based on 1973 edition of La Bible de Jerusalem. More conservative in textual base and consistent in language, updated notes.

Adapted from *All About Bibles* (Oxford, 1985) and used by permission of Oxford University Press.

FOR FURTHER READING ON THE HISTORY AND CHARACTERISTICS OF THE ENGLISH BIBLE

I. On the History of the English Bible

General Bible introductions and Bible dictionaries and encyclopedias (see *Books About the Book*, chapters 9 and 4 respectively) also have concise articles on the history of the transmission and translation of the Bible.

Bruce, F. F. *History of the Bible in English.* 3rd ed. Oxford, 1978 (1st ed. 1961). *This is the best and most thorough one-volume treatment, well illustrated with anecdotes about, and excerpts from, classic and modern English versions.*

Cambridge History of the Bible. *This is the standard set on the history of the transmission and translation of the Bible. It covers more than English versions, but concentrates on the Western world. Its three volumes are:*

    Ackroyd, Peter R., and C. F. Evans, eds. From the Beginnings to Jerome. Cambridge, 1970.

    Greenslade, S. L., ed. The West From the Reformation to the Modern Day. Cambridge, 1963.

    Lampe, G. W. H., ed. The West From the Fathers to the Reformation. Cambridge, 1969.

Herbert, A. S. *Historical Catalogue of Printed Editions of the English Bible.* ABS, 1968. *This is a chronological list of every known edition of the English Bible published from 1525 to 1961.*

Hills, Margaret T. *A Concise History of the English Bible.* 7th ed. Revised by Elizabeth J. Eisenhart et al. ABS, 1983 (1st ed. 1935). *This 61-page booklet is an excellent, though brief history of the English Bible up to 1982.*

Hills, Margaret T., ed. *The English Bible in America.* ABS, 1961. *This list concentrates on English Bibles and Testaments published in America from 1777 to 1957.*

Paine, Gustavus S. *The Men Behind the King James Version.* Baker, 1959. *As the title indicates, this book provides insight into the scholars who produced the KJV and into the making of the version itself.*

Scriptures of the World. *UBS, 1983. This is an alphabetic listing of the 1,762 languages into which at least one book of the Bible has been translated.*

Underwood, Jonathan, and Lewis A. Foster. *A History of the English Bible.* Standard, 1983. *Another brief history, with a concise guide to selecting a Bible for personal use.*

Weiss, G. Christian. *What You Should Know About Bible Translations.* Back to the Bible, 1977. *Written by a conservative to assure other conservatives that versions newer than the KJV can be trusted to communicate the Word of God, this booklet is a fine introduction for the general reader.*

II. On the Various Versions of the Bible

Adeney, Michael. "Good News for Everyone—Buying and Selling Foreign-Language Bibles." In *Bookstore Journal* (September 1983). *Intended primarily for booksellers, this article lists several major resources for acquiring many of the hundreds of foreign-language Bibles.*

Bailey, Lloyd R., ed. *The Word of God.* Atlanta: John Knox, 1982. *This book contains evaluations of nine major versions and six study Bibles by eleven scholars, all translators themselves. One of the few such titles to be done by other than evangelicals.*

Barker, Kenneth L., ed. *The NIV: The Making of a Contemporary Translation.* Zondervan, 1986. *This volume contains essays by fourteen of the NIV translators on how this version approached various translation difficulties.*

Bible for Today, The (900 Park Avenue, Collingswood, NJ 08108). *This organization carries a large variety of new and reprint books and pamphlets that support the KJV and criticize all other versions of the Bible. Their catalog is available for purchase.*

Foster, Lewis A. *Selecting a Translation of the Bible.* 2nd ed. Standard, 1983 (1st ed. 1978). *A helpful guide to selecting one of nine major versions, written from a conservative perspective.*

Hann, Robert R. *The Bible: An Owner's Manual.* Paulist, 1983. *Given the tag line "What you need to know before you buy and read your own Bible," this is a practical guide to choosing and using a version. It includes brief evaluations of nine major versions and an annotated bibliography of basic study tools.*

Kerr, William F. *The Living Bible—Not Just Another Version.* Tyndale, 1974. *Originally a paper presented to the Evangelical Theological Society, this is an evaluation of the LB; it concentrates on its positive contributions, while not ignoring its shortcomings.*

Kohlenberger, John R., III, and the editors of Oxford University Press. *All About Bibles.* Oxford, 1985. *Originally designed as a guide for booksellers but rewritten to include general readers, this 75-page booklet capsulizes much of the material of this volume.*

Kubo, Sakae, and Walter F. Specht. *So Many Versions?* 2nd ed. Zondervan, 1983 (1st ed. 1975). *One of the best and most comprehensive guides, it devotes seventeen chapters to as many* major versions of the Bible but discusses dozens more in its first and final chapters and appendix. The authors give the background and history of each version; describe its text, language, and layout; and point out its strengths as well as its weaknesses.

Lewis, Jack P. *The English Bible From KJV to NIV.* Baker, 1981. The most thorough evaluation available, covering twelve major versions, with 42-page listing of hundreds of other reviews. Like Kubo and Specht, Lewis commends and criticizes.

Nida, Eugene A. *Good News for Everyone.* Word, 1977. This is a history and a positive evaluation of Today's English Version. It also contains a brief presentation of the principles and practice of D-E translation.

Chapter 5

STUDY BIBLES: EVERYTHING YOU NEED BETWEEN TWO COVERS

The designation "study Bible" can refer to two things. In some contexts, it refers to the translation itself, to a version of the Bible suitable for study. But more often it designates a translation plus a set of materials designed to help one read and study the text. This latter designation is the subject of this chapter.

Like the existence of "so many versions," the glut of available study Bibles is at once a curse and a blessing. It is a curse in that there are so many publications commercially competing for people's attention and acquisition; it is a blessing in that this competition has necessitated the production of fuller and better study editions.

In order to help guide the reader to the study Bible that will best meet his or her needs, we will first survey the range of features that can be found in a study Bible, then we will examine the specific features of several classic and recent editions and, finally, we will look at a list of questions you can ask to narrow your choices to discover the best possible volume.

A SURVEY OF MAJOR FEATURES

Before we begin our survey of the various features of study Bibles, I want to introduce a few terms I will use for explanation and categorization. In study Bibles, as in any other type of Bible-study tool, the materials can either give an explanation or point to other portions of the text for further understanding. Helps that explain I label "subjective," because the explanation is subject to the interpreter's point of view. Helps that direct one into and

125

within the text I label "objective," because they allow the text to speak for itself.

Of course, there can be objectivity in interpretation and subjectivity in the selection of texts. I am simply trying to distinguish between those helps that tell one what to believe and those that lead one to the text to let it speak for itself. A study Bible that is primarily objective in its features can be used by anyone, regardless of theological affiliation. On the other hand, a study Bible that is primarily subjective is most useful to someone who agrees with the interpreter; it can even be offensive to someone who does not.

The subjectivity of the interpreter is usually seen in his or her *conclusions* in the comments on the text. However, the differences between the conservative and the liberal positions are often more obvious in their *introductions* to the text. For much of their difference lies in their understanding of the origin, dating, authorship, and historical setting of any book, rather than in their understanding of the teaching of its text. (I will expand on these differences below.)

Thus while I tried to avoid theological labels in relation to Bible translations, I feel it is necessary to use them in relation to Bible helps. Most versions of the Bible can be used profitably by people of any church or denomination, but many study Bibles have enough of a doctrinal or critical orientation to limit their usefulness to those who agree with a specific theological viewpoint.

The Translation Proper

The single most important feature of a study Bible is its text—that is, its translation—because the most important activity in studying the Bible is *reading* it.

Just as in regard to the choice of Bible versions, the choice of translations in a study Bible is a recent development. Most of the classics were based on and keyed to the KJV, and in fact new KJV study Bibles continue to appear. But as fewer people are choosing the KJV as their preferred translation, more are looking for study Bibles based on modern versions. Although we have recently seen the classic *Thompson Chain-Reference Bible* and *New Scofield Reference Bible* adapted to the NIV, most modern-version study Bibles are new products (though they may use recycled features).

The decade of the eighties has already witnessed an explosion in the production of new study Bibles. Now you can choose a translation before you choose the edition in which to acquire it. Thus, once you have worked through the materials in chapter 4, you are ready to continue your selection process.

I would advise putting a lot of thought into this selection. For although I recommend collecting versions for comparative study, I cannot universally recommend collecting study Bibles for this same purpose. It is neither economically nor functionally practical to do so.

One can pick up three or four paperback or used copies of the Bible in various versions for the price of one study Bible and have resources for comparative study of each verse of the Bible. But in addition to giving the text, a study Bible offers only a selection of concise, limited helps. It is meant to be a self-contained, portable library, but not the only library one should own. For the price of three or four study Bibles, one can buy three or four major reference works, each of which offers more study materials than the helps of several study Bibles combined.

One will want to spend a little to get a lot of versions for comparative study. But one will want to spend a lot to get a lifetime of information—and wear—out of a study Bible whose translation and helps are most valuable.

Introductions

A Bible introduction usually gives information about the author, readers, date, origin, and content of any book or section of the Bible. Introductions may differ in thoroughness and length (as seen in examples 1 and 2), but they may also differ in perspective.

Conservative introductions take the Bible's self-witness at face value. For example, they agree that Moses wrote all or most of the Pentateuch (the first five books of the Bible), that Paul wrote 1 and 2 Timothy and Titus, and that Peter wrote 2 Peter; this is because the books themselves say so.

However, most nonconservative or liberal scholars use criteria other than the text of the Bible to evaluate its statements and claims. Often extrabiblical sources and criticism corroborate the text. But they also raise problems that liberal scholars feel cannot be answered by the traditional understanding of the text.

OBADIAH

Author

The author's name is Obadiah, which means "servant (or worshiper) of the LORD." His was a common name (see 1Ki 18:3-16; 1Ch 3:21; 7:3; 8:38; 9:16; 12:9; 27:19; 2Ch 17:7; 34:12; Ezr 8:9; Ne 10:5; 12:25). Neither his father's name nor the place of his birth is given.

Date and Place of Writing

The date and place of composition are disputed. Dating the prophecy is mainly a matter of relating vv. 11-14 to one of two specific events in Israel's history:

1. The invasion of Jerusalem by Philistines and Arabs during the reign of Jehoram (853-841 B.C.); see 2Ki 8:20-22; 2Ch 21:8-20. In this case, Obadiah would be a contemporary of Elisha.

2. The Babylonian attacks on Jerusalem (605-586). Obadiah would then be a contemporary of Jeremiah. This alternative seems more likely.

The parallels between Ob 1-9 and Jer 49:7-22 have caused many to suggest some kind of interdependence between Obadiah and Jeremiah, but it may be that both prophets were drawing on a common source not otherwise known to us.

Unity and Theme

There is no compelling reason to doubt the unity of this brief prophecy. Its theme is that Edom, proud over her own security, has gloated over Israel's devastation by foreign powers. However, Edom's participation in that disaster will bring on God's wrath. She herself will be destroyed, but Mount Zion and Israel will be delivered, and God's kingdom will triumph.

Edom's hostile activities have spanned the centuries of Israel's existence. The following Biblical references are helpful in understanding the relation of Israel and Edom: Ge 27:41-45; 32:1-21; 33; 36; Ex 15:15; Nu 20:14-21; Dt 2:1-6; 23:7; 1Sa 21 with Ps 52; 2Sa 8:13-14; 2Ki 8:20-22; 14:7; Ps 83; Eze 35; Joel 3:18-19; Am 1:11-12; 9:12.

Since the Edomites are related to the Israelites (v. 10), their hostility is all the more reprehensible. Edom is fully responsible for her failure to assist Israel and for her open aggression. The fact that God rejected Esau (Ge 25:23; Mal 1:3; Ro 9:13) in no way exonerates the Edomites. Edom, smug in its mountain strongholds, will be dislodged and sacked. Israel will prosper because God is with her.

Outline

I. Title and Introduction (1)
II. Judgment on Edom (2-14)
   A. Edom's Destruction Announced (2-7)
      1. The humbling of her pride (2-4)
      2. The completeness of her destruction (5-7)
   B. Edom's Destruction Reaffirmed (8-14)
      1. Her shame and destruction (8-10)
      2. Her crimes against Israel (11-14)
III. The Day of the Lord (15-21)
   A. Judgment on the Nations but Deliverance for Zion (15-18)
   B. The Lord's Kingdom Established (19-21)

Example 1. NIV STUDY BIBLE, p. 1360

Thus most modern, critical, or liberal scholars (or however else you may prefer to designate nonconservative scholars) believe that a series of editors wrote the Pentateuch, that a disciple or disciples of Paul wrote the Pastoral Epistles, and that 2 Peter was written at least a half century after Peter's death.

Sometimes the differences between conservative and liberal scholarship greatly affect the understanding of the text. In the New Testament examples just cited, for instance, the apostolic

Obadiah

Introduction:
The name Obadiah means "servant of Jehovah." Nothing more is known about this prophet than this short book containing his prophecy.

Obadiah is a book of prophecy against the nation of Edom. This country had invaded and plundered Jerusalem at least four times, so Obadiah announced God's judgment against them and prophesied that their kingdom would be destroyed.

The Edomites are heard of no more after the destruction of Jerusalem in A.D. 70.

Outline of contents:
The doom of Edom (1–14)
Edom in the day of the Lord (15–21)

Example 2. YOUNG DISCOVERER'S BIBLE, p. 1433

origin of those books is in question as is biblical authority in general. On the other hand, most liberal study Bibles do take biblical authority very seriously and accept the teaching of Timothy, Titus, and 2 Peter as binding, though they may not accept the books themselves as apostolic.

Besides the New Testament letters, most books of the Bible are anonymous; so knowing the author by name has little to do with one's acceptance of the authority of these books or with one's interpretation of them. But conservative readers will still have problems with the liberals' denial of the accuracy of direct statements and the historicity of events recorded in the Scriptures, as will liberals when conservatives hold to traditional understandings in the face of seemingly contradictory evidence.

All of this serves to illustrate some of the differences in the approach and conclusions of conservative and liberal scholars and the problems of subjective materials in a study Bible. Again, as I use "conservative," "liberal," and other labels to describe the orientation of study helps, I do so to define and clarify, not to criticize. (In *Books About the Book*, chapter 9 on Bible introductions discusses more of these distinctives and lists major resources that represent and defend many perspectives and approaches to biblical study.)

Introductions usually precede the sections or books they discuss. Sometimes, as in the *Thompson Chain-Reference Bible*, the introductions are gathered together into a separate section.

Outlines

An outline displays the contents of a book. It usually appears immediately before the text. In the *Harper Study Bible*, however, the outline is actually worked into the text (see example 3). And in the *Companion Bible*, the general book outline is developed into a detailed section-by-section outline in the notes (example 4). The *Open Bible* uses charts in addition to outlines to summarize the contents of each book.

Outlines are subject to the interpreter's understanding of the structure of the book. But this is not an area of liberal-conservative or denominational debate. Differences between outlines are mostly a matter of thoroughness and detail (as seen in Examples 1 and 2).

Cross References

One of the most useful features of a study Bible for analyzing the text proper is its reference system. Cross references link verses and passages of Scripture on the basis of similar words, phrases, and concepts.

Cross references are usually found in a column beside the text, as in the *Harper Study Bible* (example 3); between two columns of text, as in the *NIV Reference Bible* (example 5); or in

THE BOOK OF

OBADIAH

I. *The judgment against Edom (1–14)*

A. *The fall of Edom predicted*

1
*1
Is 34:5;
Ezek 25:12;
Joel 3:19;
Jer 49:14;
Is 30:4;
Jer 6:4,5

The vision of Obadiah.
Thus says the Lord GOD concerning Edom—
  We have heard a report from the LORD,
  And an envoy has been sent among the nations saying,
  "Arise and let us go against her for battle"—

2 "Behold, I will make you small among the nations;
  You are greatly despised.

*3
Is 16:6;
Jer 49:16;
2 Kin 14:7;
Is 14:13-15;
Rev 18:7

3 "The arrogance of your heart has deceived you,
  You who live in the clefts of the rock,
  In the loftiness of your dwelling place,
  Who say in your heart,
  'Who will bring me down to earth?'

4
Job 20:6;
Hab 2:9;
Is 14:13-15

4 "Though you build high like the eagle,
  Though you set your nest among the stars,
  From there I will bring you down," declares the LORD.

B. *Edom's destruction to be complete*

5
Jer 49:9;
vv. 9,10;
Is 17:6

5 "If thieves came to you,
  If robbers by night—
  O how you will be ruined!—
  Would they not steal *only* until they had enough?
  If grape gatherers came to you,
  Would they not leave *some* gleanings?

Example 3. HARPER STUDY BIBLE (NASB), p. 1362

the notes, as in the *Companion Bible* (example 4). Sometimes the reference actually follows the verse and is set in the text itself, as in the *Open Bible* and the Amplified Bible (example 6). This latter format is convenient, but in my judgment it unnecessarily interrupts the flow of the text, unnaturally separates the verses into independent units, and thus makes Bible reading more difficult.

References are usually keyed to a word or phrase by means of a superscript letter or number (example 5), though some systems are keyed only to the verse itself, as are the *Open Bible*, the Amplified Bible (example 6), and The *Harper Study Bible* (example 3). The most specific reference system is found in the

131

Thompson Chain-Reference Bible, which identifies the topic that is referenced, keys it to a numbered topical index, and directs the reader to the next verse in its chain of references (example 7).

The quality of a reference system is in its thoroughness and organization. Size—that is, the number of references—can be a deceptive measure, for a system of 80,000 references may have

OBADIAH.

A¹ A a
(p. 1245)
482 or 472

1 THE vision of °Obadiah. °Thus saith °the Lord GOD °concerning Edom; ° "We have heard °a rumour from °the LORD, °and an ambassador is sent among the °heathen, °Arise ye, and let us rise up against her °in battle."

2 °Behold, I have made thee small among the ¹ heathen : thou art greatly despised.

b 3 The pride of thine heart hath deceived thee, thou that dwellest in °the clefts of the rock, whose habitation *is* high ; that saith in his heart, 'Who shall bring me down to the ground?'

4 °Though thou exalt *thyself* as the eagle, and though thou °set thy nest °among the stars, thence will I bring thee down, °saith ¹ the LORD.

B 5 °If thieves came to thee, if robbers by night, (°how art thou cut off!) would they not have stolen till they had enough? °if the grapegatherers came to thee, °would they not leave *some* grapes?

6 °How are *the things* of Esau °searched out! *how* are his hidden things sought up!

1-16 (A¹, p. 1244). EDOM. DESTRUCTION.
(Alternation and Introversion.)

A¹ | A | a | 1, 2. Remote Cause. Jehovah's Purpose
  | | b | 3, 4. Deceived by Self.
  | | B | 5, 6. Devastation.
  | A | b | 7-9. Deceived by Others.
  | | a | 10-14. Immediate Cause. Edom's Sin.
  | | B | 15, 16. Extermination.

1 Obadiah =Servant of Jehovah. Cp. 1 Kings 18
Thus saith, &c. The words of this prophecy, therefore, are not Obadiah's, but Jehovah's. Cp. *vv.* 8, 18
the Lord GOD. Heb. Adonai Jehovah. Ap. 4. VII
and II.
concerning Edom. See notes on p. 1244.
We have heard. The rhetorical difficulty may
removed by regarding these words as the words
Edom's foes. a rumour =tiding
the LORD. Heb. Jehovah. Ap. 4. II. Supply
logical *Ellipsis* (Ap. 6) : " from Jehovah [that Edom
to be attacked]". and : or, and [already].
heathen =nations.
Arise ye. These are the words of the embassage
in battle =the war.
2 Behold. Fig. *Asterismos*. Ap. 6. Calling attention
to the words of Jehovah.
3 the clefts, &c. Referring to the natural position
of the Edomites. Cp. 2 Kings 14. 7.

Example 4. COMPANION BIBLE, p. 1245

so much duplication that it cites only 40,000 unique texts, whereas a better-organized system of 60,000 may cite 45,000 unique references. The only way to evaluate a reference system satisfactorily is to spend some time using it.

As editor for the Old Testament of the *NIV Reference Bible* I spent some time using this resource. The Old Testament team took the contributions of several research teams headed by NIV

Obadiah

[1]The vision[a] of Obadiah.

1-4pp — Jer 49:14-16
5-6pp — Jer 49:9-10

This is what the Sovereign LORD says about Edom[b] —

We have heard a message from the
    LORD:
An envoy[c] was sent to the nations
    to say,
"Rise, and let us go against her for
    battle"[d] —

[2]"See, I will make you small[e] among
    the nations;
you will be utterly despised.
[3]The pride[f] of your heart has
    deceived you,
you who live in the clefts of the
    rocks[a g]
and make your home on the
    heights,
you who say to yourself,
'Who can bring me down to the
    ground?'[h]

1 [a]S Isa 1:1
[b]S Ge 25:14;
S Isa 11:14;
S 34:11; 63:1-6;
Jer 49:7-22;
S Eze 25:12-14;
S 32:29;
S Am 1:11-12
[c]Isa 18:2
[d]Jer 6:4-5
2 [e]Nu 24:18
3 [f]S Isa 16:6
[g]fn Isa 16:1
[h]S 2Ch 25:11-12
4 [i]S Isa 10:14
[j]S Isa 14:13
[k]S Job 20:6
5 [l]S Dt 4:27;
24:21; S Isa 24:13
7 [m]Jer 30:14
[n]S Ps 41:9

"will I not destroy[o] the wise men
    of Edom,
men of understanding in the
    mountains of Esau?
[9]Your warriors, O Teman,[p] will be
    terrified,
and everyone in Esau's mountains
    will be cut down in the slaughter.
[10]Because of the violence[q] against
    your brother Jacob,[r]
you will be covered with shame;
you will be destroyed forever.[s]
[11]On the day you stood aloof
    while strangers carried off his
    wealth
and foreigners entered his gates
    and cast lots[t] for Jerusalem,
you were like one of them.[u]
[12]You should not look down[v] on your
    brother
in the day of his misfortune,[w]
nor rejoice[x] over the people of Judah
    in the day of their destruction,[y]
nor boast[z] so much
    in the day of their trouble.[a]

Example 5. NIV REFERENCE BIBLE, p. 846

translators and organized these materials by computer according to the pattern established by New Testament editor Dr. Donald Madvig. In order to verify the accuracy of our programming, I manually compared many portions of our Old Testament reference system to those of existing study Bibles.

In one test case, I compared references to the concept of the "new covenant." At Jeremiah 31:31, our system listed six references, the *Ryrie Study Bible* (NASB) listed eight, the *Open Bible* (NKJV) listed three, and the *Thompson Chain-Reference Bible* listed topic "881 New Covenant" and one reference. I looked up each reference in each study Bible, listed all their references and then checked for duplication. The *NIV Reference*

Bible had a total of forty; *Ryrie*, thirty-six; *Open*, six; and *Thompson*, six. But of the NIV's forty, twenty-seven were unique; of *Ryrie's* thirty-six, only nineteen were unique; five of the *Open's* six were unique, as were all six of *Thompson's*.

This example (and all others I tested) demonstrate that the *NIV Reference Bible* has the largest overall totals with the least duplication of any system available. On the other hand, one may

THE BOOK OF OBADIAH

THE vision of Obadiah. Thus says the Lord God concerning ᵃEdom: We have heard tidings from the Lord, and an ambassador is sent forth among the nations, *saying*, Arise, and let us rise up against *Edom* to battle! [Ps. 137:7; Isa. 34:1-15; 63:1-6; Jer. 49:7-22.]

2 Behold, I will make you small among the nations, *Edom;* you shall be despised exceedingly. [Ezek. 35.]

3 The pride of your heart has deceived you, you dweller in the refuges of the rock [Petra, Edom's capital], whose habitation is high, who says in his heart, Who can bring me down to the ground?

4 Though you mount on high as the eagle, and though you set your nest among the stars, I will bring you down from there, says the Lord.

5 If thieves came to you, if robbers by night — how you are brought to nothing! — would they not steal only enough for themselves? If grape gatherers came to you, would they not leave some grapes for gleaning? [But this was done by God, not men.]

6 How are the things of Esau [Edom] searched out! How are his hidden treasures sought out!

7 All the men of your confederacy —

Example 6. AMPLIFIED BIBLE, p. 1038

prefer the specificity of the *Thompson Chain-Reference* to the thoroughness of the NIV or NASB reference Bibles. Again, only your own "hands on" experience can demonstrate to you the value and superiority of any reference system.

Notes

From the beginning of the translation of the Bible into English, notes have played an important part in communicating the meaning of the text to the reader. In most early versions, however, the notes contained as much criticism of contrary theological systems as they did commentary on the text! One of the unique features of the KJV was its deliberate omission of explanatory notes, which apparently set a precedent. For most later versions have limited their notes to alternate renderings and textual difficulties, while explanatory notes have become almost exclusively associated with study Bibles.

Author, Not Known.
53 **Analysis** of the Book.

Obadiah

587 B.C. (?)
p.p.Isa 21:11; Eze 25:12
98 Edomites
96 Prophetic Visions,
Na 1:1
67 Ambassadors

73 Humiliation (1)
36 Dishonor

p.p.2Ki 14:7
p.p.Isa 47:7; Rev 18:7
23 Pride (2)†
37 Carnal Security,
Lk 12:19
88 Self-confidence (1),
Mt 26:33
96 Self-deception

p.p.Isa 14:14; Am 9:2;
Hab 2:9
57 Eagles
70 Abasement (1)
4 Self-exaltation,
Mt 23:12

[1]The vision of Obadiah.

This is what the Sovereign LORD says about Edom—

We have heard a message
from the LORD:
An envoy was sent to the
nations to say,
"Rise, and let us go against
her for battle"—

[2]"See, I will make you small
among the nations;
you will be utterly
despised.
[3]The pride of your heart has
deceived you,
you who live in the clefts
of the rocks[a]
and make your home on
the heights,
you who say to yourself,
'Who can bring me down
to the ground?'
[4]Though you soar like the
eagle
and make your nest among
the stars,
from there I will bring you
down,"
declares the LORD.

men of understanding in
the mountains of Esau?
[9]Your warriors, O Teman,
will be terrified,
and everyone in Esau's
mountains
will be cut down in the
slaughter.
[10]Because of the violence
against your brother
Jacob,
you will be covered with
shame;
you will be destroyed
forever.
[11]On the day you stood aloof
while strangers carried off
his wealth
and foreigners entered his
gates
and cast lots for Jerusalem,
you were like one of them.
[12]You should not look down
on your brother
in the day of his
misfortune,
nor rejoice over the people
of Judah
in the day of their
destruction,
nor boast so much

p.p.Jer 49:22
990 Destruction (2)
2343 Mighty Men

p.p.Ge 27:41
p.p.Mal 1:4
2547 Violence
3049 Retribution (1)
3068 The Wicked (4)

p.p.Ge 14:16
p.p.Joel 3:3
p.p.Eze 35:10
p.p.Mic 4:11
648 Casting Lots (1)

1935 Rejoicing (4), 1Co 13:6
2201 Brotherly Love (2)
3303 Evil Speech (1)

Example 7. THOMPSON CHAIN-REFERENCE BIBLE (NIV), p. 945

Much of the time, notes simply illuminate the text with definitions of obscure or important words, explanations of customs, cross references to similar passages, enlightenment from historical backgrounds, and similar objective information (See examples 8 and 9). But as in the case of introductions, the notes often betray an alignment with a particular theological or critical approach to the text.

4:53 *believed.* Cf. the aim of this Gospel (20:31).

4:54 *the second miraculous sign.* There had, of course, already been many such signs (2:23; 3:2), but this was the second time Jesus performed a sign after coming from Judea to Galilee.

5:1 *Some time later.* An indefinite expression (cf. 6:1; 7:1). *a feast of the Jews.* Probably one of the three pilgrimage feasts to which all Jewish males were expected to go—Passover, Pentecost or Tabernacles. The identity of this feast is significant for the attempt to ascertain the number of Passovers included in Jesus' ministry, and thus the number of years his ministry lasted. John explicitly mentions at least three different Passovers: the first in 2:13,23 (see note on 2:13), the second in 6:4 and the third several times (e.g., in 11:55; 12:1). If three Passovers are accepted, the length of Jesus' ministry was between two and three years. However, if the feast of 5:1 was a fourth Passover or assumes that a fourth Passover had come and gone, Jesus' ministry would have lasted between three and four years.

5:2 *there is.* Not "was." This may mean that the pool was still in existence at the time this was being written, i.e., that John wrote before the destruction of Jerusalem. However, this falls short of proving the time of writing (see Introduction: Date). *Bethesda.* The manuscripts have a variety of names (see NIV text note), but one of the Dead Sea Scrolls seems to show that Bethesda is the right name. The site is generally identified with the twin pools near the present-day Saint Anne's Church. There would have been a colonnade on each of the four sides and another between the two pools.

5:3–4 See NIV text note. Verse 4 was doubtless inserted by a later copyist to explain why people waited by the pool in large numbers.

5:5 *invalid.* John does not say what the trouble was, but it was a form of paralysis or at least lameness.

5:6 *Do you want to get well?* The question was important. The man had not asked Jesus for help, and a beggar of that day could lose a sometimes profitable (and easy) income if he were cured. Or perhaps he had simply lost the will to be cured.

5:7 *when the water is stirred.* The man did not see Jesus as a potential healer, and his mind was set on the supposed curative powers of the water.

5:9 *the man was cured.* Ordinarily, faith in Jesus was essential to the cure (e.g., Mk 5:34), but here the man did not even know who Jesus was (v. 13). Jesus usually healed in response to faith, but he was not limited by a person's lack of it.

5:10 *the law forbids you to carry your mat.* It was not the law of Moses but their traditional interpretation of it that prohibited carrying loads of any kind on the Sabbath. The Jews had very strict regulations on keeping the Sabbath, but also had many curious loopholes that their lawyers made full use of (cf. Mt 23:4).

5:12 *this fellow.* The Jews were contrasting the authority of the law of God, which in their view prohibited the action, and that of a mere man (as they considered Jesus to be) who permitted it.

5:14 *something worse.* The eternal consequences of sin are more serious than any physical ailment.

5:16 *was doing.* The continuous action points to more than one incident, and the Jews apparently discerned a pattern. *persecuted.* John does not tell us what form the persecution took.

5:17 *My Father is always at his work.* Jesus' justification for

Example 8. NIV STUDY BIBLE, p. 1603

The notes of the New Jerusalem Bible and the New American Bible, for example, are noticeably Catholic in certain texts, *Scofield* and *Ryrie* are both conservative and dispensational, the *New Oxford Annotated* RSV and *Oxford Study Edition* of the NEB take a liberal/critical approach, and *Dake* is Pentecostal.

Beyond their interpretive distinctives, these positions can determine the tone and volume of the notes. The Catholic study Bibles tend to emphasize the historical dogmas of the Catholic church at key texts such as Matthew 16:17–19. *Scofield* and *Ryrie* emphasize distinctions between Israel and the church and literal fulfillment of prophecy (e.g., Acts 15:15–17). Notes in liberal study Bibles often counter the literal understanding of the text (e.g., Josh. 10:11) and point out stories and events they feel are contradictory or fabricated (e.g., Judg. 1; 1 Chron. 21). *Dake* gives extra attention to texts dealing with healing and spiritual gifts (e.g, Matt. 8:17; Acts 2).

Once again, theological or critical alignment in a study Bible is just fine—if one agrees with that given alignment. Those who do not agree may find themselves arguing with the notes as often as they agree with them. Although I feel that students of

---

5:22 *walked with God.* The phrase replaces the word "lived" in the other paragraphs of the chapter and reminds us that there is a difference between walking with God and merely living.

5:24 *then he was no more, because God took him away.* The phrase replaces "and then he died" in the other paragraphs of the chapter. Like Elijah, who was "taken" (2Ki 2:10) to heaven, Enoch was taken away (cf. Ps 49:15; 73:24) to the presence of God without experiencing death (Heb 11:5). Lamech, the seventh from Adam in the genealogy of Cain, was evil personified. But "Enoch, the seventh from Adam" (Jude 14) in the genealogy of Seth, "was commended as one who pleased God" (Heb 11:5).

5:27 *969 years.* Only Noah and his family survived the flood. If the figures concerning life spans are literal, Methuselah died in the year of the flood (the figures in vv. 25,28 and 7:6 add up to exactly 969).

6:1 *increase in number.* See note on 1:22.

6:2 *sons of God saw . . . daughters of men . . . and they married.* See v. 4. The phrase "sons of God" here has been interpreted to refer either to angels or to human beings. In such places as Job 1:6; 2:1 it refers to angels, and perhaps also in Ps 29:1 (where it is translated "mighty ones"). Some interpreters also appeal to Jude 6–7 (as well as to Jewish literature) in referring the phrase here to angels.

Others, however, maintain that intermarriage and cohabitation between angels and human beings, though commonly mentioned in ancient mythologies, are surely excluded by the very nature of the created order (ch. 1; Mk 12:25). Elsewhere, expressions equivalent to "sons of God" often refer to human beings, though in contexts quite different from the present one (see Dt 14:1; 32:5; Ps 73:15; Isa 43:6; Hos 1:10; 11:1; Lk 3:38; 1Jn 3:1–2,10). "Sons of God" (vv. 2,4) possibly refers to godly men, and "daughters of men" to sinful women (significantly, they are not called "daughters of

God"), probably from the wicked line of Cain. If so, the context suggests that vv. 1–2 describe the intermarriage of the Sethites ("sons of God") of ch. 5 with the Cainites ("daughters of men") of ch. 4, indicating a breakdown in the separation of the two groups.

Another plausible suggestion is that the "sons of God" refers to royal figures (kings were closely associated with gods in the ancient Near East) who proudly perpetuated and aggravated the corrupt life-style of Lamech son of Cain (virtually a royal figure) and established for themselves royal harems.

6:3 Two key phrases in the Hebrew of this verse are obscure: the one rendered "contend with" (see NIV text note) and the one rendered "for he is mortal." The verse seems to announce that the period of grace between God's declaration of judgment and its arrival would be 120 years (cf. 1Pe 3:20). But if the NIV text note reading is accepted, the verse announces that man's life span would henceforth be limited to 120 years (but see 11:10–26).

6:4 *Nephilim.* People of great size and strength (see Nu 13:31–33). The Hebrew word means "fallen ones." In men's eyes they were "the heroes of old, men of renown," but in God's eyes they were sinners ("fallen ones") ripe for judgment.

6:5 One of the Bible's most vivid descriptions of total depravity. And because man's nature remained unchanged, things were no better after the flood (8:21).

6:6 *The LORD was grieved . . . his heart was filled with pain.* Man's sin is God's sorrow (see Eph 4:30).

6:7 *I will wipe mankind . . . from the face of the earth.* The period of grace (see v. 3 and note) was coming to an end. *animals . . . creatures . . . birds.* Though morally innocent, the animal world, as creatures under man's corrupted rule, shared in his judgment.

Example 9. NIV STUDY BIBLE, p. 14

the Bible should have a diversity of interpretations represented in their collection of versions and reference books, I also feel that they should agree with their study Bible as much as possible, because it should be the most used resource in their library.

The study Bible that comes closest to being objective in its notes is the *NIV Study Bible.* Its forty-four contributors come from a wide denominational background, so the notes have no specific theological leaning; they include a variety of perspectives at once. Even though they are all evangelical, they often take the liberal view into account. Many texts that have more than one possible understanding have these possibilities listed in the notes.

"The sons of God" in Genesis 6:1–4, for example, can be seen as angels, as the godly line of Seth, or as mighty men of the ancient world. All three possibilities are outlined in the *NIV Study Bible* (example 9). This is not the only study Bible to summarize various interpretations, but it does so more regularly and more thoroughly than any other.

The notes of a study Bible are a mini-commentary; they constitute a very valuable feature, but one that can also limit the usefulness and appeal of the study Bible. I find it interesting that several widely used works, such as the *Thompson*, the *Open*, and the *Dickson* study Bibles, have no textual notes at all. Many prefer to leave this function to commentaries (discussed in detail in *Books About the Book*, chapter 11). As valuable as notes are, they are not absolutely necessary to a good study Bible.

Concordance and Index

As the cross-reference system connects key words, phrases, and concepts through the biblical text, the index or concordance lists such connections in a section separate from the text. In function, an index and a concordance are about the same. A concordance, however, is more specific in that it deals with specific words, while an index can deal with specific words and also with general subjects and concepts. Some editions, such as the *Scofield Reference Bible* and the *NIV Study Bible*, have an index to their notes.

For example, if one wants to study all the miracles of the Bible, a concordance lists all (or most) occurrences of the word *miracle* in the Bible. However, many miraculous events are called signs or wonders or have no label at all, so a list of verses containing "miracle" would only begin one's study of the concept. On the other hand, an index is limited only by its compiler's energy and skill, and can list miracles, signs, wonders, and other events regardless of the words used to describe them. (Example 10 compares the Chain Index with the concordance of the *Thompson Chain-Reference Bible*. The concordance lists all fifty-seven occurrences of the words

Ps 19:14 May the words of my mouth and the meditation of my heart be pleasing in your sight, O LORD, my Rock and my Redeemer.

1Ti 4:15 Be diligent in these matters; give yourself wholly to them, so that everyone may see your progress.

See Quietness, 2934, 2935.

2359—(2) The Righteous Delight in.

Ps 1:2 But his delight is in the law of the LORD, and on his law he meditates day and night.

Ps 39:3 My heart grew hot within me, and as I meditated, the fire burned; then I spoke with my tongue:

Ps 63:6 On my bed I remember you; I think of you through the watches of the night. (Ps 77:12)

Ps 104:34 May my meditation be pleasing to him, as I rejoice in the LORD. (Ps 119:15, 99)

Ps 119:148 My eyes stay open through the watches of the night, that I may meditate on your promises.

Ps 143:5 I remember the days of long ago; I meditate on all your works and consider what your hands have done.

MIRACLES

(A) PURPOSE FOR

2360—(1) That Men might Know the Power of the Lord (N.M.).

See Knowledge (5), **2024;** *Faith (9),* **1209.**

(2) To Witness to Christ as Messiah.

See Miracles (9), **2369.**

(3) Spurious.

See Spurious Miracles, 2232.

(B) EXAMPLES

2361—(1) By Moses and Aaron (N.M.).

Rod made serpent, Ex 4:3; 7:10.
Rod restored, Ex 4:4.
Hand made leprous, Ex 4:6, 7.
Water turned into blood, Ex 4:9, 30.
River into blood, Ex 7:20.
Frogs, Ex 8:6, 13.
Gnats, Ex 8:17.
Flies, Ex 8:21, 31.
Plague, Ex 9:3.
Boils, Ex 9:10.
Hail, Ex 9:23.
Locusts, Ex 10:13, 19.
Darkness, Ex 10:22.
Firstborn destroyed, Ex 12:29.
Sea divided, Ex 14:21.
Egyptians overwhelmed, Ex 14:26–28.
Water sweetened, Ex 15:25.
Water from rock, Ex 17:6.
Amalek vanquished, Ex 17:11.
Destruction of Korah, Nu 16:32.
Water from rock in Kadesh, Nu 20
Bronze Snake, Nu 21:8.
Aaron's rod blossoms, Nu 17:8.
2362—(2) By Joshua (N.M.).
Jordan divided, Jos 3.
Jericho taken, Jos 6.

Jeroboam's hand withered, 1Ki 13:4.
Altar split, 1Ki 13:5.
Hand restored, 1Ki 13:6.
2366—(6) By Elijah (N.M.).
Drought, 1Ki 17:1; Jas 5:17.
Meal and oil multiplied, 1Ki 17:14.
Child restored to life, 1Ki 17:22.
Sacrifice consumed by fire, 1Ki 18:38.
Captains and men slain by fire, 2Ki 1:10.
Rain brought, 1Ki 18:41.
Waters of Jordan divided, 2Ki 2:8.
2367—(7) By Elisha (N.M.).
Jordan divided, 2Ki 2:14.
Waters healed, 2Ki 2:21.
Mocking children torn by bears, 2Ki 2
Water supplied, 2Ki 3:16.
Widow's oil multiplied, 2Ki 4:5.
Pottage rendered harmless, 2Ki 4
Loaves multiplied, 2Ki 4:43.
Child raised to life, 2Ki 4:35.
Naaman healed, 2Ki 5:10.
Gehazi struck with leprosy, 2
Iron caused to swim, 2Ki 6:6
Syrians stricken, 2Ki 6:18.
Resurrection of a man, 2
2368—(8) By Isaiah (N
Hezekiah healed, 2Ki 2
Shadow put back, 2Ki
2369—(9) Of Chris
Water changed to v
Nobleman's son,
Catch of fishes
Demoniac in 4:35.
Peter's mot
Mk 1:31; Lk
Cleansing
5:13.

....as m,
his m;
m,
ity of m
m;

...ll your m.'
th all your
.h all your m';
heart and m.
a depraved m
a slave
is death,
.e to God.
f your m.
.ot
ctly united in m
ed
my m is unfruitful.
e in peace.
arthly things.
ritual m puffs him up
wn business
t change his m:

n and self-controlled

Appea
See I
1539.
Als
2
I

CONCORDANCE

MIRACLE* (MIRACLES MIRACULOUS)
(See 1540, 2232, 2360–2374, 4069.)

Ex	7: 9	'Perform a *m*,' then say to Aaron,
Mk	9:39	"No one who does a *m*
Lk	23: 8	hoped to see him perform some *m*.
Jn	7:21	"I did one *m*, and you are all
Ac	4:16	they have done an outstanding *m*,

MIRACLES* (MIRACLE)

1Ch	16:12	his *m*, and the judgments he
Ne	9:17	to remember the *m* you performed
Job	5: 9	*m* that cannot be counted.
	9:10	*m* that cannot be numbered.
Ps	77:11	I will remember your *m* of long ago
	77:14	You are the God who performs *m*;
	78:12	He did *m* in the sight
	105: 5	his *m*, and the judgments he
	106: 7	they gave no thought to your *m*;
	106: 22	*m* in the land of Ham
Mt	7:22	out demons and perform many *m*?'
	11:20	most of his *m* had been performed,
	11:21	If the *m* that were performed
	11:23	If the *m* that were performed
	13:58	And he did not do many *m* there
	24:24	and perform great signs and *m*
Mk	6: 2	does *m*! Isn't this the carpenter?
	6: 5	He could not do any *m* there,
	13:22	and *m* to deceive the elect—
Lk	10:13	For if the *m* that were performed
	19:37	for all the *m* they had seen:
Jn	7: 3	disciples may see the *m* you do.
	10:25	*m* I do in my Father's name speak
	10:32	"I have shown you many great *m*
	10:38	do not believe me, believe the *m*,
	14:11	the evidence of the *m* themselves.
	15:24	But now they have seen these *m*,
Ac	2:22	accredited by God to you by *m*,
	8:13	by the great signs and *m* he saw.
	19:11	God did extraordinary *m*
Ro	15:19	by the power of signs and *m*,

Example 10. THOMPSON CHAIN REFERENCE BIBLE (NIV), pp. 1408, 1812

"miracle," "miracles," and "miraculous" in the NIV, but the Index lists 110 miraculous events, with references to five additional related subjects.)

As with reference systems, one can evaluate the quality of an index or a concordance only by using it. Size—i.e., the number of words or subjects treated and the number of references included—is significant, but is only one factor. More important than size is selection. When E. W. Goodrick and I assembled the *NIV Handy Concordance*, which appears in all study editions of the NIV, we separately went through a computer listing of every reference to every major word in the Bible in order to choose the most important words and the most important and most familiar texts to represent them. This resulted in not only the largest concordance ever bound into a Bible, but also, we hope, the best selection of references in such a concordance.

The words of a concordance are the very words of the version it is based on, but an index is not limited in vocabulary. In evaluating a subject index to a modern version, one should be sure it is not in "King James" English, which might indicate it was simply transplanted from an older work. Nelson's Biblical Cyclopedic Index to the *Open Bible* and *New Catholic Study Bible* is basically the same in each. But the vocabulary has been adapted to the four versions it indexes. In to the *New Catholic Study Bible* it includes references to the apocrypha as well.

(*Books About the Book* examines more thoroughly the evaluation and use of concordances and indexes in chapters 5 and 6, which deal with topical Bibles and concordances.)

Dictionary

Another alphabetically organized feature of many study Bibles is the dictionary. A Bible dictionary, like a language dictionary, defines key technical words. But like an encyclopedia, it goes beyond definition to give explanatory articles about Bible people, places, events, and subjects. Its information is drawn primarily from the biblical text and is often supplemented by historical, archaeological, and other biblical reference works.

Many study Bibles have only limited dictionary features, often integrated with their concordance or index (see examples

10 and 11). In the *Master Study Bible*, on the other hand, the dictionary is a major feature, comprising more than half of its one thousand pages of reference materials. The *Hebrew-Greek Key Study Bible* has brief dictionaries of the biblical languages.

Full-sized Bible dictionaries (discussed in *Books About the Book*, chapter 4) can have a conservative or liberal or even a denominational slant. But the dictionaries of study Bibles are

Dictionary-Concordance

Aaron—the brother of Moses; he served as Moses' spokesman before Pharaoh (Ex 4:14-16,27-31; 7:1-2); Israel's first high priest (Ex 28:1; Nu 17; Heb 5:1-4).

Abba—the word for *father* in Aramaic, one of the three languages Jesus spoke.
    Ro 8:15 And by him we cry "*A*, Father."
    Gal 4:6 the Spirit who calls out, "*A*, Father"

Abel—the second son of Adam (Ge 4:2); he offered the proper sacrifice to God (Ge 4:4; Heb 11:4), but was murdered by his brother Cain (Ge 4:8; Mt 23:35; 1Jn 3:12).

abhor—to hate or to turn away from.

Abigail—the wife of Nabal; she helped save David's life (1Sa 25:14-35) and later became his wife (1Sa 25:36-42).

abolish—to destroy completely; to put an end to.

abomination—a thing to be hated.

abound—to be more than enough; to overflow.

acquit—to free from punishment or blame.

acts—deeds.
    Ps 150:2 Praise him for his *a* of power
    Isa 64:6 all our righteous *a* are like filthy

Adam—the first man God created (Ge 1:26-2:25); he sinned by disobeying God (Ge 3) thereby bringing all people under the curse of sin (Ro 5:12-21).

admonish—to give warning or advice in a caring way.

adorn—to make more beautiful.

adultery—having sexual relations with someone other than one's husband or wife.
    Ex 20:14 You shall not commit *a*
    Mt 5:28 lustfully has already committed *a*

adversary—enemy; opponent.

advocate—1. (*v.*) to speak in favor of. 2. (*n.*) someone who speaks in another person's defense. Jesus is our advocate.

affliction—trouble or pain that lasts a long time.
    Ro 12:12 patient in *a*, faithful in prayer.

Example 11. YOUNG DISCOVERER'S BIBLE, p. 1943

too brief in scope and length to have a distinct interpretive orientation. The major criterion for evaluating the dictionary features of a study Bible is thoroughness.

Be sure to check the length of a Bible dictionary, the number of words it treats, and the average length of the articles. Compare the article titles with the headings of the concordance or index to see how much overlap there is. Read several articles to determine the nature of the dictionary's coverage. If the dictionary simply summarizes biblical information, it adds little to the function of the concordance or index—and this is why many study Bibles integrate these features.

Maps

Most Bibles contain a set of maps. And most of these maps are of good content and quality.

Maps are extremely important to reading and studying the Bible because few people have an adequate knowledge of biblical geography for forming a mental picture of all the movement described in narrative passages. It is valuable to have a basic geographic orientation when reading Joshua, the Gospels, or Acts, for example, and it is significant to know that Jonah, although told by God to go to Nineveh, went 180 degrees in the opposite direction toward Tarshish.

Most study Bibles have eight to twelve pages of pastel-colored maps that provide a general orientation to biblical history and geography. But recent editions have taken their cartography more seriously. Oxford study Bibles, for example, use natural colors to show water, desert, vegetation, and relief and are outstanding in their detail and accuracy. The *NIV Pictorial Family Bible* and the *NIV Study Bible* have, in addition to their general maps, dozens of event-oriented maps spread throughout the text on the same page where the action is taking place (see example 12).

The maps in a Bible may be evaluated by quantity, quality, and accessibility. Quantity relates to the number of maps, the number of locations identified on each, and the number of events represented. Quality relates to accuracy, artistic design, and possibly use of color. Accessibility relates to how easy the maps are to find and use. Many sets of maps are indexed so that one can easily locate countries, cities, and natural landmarks. (The function and use of maps in Bible study are detailed in chapter 8 of *Books About the Book*.)

Charts and Other Illustrations

Concordances, indexes, and dictionaries collate biblical data into alphabetically organized lists and articles. Charts gather and display biblical and historical data in a more visual form.

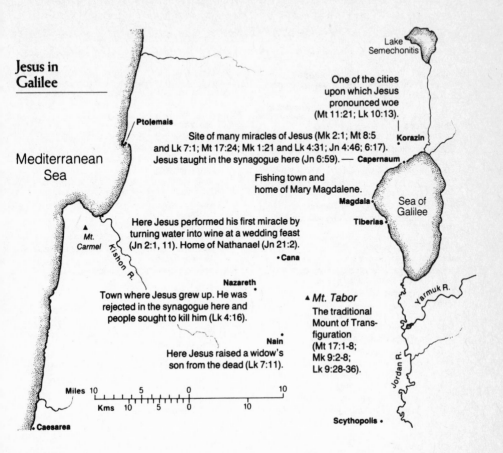

Example 12. NIV STUDY BIBLE, p. 1606

The *Thompson Chain-Reference Bible* was one of the first to make extensive use of charts in outlining biblical history, character studies, and topical information. As mentioned earlier, the *Open Bible* and the *New Catholic Study Bible* use charts to diagram and summarize the contents of each book of the Bible. The *NIV Study Bible* (example 13) has three dozen charts that gather together biblical materials and integrate them with historical and cultural information. The *NIV Pictorial Family Bible* makes excellent use of color in its charts, maps, and photographic illustrations.

Charts can be evaluated by the detail and significance of

Jewish Sects

PHARISEES

Their roots can be traced to the second century B.C.—to the Hasidim.

1. Along with the Torah, they accepted as equally inspired and authoritative, all material contained within the oral tradition.
2. On free will and determination, they held to a mediating view that made it impossible for either free will or the sovereignty of God to cancel out the other.
3. They accepted a rather developed hierarchy of angels and demons.
4. They taught that there was a future for the dead.
5. They believed in the immortality of the soul and in reward and retribution after death.
6. They were champions of human equality.
7. The emphasis of their teaching was ethical rather than theological.

SADDUCEES

They probably had their beginning during the Hasmonean period (166-63 B.C.). Their demise occurred c. A.D. 70 with the fall of Jerusalem.

1. They denied that the oral law was authoritative and binding.
2. They interpreted Mosaic law more literally than did the Pharisees.
3. They were very exacting in Levitical purity.
4. They attributed all to free will.
5. They argued there is neither resurrection of the dead nor a future life.
6. They rejected a belief in angels and demons.
7. They rejected the idea of a spiritual world.
8. Only the books of Moses were canonical Scripture.

ESSENES

They probably originated among the Hasidim, along with the Pharisees, from whom they later separated (I Maccabees 2:42; 7:13). They were a group of very strict and zealous Jews who took part with the Maccabeans in a revolt against the Syrians, c. 165-155 B.C.

1. They followed a strict observance of the purity laws of the Torah.
2. They were notable for their communal ownership of property.
3. They had a strong sense of mutual responsibility.
4. Daily worship was an important feature along with a daily study of their sacred scriptures.
5. Solemn oaths of piety and obedience had to be taken.
6. Sacrifices were offered on holy days and during sacred seasons.
7. Marriage was not condemned in principle but was avoided.
8. They attributed all that happened to fate.

ZEALOTS

They originated during the reign of Herod the Great c. 6 B.C. and ceased to exist in A.D. 73 at Masada.

1. They opposed payment of tribute for taxes to a pagan emperor, saying that allegiance was due only to God.
2. They held a fierce loyalty to the Jewish traditions.
3. They were opposed to the use of the Greek language in Palestine.
4. They prophesied the coming of the time of salvation.

Example 13. NIV STUDY BIBLE, p. 1476

their contents. They should supplement rather than overlap the other study features of the Bible. And they should communicate significant data rather than simply decorate the page.

Special Essays and Articles

Most study Bibles have special articles on such subjects as how to understand the Bible. They also have theological themes, the history of Bible translation, outlines of biblical history and archaeology, and so on. In fact, many study Bibles are simply text or reference Bibles with a set of essays bound into the front or back of the book. Some Bible publishers even produce "study Bibles" by including a set of articles by a ministry organization or special interest group, and that organization then uses that Bible for promotions and fund raising.

In my judgment, the inclusion of a handful of articles in a text or basic reference Bible does not create a study Bible. On the other hand, many legitimate study Bibles do have a valuable collection of general essays, often by a group of recognized scholars, and these supplement well the research features of the book.

You can almost evaluate the articles in a study Bible by the table of contents. Their titles and number of pages alone may indicate how useful they will be and how often you might consult them. Some are so brief or general that you may read them only once or not at all—and why should you have to continue carrying them around in your Bible? But if they contain facts, insights, or principles of interpretation that you will consult over and over, they are worth having at your fingertips.

Harmony of the Gospels and Old Testament History

The life of Christ is presented in four Gospels, and the history of the Old Testament in several books, including the Prophets. Many study Bibles organize the events of the Gospels into a roughly chronological outline, showing both the parallels and unique accounts of each. This parallel outline is called a harmony. Some more recent study Bibles do the same for Old Testament parallels.

A harmony of the Gospels is usually a separate section and is usually an outline listing events and biblical references. The *Master Study Bible* is unique in that it not only outlines the life of Christ but also gives the full text of all four Gospels in this harmonistic form. The *Open Bible* and the *NIV Study Bible* integrate their harmonies of the Old Testament and Gospels into the text by listing parallel references under the subheadings. (Example 14 compares these two formats.)

This section has discussed features one is likely to find in most major study Bibles. But of course, not all are the same in contents. Features that are less pervasive or are even unique to certain volumes will be discussed in the following survey of major study Bibles.

John the Baptist Prepares the Way

1:2–8pp — Mt 3:1–11; Lk 3:2–16

1 The beginning of the gospel about Jesus Christ, the Son of God.[a] [a]

2It is written in Isaiah the prophet:

"I will send my messenger ahead of
you,
who will prepare your way"[b] [b]—
3"a voice of one calling in the desert,
'Prepare the way for the Lord,
make straight paths for him.' "[c] [c]

4And so John[d] came, baptizing in the
desert region and preaching a baptism of
repentance[e] for the forgiveness of sins.[f]
5The whole Judean countryside and all the
people of Jerusalem went out to him. Con-

1:1 [a]S Mt 4:3
1:2 [b]Mal 3:1; Mt 11:10; Lk 7:27
1:3 [c]Isa 40:3; Jn 1:23
1:4 [d]S Mt 3:1 [e]ver 8; Jn 1:26, 33; Ac 1:5,22; 11:16; 13:24; 18:25; 19:3,4 [f]Lk 1:77
1:6 [g]2Ki 1:8 [h]Lev 11:22
1:7 [i]Ac 13:25
1:8 [j]Isa 44:3; Joel 2:28; Jn 1:33; Ac 1:5; 2:4; 11:16; 19:4-6
1:9 [k]S Mt 2:23

8I baptize you with[d] water, but he will
baptize you with the Holy Spirit."[j]

The Baptism and Temptation of Jesus

1:9–11pp — Mt 3:13–17; Lk 3:21,22
1:12,13pp — Mt 4:1–11; Lk 4:1–13

9At that time Jesus came from Naza-
reth[k] in Galilee and was baptized by
John[l] in the Jordan. 10As Jesus was coming up out of the water, he saw heaven
being torn open and the Spirit descending
on him like a dove.[m] 11And a voice came
from heaven: "You are my Son,[n] whom I
love; with you I am well pleased."[o]
12At once the Spirit sent him out into
the desert, 13and he was in the desert forty
days,[p] being tempted by Satan.[q] He was
with the wild animals, and angels attended
him.

C. The Christ of Obscurity
(see *4308b*)

HARMONY OF THE GOSPELS

	Matthew	Mark	Luke	John	Referen in other bo
Preliminary Events					
a. The angel Gabriel appears to Zechariah			1:5–22		
b. Mary visits Elizabeth			1:39–56		
c. Birth of John the Baptist			1:57–80		
d. An angel appears to Joseph	1:18–25				
Birth Foretold by an Angel					
38. The annunciation to Mary			1:26–38		
In Infancy					
39. Birth of Jesus			2:1–7		
40. Visit of the shepherds			2:8–17		
41. The presentation in the temple			2:22–24		
The words of Simeon and Anna			2:25–38		
42. The visit of the Magi	2:1–12				
43. The escape into Egypt	2:13–15				
44. The return to Nazareth	2:19–23		2:39		
His Youth					
45. His visit to the temple when twelve years old			2:41–50		
46. Silent years; no events recorded			2:51–52		
D. The Ministering Christ					
(1) The Year of Inauguration (First year of ministry) (see **4308c**)					
The ministry of John the Baptist	3:1–12	1:1–8	3:1–18		
47. The baptism of Jesus	3:13–17	1:9–11	3:21–22		Col 2:12
48. The temptation of Jesus	4:1–11	1:12–13	4:1–13		
The testimony of John the Baptist				1:19–36	
49. Five disciples called				1:35–49	
50. Water made wine, the first miracle				2:1–11	
51. The first Passover				2:13–25	
52. The temple cleansed				2:13–17	
53. The discourse on the new birth				3:1–21	
54. **The early Judean ministry**				3:22	
55. The water of life				4:4–26	
56. The revival in Samaria				4:28–42	

Example 14. NIV STUDY BIBLE, p. 1493 (top), and THOMPSON CHAIN REFERENCE BIBLE (NIV), p. 1589

A SURVEY OF MAJOR STUDY BIBLES

In the preceding chapter I commented on forty-nine of the more than fifty currently available translations. Although there are more than one hundred study Bibles on the market, fewer than forty study editions of ten major versions have enough features to attract our consideration. The preceding survey and the evaluation outline that follows give the bases for reviewing any study Bibles that I have skipped or that have appeared since this book went to press.

This survey is organized by version and by chronological order. First, it follows the order of publication of the versions, from KJV to NKJV. And the study editions are discussed under each version in the order of their appearance. The study editions of modern versions that are adapted from older volumes are listed, but the description of their features will be found under the original.

Study Bibles: King James Version

NEWBERRY REFERENCE BIBLE (1893; KREGEL REPRINT, 1973)

Originally published in two parts as *The Englishman's Hebrew Bible* (1890) and *The Greek-English New Testament* (1893), the *Newberry Reference Bible* was one of the first study Bibles that attempted to communicate nuances of the original languages to English readers.

Editor Thomas Newberry devised an elaborate system of symbols to indicate the number, moods, and tenses of Greek and Hebrew words and to mark the use of articles and pronouns. Introductions to both Testaments explain the symbols and the essentials of syntax they identify. Also included are forty-three pages of aids to Bible study, an eighty-six-page concordance, and sixteen pages of maps.

Now more than a century old, this work is still useful, but is dated both in translation and in its understanding of the biblical languages. Moody's forthcoming *Discovery Bible* could be considered a modern equivalent to this ground-breaking volume.

THOMPSON CHAIN-REFERENCE BIBLE (1908, KIRKBRIDE, FOURTH IMPROVED EDITION, 1964)

One of the best-organized and most popular of all study Bibles is the *Thompson Chain-Reference Bible*. It first appeared in 1908 following eighteen years of research by Methodist minister Frank Charles Thompson. Thompson and his wife, Laura, expanded the materials through four editions before his death in 1944.

The heart of this work is its unique chain-reference system. Thompson developed a chain index of more than four thousand biblical subjects; it forms a 196-page topical Bible and Bible dictionary immediately following the biblical text. Then, rather than simply sprinkling the margins with cross references, he lists the specific topics in each verse, with their index number, and often identifies the next biblical reference in the chain. By turning to the numbered topic in the back or following the references through the text, the reader is led in a well-organized thematic study.

This Bible also contains more than fifty additional features in its eight "departments," including introductions and outlines of each book, character studies, dozens of historical and topical charts and diagrams, a fifty-eight-page archaeological dictionary, and an eighty-page concordance, all of which are keyed by number to the text and index.

The Kirkbride Bible Company cooperated with Zondervan in releasing the NIV edition of the *Thompson Chain-Reference Bible* in 1983. Because of its organization as an index to the biblical text, with little interpretive bias, this remains a valuable work for personal and devotional Bible study.

SCOFIELD REFERENCE BIBLE (OXFORD, 1909, 1917) AND NEW SCOFIELD REFERENCE BIBLE (OXFORD, 1967)

Perhaps no study Bible has been so widely used or so strongly criticized as the *Scofield Reference Bible*. Its wide use results from its excellent organization, its high view of inspiration and the unity of Scripture, and its interpretive scheme. The interpretive scheme, "dispensational," has also generated most of its criticism.

Dispensationalists teach that God has dealt with humanity

according to a grand scheme that has been gradually revealed and worked out through a succession of covenants and dispensations. Students must "rightly divide the word of truth" (2 Tim. 2:15) by reading each section of the Bible from the perspective of its proper dispensation and not assigning promises and regulations from one dispensation to another.

Although most accept the concept of progressive revelation and of different dispensations, especially distinguishing the Old Covenant from the New, critics of dispensationalism feel it cuts the Bible into too many pieces, teaches different ways of salvation, and wrongly expects a literal future fulfillment of prophecies relating to Israel. Some even treat it as heresy. However, dispensationalism has become a popular and accepted teaching, especially among American evangelicals, due in no small way to the popularity of the *Scofield Bible.*

Each book of the Bible is preceded by a concise introduction. Outlines are in the text as subheadings. The compact reference system points out unifying themes and major conceptual parallels. The notes are primarily intended to show the dispensational view of the nature and interrelation of the covenants and dispensations and to emphasize messianic and national prophecies. Key concepts in the notes are identified in an index, followed by a 162-page concordance and twelve maps.

The original edition was a pioneering work by C. I. Scofield, who was advised by a panel of editors. As dispensational theology spread and developed, a new edition was called for to update and revise the original. The revision was done by nine editors, chaired by E. Schuyler English. Their updating of the notes also served to emphasize that dispensationalism teaches only one way of salvation (by faith), and that dispensations were not absolute divisions but could overlap. They greatly expanded the reference system. They further revised the KJV text, relegating archaic words to the margin and replacing them with more contemporary vocabulary—in a sense, this text became the first "New King James Version." In 1984 an NIV edition of the *New Scofield Reference Bible* was published by Oxford.

Both new and old editions of the *Scofield Reference Bible* continue to be used and appreciated by readers who accept their teaching. Many, however, prefer the *Ryrie Study Bible,* which, though clearly dispensational, is less theological and has more (and more varied) helps.

COMPANION BIBLE (1910; ZONDERVAN REPRINT 1972)

Originally published in six volumes, this massive work of more than 2,150 pages contains reams of valuable, though sometimes eccentric, study helps. Each book is introduced and outlined, but each section and paragraph is also outlined in further detail in the notes that parallel the text. The notes themselves contain explanatory, topical, linguistic, and historical insights and are keyed to detailed studies in the 198 appendixes that follow the text.

The editor, E. W. Bullinger, was monumentally prolific, this being only one of his seventy-seven reference books, several of which appear in condensed form as appendixes. In theological circles, however, Bullinger is primarily remembered for having founded "ultra-dispensationalism," which teaches that not only the Old Testament but also several letters of the New Testament are not applicable to Christians today. His idiosyncracies can be seen in some of the study helps, but they are not blatant or promoted.

In spite of some eccentricities, the *Companion Bible* remains useful for its detailed analysis of the biblical text, both in English and in the originals.

DICKSON NEW ANALYTICAL STUDY BIBLE (1936, WORLD [NINTH?] REVISED EDITION, 1973)

This popular study Bible first appeared in 1936 from the John A. Dickson Publishing Company and was sold exclusively for almost fifty years on a door-to-door basis. It is now available in bookstores from World Bible Publishers.

The *Dickson New Analytical Study Bible* has about 800 pages of well-designed helps. A general introduction to the Bible and a 184-page Bible dictionary precede the text. Each book has an introduction and an analytical chart and is followed by a discussion of the outstanding facts of that book. The volume concludes with, among other features, a 42-page topical Bible and a 117-page concordance. A 17,000-entry general index ties together all of these features.

The text is without notes, but each chapter has a summary of major events or concepts. The cross references follow each verse, rather than being in a separate column. This gives ready references, but it unnecessarily fragments the text into individual verses as though they were self-contained units. Very helpful is the inclusion of 5,500 words and phrases from the Revised Version to update or clarify KJV vocabulary, explaining, for example, that "charity" in 1 Corinthians 13 is actually "love." These follow the KJV rendering and are set in brackets to distinguish them from the KJV.

For its updating of the text and its helpful, primarily objective features, this is an excellent study Bible for those who wish to maintain the KJV as their primary version.

PILGRIM STUDY BIBLE (OXFORD, 1948)

At the suggestion of Ruth Hill Munce, the *Scofield Reference Bible* was simplified and adapted to the needs of young readers. This was accomplished by a panel of thirty-nine editors, under editor-in-chief E. Schuyler English, over a ten-year period. The result was the *Pilgrim Study Bible*.

Each book has a brief introduction and outline. Words, phrases, and major theological themes of the text are explained in a set of notes. These notes also contain cross references. A fifty-page index to the text and notes precedes the concordance and maps. All words and concepts that are explained in the notes are starred in the index, in the notes, and even in the text.

This well-edited work has been widely used to raise children on the KJV and dispensational theology and will certainly continue to do so as long as both remain popular. I hope that we will soon see similarly useful starter study Bibles based on modern versions.

DAKE'S ANNOTATED REFERENCE BIBLE (DAKE, 1961 [NT], 1963)

One of the few Pentecostal study Bibles, *Dake's* is very popular in charismatic circles. It is the product of forty-three years of study and is one of the few study Bibles that has more words in its helps than in the Bible.

Most of Finis Jennings Dake's materials are set in two columns, which appear on each set of facing pages beside the two columns of biblical text. His introduction claims 500,000 cross references, 35,000 notes and comments, 8,000 outlines, and 2,000 illustrations. Many of these materials are lists of observations from the text, but much is interpretive, with emphasis on prophecy, healing, and the miraculous.

This work contains a great deal that is speculative and eccentric, such as Dake's strong teaching on racial segregation (e.g., p. 148 [OT] and 159 [NT]) and his dogmatism on just about every subject he addresses. But it also contains a great deal of valuable biblical study that will yield many insights to discerning readers.

OPEN BIBLE (NELSON, 1975; EXPANDED EDITION, 1985)

The *Open Bible* first appeared in 1975 and in the next decade was adapted to two additional versions and released in expanded editions. It is a revision of the *New Encyclopedic Reference Bible*, published in 1964 by Royal Publishers and distributed by Zondervan until 1984. Twenty-five contributors are listed.

The table of contents lists thirty-three features. The major features are the "Biblical Cyclopedia Index" (a 300-page topical Bible/concordance), lengthy book introductions and outlines, Christian Life Study Outlines in the New Testament, and concordance. Alternate translations and cross references are given at the end of each verse, though the space limitations of this format preclude an adequate reference system. Other features include an outline harmony of the Gospels and articles on biblical backgrounds.

The NASB edition of 1979 had its own reference system and concordance, and its cyclopedic index was modified for vocabulary and spelling. The NKJV edition of 1983 was called an expanded edition because of lengthened book introductions with analytical charts to illustrate their outlines and because the study outlines had been expanded to include the Old Testament. Eighteen contributors to this new edition are listed. In 1985, expanded editions of the KJV and NASB were released with one additional feature—a twenty-four-page "Visual Survey of the Bible," which appeared in 1986 in the NKJV format.

The *Open Bible* is currently immensely popular, possibly because it has no sectarian slant; it is easy to use; and its helps are relatively brief. Although not as thorough as most other major study Bibles, it is a useful guide to basic biblical research.

RYRIE STUDY BIBLE (MOODY, 1976 [NT], 1978)

The *Ryrie Study Bible* appeared in 1976 in both KJV and NASB editions, in the New Testament only. The whole Bible edition was published in 1978, the NKJV edition in 1985, and the NIV edition in 1986.

Book introductions are full and strongly defend the conservative understanding. Outlines both precede the text and are worked into it as subheadings. Notes contain explanatory, historical, cultural, and doctrinal insights. Although Ryrie follows the dispensational understanding of the *Scofield* and *Pilgrim Study Bibles*, he does not promote it as emphatically as these other works do. Other helps include an outline harmony of the Gospels, a large reference system, and a concise topical index and concordance.

Unique to this study Bible is its twenty-two-page synopsis of Bible doctrine. This work outlines major elements of theology and lists the interpretations of several major systems at each point (though, of course, always arguing for its own).

An immensely popular work, the *Ryrie Study Bible* is widely used and appreciated by readers from many denominational affiliations.

NAVE'S STUDY BIBLE (BAKER, REVISED EDITION, 1978)

Famous for his *Topical Bible*, Orville Nave's *Study Bible* is also a major topical index to the Scripture. The date of the original is not given in Baker's 1978 revised reprint, though it must have been just after the turn of the century, as it includes readings from the ASV.

The text is flanked by two columns that, like those of the *Thompson Chain-Reference Bible*, identify a topic and give the location of an index of related Scriptures. Rather than being in the back, however, these topical discussions are spread throughout the Bible at the bottom of the pages. An eighty-one-page index and concordance lists all topics and subtopics and indicates the page on which the article in question is located.

In addition to its built-in topical Bible, there are indexes to major theological themes and to cross references, a glossary of biblical words, and an indexed set of maps. Although it has only one major feature, *Nave's Study Bible* is the most thorough topically organized study Bible in print.

MASTER STUDY BIBLE (HOLMAN, 1983)

This work is unusual in that the modern version edition (NASB, 1981) came out before its KJV edition. Although a new product, it contains materials gathered from a number of earlier works. Holman Bible Publishers is one of the few publishers candid enough to admit this of their study Bible by listing ten copyright dates for these materials.

The first half of the book contains the biblical text with lengthy outlines, useful introductions, and a full cross-reference system. But from page 1286 on, there are over 900 pages of helps. Prominent among them is a 555-page Bible encyclopedia, the largest dictionary ever included in a study Bible. The Gospel harmony is not only in outline form but also presents the full text of all four Gospels with explanatory notes. A topical listing of the teaching of Christ, historical charts, general essays, a concordance, and maps round out the features of this volume.

The *Master Study Bible*, with one thousand pages of new and classic contributions from more than eighty scholars, is one of the more useful volumes for thorough English Bible research.

HEBREW-GREEK KEY STUDY BIBLE (AMG/BAKER, 1984)

Another recent study Bible that blends old and new is Spiros Zodhiates' *Hebrew-Greek Key Study Bible*. As the title indicates, its distinction is the communication of insights from the original languages to the English reader.

Several key words in each verse are underlined and footnoted to the numbering system in Strong's *Exhaustive Concordance to the Bible*. Strong's Hebrew and Greek dictionaries are reproduced in the back of the book. By using the numbers, an English reader can get a concise definition of the original word and also see its range of translation in the KJV.

Zodhiates has also included three major features of his own. First, a 170-page section of similarly numbered "Lexical Aids" expands on Strong's definitions of key words. Second, he has noted key aspects of Greek grammar with a system of abbreviations. Third, he has provided explanatory notes for difficult and important passages.

This work was greeted with enthusiastic response when it was first released. In my judgment, however, those who use it will spend a great deal of time flipping pages and matching numbers to come up with a reading similar to what may already be found in a modern translation. A contemporary study Bible and an English-based dictionary of Bible words, such as Richards' *Expository Dictionary of Bible Words* (Zondervan, 1985), will yield greater insights with less time invested.

Study Bibles: Revised Standard Version

HARPER STUDY BIBLE (ZONDERVAN, 1964)

There are two major study editions of the RSV, one conservative and one liberal. Both continue to be widely used. The former is the work of a single editor, Harold Lindsell. This work was released by Harper & Row in 1964 but has been published by Zondervan since 1965.

Book introductions precede the text as do general outlines, which are expanded in detail in the text itself. References are in a single side column, and explanatory, historical, and theological comments are in notes at the bottom of the page. These notes are indexed by subject in a 12-page section. The 191-page concordance was edited by Eugene A. Nida.

This work formed the basis of the *Lindsell Study Bible* (LB, 1980 [its title was changed to the *People's Study Bible* in 1986]) and was adapted to the NASB in 1985. With the impending revision of the RSV, the future of current RSV study Bibles seems uncertain. But the *Harper Study Bible* will certainly live on with or without its RSV edition.

NEW OXFORD ANNOTATED BIBLE WITH THE APOCRYPHA (OXFORD, EXPANDED EDITION, 1977)

This is not only the best-selling RSV study Bible, but also a standard textbook for the Bible curricula at many universities and divinity schools. Its materials have gone through three editions, including expansion of contents to include more apocryphal books than any other English Bible. The Apocrypha has its own section and is also published separately.

Herbert G. May and Bruce M. Metzger were general editors of this work. Contributions came also from twenty other scholars—Protestant, Catholic, and Orthodox. In addition to general introductions to both Testaments and the Apocrypha, each book has its own concise introduction. Explanatory, historical, and literary notes are at the bottom of the page. Cross references are included in the notes. Eight general essays and separate indexes to the notes of the Protestant canon and the Apocrypha follow the text. A set of twelve indexed maps concludes the volume.

A classic work for nonconservative students of the Bible, the *New Oxford Annotated Bible* will be adapted to the revised RSV or at least will set the standard for an academic edition of the revised RSV.

NEW ENGLISH BIBLE: OXFORD STUDY EDITION (OXFORD, 1976)

The NEB currently accounts for less than 1 percent of the United States market, with most of its sales coming from the *Oxford Study Edition*. Twenty-nine contributors under general editor Samuel Sandmel represent liberal Protestant, Catholic, and Jewish scholarship.

The format is identical to that of Oxford's RSV study Bible, except that the Apocryphal books are between the Testaments, and for the notes of all three sections there is only one index. Each book has a brief introduction and textual notes, with relatively few cross references. There are four special articles, the longest of which is "Literary Forms of the Bible." Nine indexed maps complete the features.

THE JERUSALEM BIBLE (DOUBLEDAY, 1966) AND *NEW JERUSALEM BIBLE* (DOUBLEDAY, 1985) AS STUDY BIBLES

The JB and NJB were both translations and study Bibles from their beginning. Their major study features are introductions, cross references, and annotations. These materials, as well as the original French translations, were produced by the *Ecole biblique* in Jerusalem. Of the two, the NJB is a more useful version for study and its notes are twenty years more up-to-date.

Each section of the Bible (e.g., Pentateuch, Prophets, Gospels) is given its own introduction. Specific book introductions are a part of this general literary and historical treatment. The critical approach is similar to that of the Oxford study Bibles. The cross references and notes, however, are more numerous and more thorough. The notes do occasionally have a distinct Catholic flavor (e.g., p. 1969), but most often they represent a widely acceptable critical approach.

The quality of translation and notes of the NJB, coupled with the uncertain future of the RSV and NEB, may possibly make it the first choice among nonconservative students of the Bible.

Study Bibles: New American Standard Bible

RYRIE STUDY BIBLE (MOODY, 1976 [NT], 1978)

MASTER STUDY BIBLE (HOLMAN, 1981)

OPEN BIBLE: EXPANDED EDITION (NELSON, 1979, 1985)

HARPER STUDY BIBLE (ZONDERVAN, 1985)

The NASB was introduced in 1971 with cross references and a concordance. Its first full-fledged study edition was the *Ryrie Study Bible*, completed in 1978. This was followed by the *Open Bible* in 1979, the revised or "Expanded Edition" of which appeared in 1985. The NASB edition of the *Master Study Bible* was published in 1981, and the *Harper Study Bible* in 1985. As these formats are discussed under the KJV (or RSV), we do not need to reiterate their features here. They differ only in their reference system, concordance, and key-word vocabulary.

CAMBRIDGE STUDY BIBLE (CAMBRIDGE, 1981)

The *Cambridge Study Bible* is among the best-bound and most portable editions of the NASB. Besides the standard reference system and concordance, this edition features brief introductory outlines of each book, a useful 122-page Bible dictionary, and eight maps.

TOPICAL CHAIN STUDY BIBLE (NELSON, 1983)

This is a multicolored study edition modeled after the *New Marked Reference Bible* (1928, 1956; Zondervan reprint, 1964). The text is color-highlighted according to four main topics, each of which is further subdivided into 107 topics. The standard

NASB reference system is on one side of the text, the topical chain system is on the other. This work contains 789 topical and devotional essays, which are spread throughout the volume at the bottom of the pages.

The color scheme creates an inflexible and rather limited framework on the page and fragments the text in such a way as to make Bible reading difficult. I recommend, instead, a study Bible with more (and more varied) features, in which you can do your own color coding.

STARTER STUDY BIBLE (WORLD, 1985)

Several youth-oriented Bibles appeared in the eighties following the pioneering edition of the LB: *The Way* (1972). Most of these editions for children or youth are simply standard versions with lots of pictures and some brief essays or devotionals. The *Starter Study Edition* of the NASB has a bit more substance than the others.

Charles C. Ryrie contributed the twenty-page preface and the book introductions. The fifty-two-page Bible dictionary is helpful, but it contains some KJV words not found in the NASB.

DISCOVERY BIBLE (MOODY, 1986 [NT])

This New Testament reference work was announced in 1985 but was not available for review when this book went to press. It is similar in format and goals to the *Newberry Reference Bible*, employing a system of symbols and annotations to communicate nuances of the Greek verb and sentence structure. The publishers are planning to produce a companion volume that will outline in detail the syntax of New Testament Greek for those using the *Discovery Bible* for interpretation.

PEOPLE'S STUDY BIBLE (TYNDALE, 1980, 1986)

The LB has seen several formats and editions. The first substantial reference edition, the *Lindsell Study Bible*, was edited by Harold Lindsell from his *Harper Study Bible* (see p. 155). An expanded edition appeared in 1986 as the *People's Study Bible* in LB and KJV translations.

One very valuable feature of this work involves Lindsell's

notes on the LB itself. On almost every page he gives more "literal" renderings of key phrases and uses the term *implied* to note where the paraphrase has gone beyond the wording of the originals. Those who wish to read and study from the LB should strongly consider working with this fine study Bible.

LIFE APPLICATION BIBLE (TYNDALE, 1987 [?])

Tyndale released the Gospel of Mark in the *Life Application Bible* in 1986, pointing toward a whole Bible in late 1987. The study materials were developed by Youth for Christ International and include introductions and outlines, in-text maps and charts, cross references, character studies, and life application-oriented notes.

TODAY'S ENGLISH VERSION: THE NEW CATHOLIC STUDY BIBLE: ST. JEROME EDITION (NELSON, 1985)

The first major study edition of the TEV is surprising in many ways. First, it is a Catholic study Bible. Second, since it is both Catholic and critical in its approach to the text, it is surprising to find it coming from the Catholic Bible Press of Thomas Nelson, a very conservative Protestant publishing house.

Sixteen Catholic scholars and educators contributed the materials to this work. Each book of the Bible, including twelve deuterocanonical and three apocryphal, has an introductory survey and outline similar in appearance to those of the *Open Bible*. In content, however, these introductions are similar to the critical approach of the Oxford study editions and the Jerusalem Bible. It also has the biblical cyclopedic index of the *Open Bible*, with vocabulary and references adapted to the TEV and the deuterocanonical books. Also included are several general articles on Bible study, background, and history.

This should prove a useful resource for Bible reading and study on a more basic level than that of the NJB.

Study Bibles: New International Version

NIV PICTORIAL FAMILY BIBLE (ZONDERVAN, 1980)

The first study editions of the NIV were not originals but were adapted from previously done, well-accepted works. The

NIV Pictorial Family Bible was based on a TEV edition published in England in 1978.

Over five hundred color photographs and thirty-seven color maps are spread throughout the volume, set within the passages they serve to illustrate. Dozens of historical, biographical, and topical essays, illustrated with one hundred charts and illustrations, are also inserted at appropriate places, such as the panoramic view of Gilead on page 262.

The readable NIV coupled with an attractive and functional layout makes this volume especially useful for young or new Bible readers.

THOMPSON CHAIN-REFERENCE BIBLE (KIRKBRIDE/ZONDERVAN, 1983)

Although a standard work for most of the century, the *Thompson Chain-Reference Bible* had never been adapted to a modern version until Kirkbride and Zondervan cooperated on the NIV edition. The layout, format, and information of the original (described on p. 148) were left unchanged, excepting those words and subjects that were altered to match NIV vocabulary by editor David Douglass. The marginal and chain references were also computer-checked for accuracy and all of the maps, charts, and diagrams were redrawn by Hugh Claycombe. The NIV edition, of course, has its own concordance, which E. W. Goodrick and I edited; with its 35,000 references, this is the largest concordance in any study Bible.

This combination of a proven reference system and the best-selling modern version is valuable for topical and devotional study.

OXFORD NIV SCOFIELD STUDY BIBLE (OXFORD, 1984)

Another proven study system was made available in an NIV edition by Oxford. Clarence E. Mason, W. Sherrill Babb, and Paul S. Karleen of Philadelphia College of the Bible adapted the notes of the 1967 edition of the *New Scofield Study Bible* (see pp. 148–49) to NIV vocabulary and verified the cross references. This edition also includes the NIV concordance and Oxford's well-known Bible maps.

The NIV edition of the *New Scofield Reference Bible* is an excellently designed and manufactured study Bible that will give a lifetime of use to those who appreciate its theological distinctives.

NIV STUDY BIBLE (ZONDERVAN, 1985)

The NIV Study Bible, as the name implies, was created specifically for the New International Version. It was edited by Kenneth L. Barker. Its forty-four contributors, thirty-seven of whom were NIV translators, represent a wide denominational spectrum of international evangelicalism. A unique element of its materials, besides their volume, is that they represent no single theological alignment. The notes often present more than one possible understanding and, where they differ, present both the conservative and liberal positions on introduction, historicity, and dating (see pp. 127, 129).

Most study Bibles put their notes and references on the same page as the relevant text. In the NIV Study Bible, forty-six maps and thirty-seven charts are also interwoven into the text. The notes, maps, and charts are also accessible through fifty pages of indexes and the tables of contents. Dr. Donald Madvig and I developed the reference system, which appears also in the NIV Reference Bible. With over 100,000 references, it is the largest and perhaps the best organized reference system in all of the study Bibles (see pp. 136–38). The NIV concordance, discussed above, is also included before the sixteen color maps.

The NIV Study Bible is currently the most thorough and up-to-date of all study Bibles. The quality of its features and the inclusiveness of its notes recommend it to any reader, regardless of theological affiliation.

YOUNG DISCOVERER'S BIBLE AND NIV FAMILY BIBLE (ZONDERVAN, 1985)

Two other editions of the NIV appeared in 1985. The Young Discoverer's Bible, like the Starter Study Bible, is aimed at youth, with concise introductions and a valuable dictionary-concordance. The NIV Family Bible is more than a coffee-table keepsake. Its large print, the reference system of the Harper Study Bible, the NIV Handy Concordance, and hundreds of color photographs and classic artworks make it very functional for family devotions and personal study.

THE STUDENT BIBLE (ZONDERVAN, 1986)

An innovatively and realistically designed study edition of the NIV was released by Zondervan in early 1986. Edited by Philip Yancey and Tim Stafford, *The Student Bible* is intended as a reading Bible for all ages and all levels of commitment. Three "tracks" or levels of Bible-reading schedules provide two-week introductory exposures to key biblical texts, a six-month sampling from each book, and a three-year comprehensive reading plan. Book introductions and "insight" and "highlight" sections help explain and apply the text. A brief subject guide rounds out its features.

NIV NEW TESTAMENT: AN ECUMENICAL BIBLE STUDY EDITION (PAULIST, 1986)

Paulist Press produced the first Catholic/Ecumenical edition of the NIV. Introductions, from a critical perspective, and questions for reflection prepared by several Catholic scholars precede the text of the New Testament.

RYRIE STUDY BIBLE (MOODY, 1986)

The NIV edition of the *Ryrie Study Bible* (discussed above) was released in late 1986. Ryrie's study materials will accompany the text, reference system, and concordance of the NIV.

THE SERENDIPITY BIBLE STUDY BOOK (ZONDERVAN, 1986)

This unique study Bible contains the complete text of the NIV New Testament surrounded by a wealth of materials for personal and group Bible studies. Each page of the text is paralleled by a column of questions and comments designed to begin discussion, examine the text, and apply insights to life; these helps for active study are designated "Open," "Dig," and "Reflect," respectively. Forty-eight of the studies center on the life of Christ. Ten six-part topical studies provide for as many as 120 sessions. *The Serendipity Bible Study Book* was edited by Lyman Coleman, Denny Rydberg, Richard Peace, and Gary Christopherson.

CONCORDIA SELF-STUDY BIBLE (CONCORDIA, 1986)

Four Lutheran scholars, under General Editor Robert G. Hoerber, added notes and introductory comments from a Lutheran perspective—and from Luther himself—to the *NIV Study Bible* to create this valuable volume. Materials unique to Concordia's edition are marked with a dagger (†) and are most noticeable at texts foundational to Lutheran theology (e.g., Mark 14:22, 24; Acts 2:38).

Study Bibles: New King James Version

OPEN BIBLE: EXPANDED EDITION (NELSON, 1983, 1986)

Just a year after the completion of its NKJV, Nelson published the Expanded Edition of the *Open Bible*. As mentioned above (p. 152), this revised format added charts and visuals to the book introductions and expanded the Christian Life Study Outlines into the Old Testament. The NKJV edition also has its own reference system and concordance, as well as a cyclopedic index adapted to NKJV vocabulary.

RYRIE STUDY BIBLE (MOODY, 1985)

Moody brought out the second major study edition of the NKJV by adapting their *Ryrie Study Bible* (see p. 153). The cross-reference system in this edition is the fullest produced to date for the NKJV.

THE CHRISTIAN LIFE BIBLE (NELSON, 1985)

The first major study edition unique to the NKJV was *The Christian Life Bible*, edited by Porter L. Barrington and having seventy contributors. Barrington was responsible for the Christian Life study outlines of the *Open Bible*, expanding them into fifty-two master outlines for this work. A forty-page section in the front of the book lists and summarizes these outlines, which are distributed throughout the text. They are primarily theological studies from a conservative and dispensational perspective.

Other features include three essays, a brief dictionary of people and places, a 123-page concordance and indexes to the outlines, and nine maps. With its emphases on evangelism, Christian life, and theological themes, this work will appeal primarily to conservative readers.

Study Bibles: Chronological Editions

There are dozens, if not hundreds, of other study Bibles that contain only a few pages of helps or that are reference Bibles with inserts prepared by individuals or groups for use within their own circles and as fund-raisers. These are easy enough to evaluate after the pattern I will outline shortly. But I will touch on one additional category of specialized study Bibles, the chronological Bible. These works attempt to arrange the biblical text in consecutive order, often supplying dates and other introductory information. They do not (or should not) present themselves as replacements for a canonically organized Bible, but as a supplementary edition for reading and for study.

THE REESE CHRONOLOGICAL BIBLE (1977; BETHANY, 1980)

THE NEW CHRONOLOGICAL BIBLE (WORLD, 1980)

THE KLASSEN CALENDARIZED STUDY BIBLE (NEW LEAF, 1982)

These three volumes are all based on the KJV text and are somewhat interrelated. *The Reese Chronological Bible* uses the dating scheme of Frank R. Klassen, who later put out his own, similar work. Unique to Klassen's work is a sixty-four-page color insert, "Chronology of the Bible," and seven chronological charts. In both, however, the dating is often specific to the very day and year and regularly disagrees with widely accepted chronologies. All include the full text of the KJV, sometimes setting parallel passages in parallel columns, as in Kings and Chronicles, but more regularly running them back-to-back.

NARRATED BIBLE (HARVEST, 1984)

The most useful and best designed of the chronological Bibles is the *Narrated Bible*. Editor F. LaGard Smith arranged the text of the NIV into a general chronology but further organized the laws of Exodus through Deuteronomy and the

Proverbs into topics and subtopics—very convenient for thematic study. Parallel passages are combined into one conflate account. The Gospels, for example, are organized into one life of Christ, with the unique contributions of each indicated by abbreviations.

The text is further divided into 365 sections to facilitate a yearly reading schedule. The title comes from the "narration" that precedes and sometimes follows each section and episode. In these the editor gives historical, cultural, and devotional insights. The publisher wisely printed the narration in burgundy ink so that new readers would not confuse it with the biblical text. Three indexes identify the 365 reading sections, the major events of biblical history, and the page location of each verse or passage of the Bible.

This innovative and well-designed Bible is very useful for reading and for historical and topical study. But again, neither this nor any other chronological Bible can substitute for reading the text in its canonical order and form.

HOW TO CHOOSE A STUDY BIBLE

The most important decision one must make when choosing a study Bible is the choice of translation. As we outlined that procedure in chapter 4 (pp. 107-14), we saw that once you evaluated your needs, abilities, and purpose, the choice was narrowed to five or six primary possibilities. After personal evaluation and the choice of a version, the choices in study Bibles are also narrowed to a handful. On the other hand, if you cannot decide between two or three translations, the study edition itself may settle the issue.

The following outline constitutes a process of elimination. You must first decide if you want the study helps to explain the text or if you want to go after the information yourself. Although most study Bibles have both types of features, they tend to lean toward one or the other. Those who want explanations must decide on the theological perspective of the annotations. Those who want research tools must decide which features will give them the functions they need.

As in the case of translations, this outline does not list every possibility. It is limited to major resources and reflects my personal preferences. Again, you must spend some time in these works and make the choice your own. No secondhand recommendation, no matter how well-informed or well-intentioned, can substitute for firsthand evaluation.

Selecting a Study Bible: Determine the Approach

New students of the Bible or those who simply want help to understand what they read may prefer an edition that majors in annotations to the text. Their first choice is in the matter of general theological orientation; that is, whether the stance is conservative or nonconservative (liberal). For those who choose a conservative orientation, the second choice may involve a more specific theological alignment. The more experienced students or those who want to dig for their own answers may skip ahead to the next outline on research-oriented study Bibles.

Selecting a Study Bible: Outline of Annotated Bibles

A. Nonconservative/Liberal Orientation
   1. *New Jerusalem* or *Jerusalem Bible*
   2. *New Oxford Annotated Bible* (RSV)
   3. *Oxford Study Edition* (NEB)

B. Conservative Orientation
   1. Without Specific Theological Alignment:
      a. *NIV Study Bible*
      b. *Harper Study Bible* and *People's Study Bible* (RSV, NASB, KJV, LB)
   2. With Theological Alignment
      a. Dispensational (see pp. 148–49)
         1) *Ryrie Study Bible* (KJV, NIV, NASB, NKJV)
         2) *Scofield Reference Bible* and *New Scofield Reference Bible* (KJV, NIV)
         3) *Companion Bible* (KJV)
         4) *Pilgrim Study Bible* (KJV)
      b. Lutheran: *Concordia Self-Study Bible* (NIV)
      c. Pentecostal and Dispensational: *Dake's Annotated Reference Bible* (KJV)

Selecting a Study Bible: Research-Oriented Bibles

The major features that can make up a study Bible were discussed earlier in the chapter (pp. 125–46). The most valuable of these features for the direct study of the text are the cross-references, topical index, concordance, harmony of Old Testament and Gospel parallels, and book outlines. Dictionaries define and briefly discuss people, places, events, and words. Introductions, articles, and essays discuss historical, background, and interpretive issues. Maps supply a geographic and historic orientation. Charts and illustrations summarize and diagram historical events and topical studies.

The following outlines list each major feature, in the order discussed on pages 125–46, and those study Bibles that I believe to be the best and most thorough in each area. Chart 8 summarizes most of the editions discussed on pages 147–65, but is basically a simple checklist for comparison. Again, you must evaluate these features personally to determine their usefulness and value to yourself.

Selecting a Study Bible: Outlines of Research Features

A. Book Introductions
1. *NIV Study Bible / Concordia Self-Study Bible*
2. *Open Bible: Expanded Edition* (KJV, NASB, NKJV)
3. *New Jerusalem* (liberal)
4. *Ryrie Study Bible* (KJV, NIV, NASB, NKJV)
5. *Harper* and *People's Study Bibles* (RSV, NASB, KJV, LB)

B. Book Outlines
1. *Companion Bible* (KJV)
2. *NIV Study Bible / Concordia Self-Study Bible*
3. *Harper Study Bible* and *Lindsell Study Bible* (RSV, NASB, LB)
4. *Open Bible: Expanded Edition* (KJV, NASB, NKJV)

C. Cross References
1. *NIV Study and Reference Bibles*
2. *Thompson Chain-Reference Bible* (KJV, NIV)
3. *Ryrie Study Bible* (KJV, NIV, NASB, NKJV)
4. Any NASB Reference Bible (except the *Open Bible*)

D. Concordance
1. Any NIV study Bible
2. *Scofield Reference Bible* or *New Scofield Reference Bible* (KJV)
3. *Thompson Chain-Reference Bible* (KJV, NIV)
4. *Dickson New Analytical Study Bible* (KJV)
5. *Harper Study Bible* (RSV)

E. Topical Index
1. *Nave's Study Bible* (KJV)
2. *Thompson Chain-Reference Bible* (KJV, NIV)
3. *Open Bible: Expanded Edition* (KJV, NASB, NKJV) and *New Catholic Study Bible* (TEV)
4. *Dickson New Analytical Study Bible* (KJV)
5. *People's Study Bible* (LB, KJV)

F. Dictionary
1. *Master Study Bible* (KJV, NASB)

2. *Dickson New Analytical Study Bible* (KJV)
3. *Cambridge Study Edition* (NASB)
4. *Hebrew-Greek Key Study Bible* (biblical languages only [KJV])

G. Maps
1. *NIV Study Bible / Concordia Self-Study Bible*
2. *NIV Pictorial Family Bible*
3. *Any Oxford study Bible*
4. *Thompson Chain-Reference Bible* (especially NIV)

H. Charts
1. *NIV Study Bible / Concordia Self-Study Bible*
2. *Thompson Chain-Reference Bible* (especially NIV)
3. *NIV Pictorial Family Bible*
4. *Open Bible: Expanded Edition* (KJV, NASB)

I. Harmonies of the Gospel and Old Testament Parallels
1. *Master Study Bible* (KJV, NASB)
2. *NIV Study Bible / Concordia Self-Study Bible*
3. *Open Bible: Expanded Edition* (KJV, NASB, NKJV) and *New Catholic Study Bible* (TEV)
4. *Thompson Chain-Reference Bible* (KJV, NIV)
5. *Ryrie Study Bible* (KJV, NIV, NASB, NKJV)

AN ALPHABETICAL LIST OF STUDY BIBLES SURVEYED IN THIS CHAPTER

KING JAMES VERSION

Companion Bible (1910, Zondervan reprint, 1972)
Dake's Annotated Reference Bible (Dake, 1963)
Dickson New Analytical Study Bible (1931, World, 9th [?] edition, 1973)
Hebrew-Greek Key Study Bible (AMG/Baker, 1984)
Klassen Calendarized Study Bible (New Leaf, 1982)
Master Study Bible (Holman, 1983)
Nave's Study Bible (1901[?], Baker revision, 1978)
New Chronological Bible (World, 1980)
New Marked Reference Bible (1928, Zondervan reprint, 1972)
New Scofield Reference Bible (Oxford, 1967)
Newberry Reference Bible (1893, Kregel reprint, 1973)
Open Bible: Expanded Edition (Nelson, 1975, 1985)
People's Study Bible (Tyndale, 1986)
Pilgrim Study Bible (Oxford, 1948)
Reese Chronological Bible (Bethany, 1980)
Ryrie Study Bible (Moody, 1978)
Scofield Reference Bible (Oxford, 1917)
Thompson Chain-Reference Bible (Kirkbride, 4th Improved Edition, 1964)

REVISED STANDARD VERSION

Harper Study Bible (Zondervan, 1964)

New Oxford Annotated Bible (Oxford, 1977)

NEW ENGLISH BIBLE

Oxford Study Edition (Oxford, 1976)

JERUSALEM BIBLE AND NEW JERUSALEM BIBLE

Standard editions (Doubleday, 1966, 1985)

NEW AMERICAN STANDARD VERSION

Cambridge Study Bible (Cambridge, 1981)
Discovery Bible: New Testament (Moody, projected 1987)
Harper Study Bible (Zondervan, 1985)
Master Study Bible (Holman, 1981)
Open Bible: Expanded Edition (Nelson, 1979, 1985)
Ryrie Study Bible (Moody, 1978)
Starter Study Bible (World, 1985)
Topical Chain Study Bible (Nelson, 1983)

LIVING BIBLE

Life Application Bible (Tyndale, projected 1987)
People's Study Bible (Tyndale, 1980, 1986)

TODAY'S ENGLISH VERSION

The New Catholic Study Bible: St. Jerome Edition (Nelson, 1985)

NEW INTERNATIONAL VERSION

Concordia Self-Study Bible (Concordia, 1986)
Ecumenical Study Edition ([NT] Paulist, 1985)
Narrated Bible (Harvest, 1984)
NIV Family Bible (Zondervan, 1985)
NIV Pictorial Family Bible (Zondervan, 1980)
NIV Reference Bible (Zondervan, 1984)
NIV Study Bible (Zondervan, 1985)
Oxford NIV Scofield Study Bible (Oxford, 1984)
The Serendipity Bible Study Book ([NT] Zondervan, 1986)
The Student Bible (Zondervan, 1986)
Thompson Chain-Reference Bible (Kirkbride/Zondervan, 1983)
Young Discoverer's Bible (Zondervan, 1985)

NEW KING JAMES VERSION

Christian Life Bible (Nelson, 1985)
Open Bible: Expanded Edition (Nelson, 1983)
Ryrie Study Bible (Moody, 1985)

Chart 8
16 MAJOR STUDY BIBLE FORMATS
(In Order of Publication)

STUDY BIBLE (Author/Editor) [Date]	VERSION	PUBLISHER	Book Introductions	Book Outlines	Cross References (Approximate Number)	Textual Notes	Dictionary/Encyclopedia (Number of pages)	Index [I]/Concordance [C] (Number of Pages)	Maps [M]/Maps with Index [MI] (Number of Maps)	Charts / Illustrations	Harmony of Gospels: Outline [O] With Full Text [T]	Text Features: Self-Pronouncing [SP] Red Letter [RL]	Total Pages	OTHER FEATURES
THOMPSON CHAIN-REFERENCE BIBLE (Frank C. Thompson) [1908/1964, 4th ed.]	KJV	Kirkbride (both editions)	X	X	38,000 Margin 40,000 Index		♦♦	I 204 C 80	MI 12	C	O	RL SP	1637	4200 Subject Topical Reference System tied to Marginal System and alphabetic index; Archaeological Dictionary; historical and topical charts and illustrations; Guide to Bible reading and study.
(David R. Douglass) (NIV editor) [1983]	NIV	Zondervan (NIV)	X	X	" "		♦♦	I 266 C 176	MI 14	C I	O	RL	1900	♦♦ Dictionary in Index.
SCOFIELD REFERENCE BIBLE (C.I. Scofield + 8) [1909, 1917]	KJV	Oxford	X	X	40,000	X		C 161	MI 12			RL	1542	Notes are explanatory and interpretive (conservative, dispensational). Notes are indexed. Established the format for most other Study Bibles of the 20th Century (See below, New Scofield Reference Bible.)
COMPANION BIBLE (E.W. Bullinger) [1910]	KJV	Zondervan	X	X	50,000	X		I 7	M	X			2150	Notes are explanatory and topical; outlines extend to the paragraph level. 198 "Appendixes" of historical, topical and word studies.

Title	Version	Publisher						MI	C	O			Notes
DICKSON NEW ANALYTICAL STUDY BIBLE (John A. Dickson) [1936, 1973]	KJV	World	X	X	41,000	184	I 42 / C 117	MI 10			SP	1834	Text has 5,500 words and phrases from ASV. Outlines are in chart form. Each book is followed by a summary of "Outstanding Facts." 17,000-entry Index to all features.
PILGRIM STUDY BIBLE (E. Schuyler English + 37) [1948]	KJV	Oxford	X	X	10,000		I 50 / C 150	MI 4			SP RL	1894	Annotated for new or young believers. Notes are explanatory and interpretive (conservative, dispensational); based on Scofield. Notes are indexed. References are in the notes.
HARPER STUDY BIBLE (Harold Lindsell) [1964]	RSV	Zondervan	X	X	60,000		C 191	MI 16	C	O	SP	2109	Notes are explanatory and interpretive (conservative, Protestant). Outlines are in the text as subheads. Good introductions and cross references. Brief index to the notes. (See below, Lindsell Study Bible.)
	NAS [1985]		X	X	60,000		C 125	MI 16	C	O	RL	1757	
NEW SCOFIELD REFERENCE BIBLE (E. Schuyler English + 8) [1967] (Mason, Babb, Karleen) [NIV, 1984]	KJV	Oxford	X	X	45,000		C 188	MI 9			RL	1602	Revision of 1917 ed.; NIV edition slightly revises 1967 ed. Notes are explanatory and interpretive (conservative, dispensational) and are indexed. Reference system enlarged from 1917 ed. KJV edition updates archaic language. New Oxford Bible Maps.
	NIV		X	X	45,000		C 215				RL	1592	
OPEN BIBLE: EXPANDED EDITION (More than 25 contributors) [1975] [1st KJV ed.]	KJV [1985]	Nelson	X	X	28,000		I 298 / C 62	MI 9	C	O	SP RL	1705	Text offers some alternate translations. 28 Study Outlines and a Guide to Christian Workers. Lists of Parables, Miracles, and Prophecies of Christ. Index is the same in all versions, but vocabulary is adapted; concordances and cross references are unique to each. Charts are used in addition to book outlines; A 24-page Visual Survey of the Bible.
	NAS [1985]				30,000		I 287 / C 96	MI 9	C	O	RL	1747	
	NKJV [1983, 1986]				23,000		I 294 / C 64	MI 9	C	O	RL	1802	

STUDY BIBLE (Author/Editor) [Date]	VERSION	PUBLISHER	Book Introductions	Book Outlines	Cross References (Approximate Number)	Textual Notes	Dictionary/Encyclopedia (Number of pages)	Index [I]/Concordance [C] (Number of pages)	Maps [M]/Maps with Index [MI] (Number of Maps)	Charts/Illustrations	Harmony of Gospels: Outline [O] With Full Text [T]	Text Features: Self-Pronouncing [SP] Red Letter [RL]	Total Pages	OTHER FEATURES
RYRIE STUDY BIBLE (Charles C. Ryrie) [1978]	KJV	Moody	X	X	70,000	X		C 116	MI 11	C	O	RL	2127	Notes are explanatory and interpretive (conservative, dispensational). Outlines precede each book and are in the text as subheads. 72 pages of additional helps, including an Synopsis of Doctrine and Subject Index to the notes.
[1985]	NAS		X	X	70,000	X		C 96	MI 11	C	O	RL	2116	
	NKJV		X	X	70,000	X		C 95 NAS	MI 11	C	O	RL	2148	
[1986]	NIV		X	X	100,000	X		C 164	MI 15	C	O	RL	2016	NIV edition has larger cross-reference system and concordance; more detailed maps.
OXFORD STUDY EDITION (Samuel Sandmel + 28) [1976]	NEB	Oxford	X		15,000	X			MI 9				1743	With Apocrypha. Notes are explanatory and interpretive (liberal, scholarly); references are in the notes. Brief index to notes.
NEW OXFORD ANNOTATED BIBLE (Herbert G. May, Bruce M. Metzger + 20) [1977]	RSV	Oxford	X		15,000	X			MI 14			SP	1968	Includes Apocrypha (with 3–4 Maccabees and Psalm 151). Notes are explanatory and interpretive (liberal, scholarly); references are in notes. Brief index to notes. 42 pages of essays of biblical backgrounds.

Title	Version	Publisher											Notes
LINDSELL STUDY BIBLE (Harold Lindsell) [1980]	LB	Tyndale	X	X	46,000		C 95	MI 6	C			1619	Harper SB revised and expanded for LB. Notes are explanatory and interpretive (conservative, Protestant) and critique the paraphrase. Outlines are in the text as subheads. Brief index to the notes.
MASTER STUDY BIBLE (75 Contributors) [1981/1983]	NAS	Holman	X	X	70,000	662	C 96	MI 8	C	T	RL	2392	Full introductions and outlines in text and dictionary. Teachings of Jesus by Subject (with Text). Guide to Bible Study and Plan of Bible Reading. Essays on Bible backgrounds. Separate pronunciation guide in KJV.
	KJV		X	X	40,000	554	C 92	MI 7	C	T	SP RL	2224	
NEW CATHOLIC STUDY BIBLE (16 contributors) [1985]	TEV	Nelson	X	X	7,000		I 284	MI 9	C	O		1625	Introductions use visuals and charts from the Open Bible, but from a moderately liberal Catholic perspective. 12 historical and interpretive essays. Apocrypha.
CHRISTIAN LIFE BIBLE (Porter L. Barrington + 70) [1985]	NKJV	Nelson	X	X	23,000		C 123	MI 9				1520	52 primarily doctrinal Study Outlines precede the text and are spread through the Bible. 3 essays on history, evangelism and backsliding. Brief subject index.
NIV STUDY BIBLE (Kenneth L. Barker + 45) [1985]	NIV	Zondervan	X	X	100,000		C 153	MI 62	C	O	RL	20,000	Full introductions and outlines. 20,000 textual notes often list comparative interpretations. Notes, 62 maps and 35 charts are all indexed. 5 general essays.
Concordia Self-Study Bible [1986]		Concordia											Concordia Self-Study Bible adds notes and introductory materials from a Lutheran perspective (marked by †).

Adapted and expanded from "Study Bible Comparison Chart" and used by permission of Holman Bible Publishers.

Chapter 6

PUTTING IT ALL TOGETHER: A SURVEY OF BIBLE FORMATS AND BINDINGS

If we would tabulate all the ways that Bibles can differ—in text, content, translation, study features, size, shape, and color—and work out all their potential combinations, we would come up with well over 100,000 unique products. (I suppose some booksellers feel there are really that many available!) Actually, there are far fewer, but still there are thousands from which to choose. How, then, shall we make our choice?

Chapter 4 outlined the process of choosing a Bible translation, and chapter 5 outlined the process of choosing a study edition. Once one has chosen the *content* of his Bible, there remains only the selection of its *form*—its size and binding.

When I began my work as a bookstore clerk, we had an entire wall devoted to Cambridge Bibles, KJV only, because of their great range in size, paper, binding quality, and color. I could spend an hour attempting to explain the terminology relating to various type-styles and leathers, yet all of the contents were essentially the same.

With the explosion of translations and study formats came an implosion of size and binding formats, an economic necessity for both publishers and booksellers. Still, choices do exist. The greatest variety of choices involve bindings, quality, and color. Most text or reference Bibles have a variety of sizes, whereas most study Bibles do not.

The following survey of potential formats is not exhaustive. For example, it does not cover every form in which a KJV text Bible is printed and it does not define all publishers' trademarked terminology for similar features. It is limited because it emphasizes modern versions and study Bibles. A more exhaustive listing of formats and terminology is given in Oxford's *All About Bibles* (1985).

LAYOUT

Layout deals with page design—that is, the way the text is presented. As I mentioned in my survey of translations in chapter 3, from the Geneva Bible of 1560 to the RV of 1885, most Bibles had essentially the same layout: double-column texts with each verse numbered and indented as though it were an individual entity.

But beginning in the late nineteenth century—with such versions as Darby, Rotherham, and the ASV—paragraphing, poetic indentation, and one-column texts were introduced. Most modern versions (excepting the NKJV and most editions of the NASB) have followed their lead. Although some people complain about paragraph layout, which makes locating verses slightly more difficult, this definitely aids understanding and helps prevent isolating verses from their contexts.

No study Bible and few text Bibles actually give a choice in layout, though the NIV is available in both single- and double-column editions. When there is a choice, a given layout may make one edition more readable than another.

TYPE SIZE AND COLOR

Another important factor in settling on an edition of the Bible is its type size. Most people seem to want a pocket-sized, giant-print Bible with full study helps! The reality of the situation, of course, is that the larger the type size and the greater the number of features, the larger and bulkier the Bible. Although a knowledge of different type sizes and typefaces may be valuable when shopping for a KJV, most versions have at least a compact, a standard, and a large and/or giant-print layout (see example 15).

Print size is measured in points (a point is 1/72 of an inch). Normal-sized print—such as is found in most newspapers, magazines, and books—is usually an 8- to 10-point type size. Those who desire a compact Bible or Testament must be willing and able to read the tiny 4- to 5-point script. Study Bibles often use 6- to 7-point type to save space and still be readable.

Example 15. FIVE SAMPLES SHOWING SOME OF THE TYPE SIZES AVAILABLE IN NIV BIBLES

IN the beginning *a* was the Word, and the Word was *b* with God, *c* and the Word was God.
2 *d* The same was in the beginning with God.
3 *f* All things were made by him; and without him was not any thing made that was made.
4 *h* In him was life; and *i* the life was the light of men.
5 And *l* the light shineth in darkness; and the darkness comprehended it not.

A.D. 29
—
a Prov. 8. 22.
Col. 1. 17.
b Prov. 8. 30.
1 John 1. 2.
c 1 John 5. 7.
d Gen. 1. 1.
e Luke 3. 15.
Acts 13. 25.
f Ps. 33. 6.
Eph. 3. 9.
Col. 1. 16.
g Mal. 4. 5.
h ch. 5. 26.
i ch. 9. 5.
k Deut. 18. 15.

John, when the Jews sent priests and Levites from Jerusalem to ask him, Who art thou?
20 And *e* he confessed, and denied not; but confessed, I am not the Christ.
21 And they asked him, What then? Art thou *g* Elias? And he saith, I am not. Art thou *k* that prophet? And he answered, No.
22 Then said they unto him, Who art thou? that we may give an answer to them that sent us. What sayest

Tiny print (6 points) KJV Compact Bible

The Word Became Flesh

1 In the beginning was the Word, and the Word was with God, and the Word was God. ²He was with God in the beginning.
³Through him all things were made; without him nothing was made that has been made. ⁴In him was life, and that life was the light of men. ⁵The light shines in the darkness, but the darkness has not understood *a* it.
⁶There came a man who was sent from God; his name was John. ⁷He came as a witness to testify concerning that light, so that through him all men might believe. ⁸He himself was not the light; he came only as a witness to the light. ⁹The true light that gives light to every man was coming into the world. *b*

Small print (8 points) NIV Pew Bible

The Word Became Flesh

1 In the beginning was the Word, and the Word was with God, and the Word was God. ²He was with God in the beginning.
³Through him all things were made; without him nothing was made that has been made. ⁴In him was life, and that life was the light of men. ⁵The light shines in the darkness, but the darkness has not understood *a* it.
⁶There came a man who was sent from God; his name was John. ⁷He came as a witness to testify concerning that light, so that through him all men might believe. ⁸He himself was not the light; he came only as a witness to the light. ⁹The true light that gives light to every man was coming into the world. *b*

Medium print (9 points) Revised NIV Worship Bible

The Word Became Flesh

1 In the beginning was the Word, and the Word was with God, and the Word was God. ²He was with God in the beginning.

³Through him all things were made; without him nothing was made that has been made. ⁴In him was life, and that life was the light of men. ⁵The light shines in the darkness, but

Large print (12 points) Young Discoverer's Bible

The Word Became Flesh

1 In the beginning was the Word, and the Word was with God, and the Word was God. ²He was with God in the beginning.

³Through him all things were made; without him nothing was made that has been made. ⁴In him was life, and that life was the light of men. ⁵The light shines in the darkness, but the darkness has not understood[a] it.

⁶There came a man who was sent from God; his name was John. ⁷He came as a witness to testify concerning that light, so that through him all men might believe. ⁸He himself was not the light; he came only as a witness to the light. ⁹The true light that gives light to every man was coming into the world.[b]

Giant print (14 points) NIV Giant Print Bible

Most people do not consider shopping for large- or giant-print layouts, believing them to be only for elderly or sight-impaired readers. But the larger print is very inviting to any reader and is especially useful for communicators who read the Bible in public.

For evaluating the type used in a Bible, it is not necessary to know the exact size of the print or whether its name is derived from a jewel (Ruby), from a French word (Nonpariel), or from the church-service books that used a particular typeface (Long Primer). However, it is necessary to spend some time reading the text in good light and in mediocre light to determine its readability with more than just a glance. I have had more than a few customers who had to exchange Bibles, even foregoing a desired edition, because they simply could not read the type size for any length of time.

RED-LETTER BIBLES

Some Bibles give a choice in the color of some of their type. I mean, of course, red-letter editions—Bibles that print the words of Jesus in red ink. The use of different colors of ink to mark different speakers or events dates back centuries to hand-written illuminated manuscripts, but the red-letter Bible is a twentieth-century invention.

Some publishers limit the red verses to the Gospels, ignoring, for example, Acts 20:35 and parts of Revelation 1 to 3. Most differ in John, where it is often unclear when Jesus' speaking ends and John's commentary begins, as in chapter 3. Some critics of the red-letter device point out that red is hard on the eyes. But a more serious criticism of it is that it tends to give the impression that the red text is more fully inspired or more valuable than the black. I agree with this criticism. The red-letter format serves no useful purpose, is distracting, and can do the reader a disservice. I do not recommend it.

TRIM SIZE

Trim size is a printer's term for the dimensions of the page once a book has been collated, bound, and trimmed. The size of the print often determines the dimensions of a Bible. Those who desire a specific size of Bible must accept the size of the type in which it is set.

Compact or pocket-size Bibles are small and thin enough to fit in a pocket or handbag. The size of the type is usually 4- to 6-point; the trim size, about 3″ by 4½″ to 3½″ by 5¼″.

Handy or personal-size Bibles are portable and easy-to-read, using 7- to 8-point type. The trim size of approximately 5¼″ by 7⅝″ has enough room for references and notes.

Standard or reference-size Bibles are about 5¾″ by 8⅝″ with 9- to 10-point type. This is a most popular and readable format, which also has the greatest variety of binding styles. Most study Bibles are produced in this size.

Large-print, giant-print, family, and pulpit Bibles can vary in size from 6½″ by 9³⁄₁₆″ to 8½″ by 11″. Large-print and family Bibles are set in 11- to 12-point type; giant-print and pulpit Bibles can use 16- to 18-point type. Wide-margin Bibles use a large trim size with a smaller layout in order to create one- to one-and-a-half-inch margins for notes. The *New Scofield Bible* and the *Thompson Chain-Reference Bible* are among a few study Bibles available in a large trim size with a more readable type size.

BIBLE AND INDIA PAPERS

Although one rarely has a choice of paper quality when selecting a Bible, it is interesting to be aware of the high quality of Bible paper (which accounts for more than half the cost of the Bible).

Bibles contain 1,000 to 2,500 pages, as many as four times the number one would find in a novel of average length. If a Bible were printed on standard paper, as many early Bibles were, it could be four to six inches thick! Thus most Bibles are printed on very thin yet very strong paper.

In addition, Bible paper should be an "off shade" of white to avoid glare and too sharp a contrast with the black type. (The original New Testament of the NIV used brown ink on a light tan paper, and many regret that the whole Bible did not follow suit.) Further, the paper must be opaque so that the printing on the reverse side of the page does not show through.

Bible papers are comparably economical and are lightweight, 1,100 to 1,200 pages making up an inch of thickness. This quality paper is used in most paperback, hardback, and lower-grade leather bindings.

India paper, which appears under many trade names, is the finest Bible paper made. It is extremely opaque, takes print well, and is strong; yet it is so thin that 1,500 to 1,600 pages equal one inch! All higher-quality leather Bibles are printed on India paper.

Writing-quality paper is a Bible paper or India paper used in wide-margin and looseleaf Bibles. It can take ink from a ballpoint or fountain pen without excessive blotting or show-through.

BINDING FABRICS AND STYLES

As with type and trim sizes, the widest variety of binding materials and styles are found in KJV Bibles. Most versions and study Bibles, however, do offer several options.

Generally, the more expensive the binding, the longer the Bible will last. A lifetime Bible is usually bound in and lined with quality leather. To save money, students and others might prefer a cloth or hardback binding. Paperbound Bibles should be considered only for economic necessity, for mass distribution, or for collecting translations for comparative study. The following section deals with bindings.

Nonleather Bindings

Paper or kivar. Kivar is a latex- or plastic-impregnated paper that repels water and wears better than uncoated paper. Paper bindings are usually limited to award Bibles and inexpensive Bible-society printings.

Cloth or buckram. These standard bookbinding materials are made of pyroxylin-coated cotton or synthetics and are moisture-resistant and long wearing. A rigid binding is recommended for Bibles that must stand on a shelf or that will see lots of hard use and many kinds of weather.

Imitation leather, Leatherflex, or Moroccoette. This binding is also pyroxylin-coated cloth but is grained like leather and is usually flexible. It resists scuffing but is not nearly as durable as genuine leather. Other names for this type of binding include Buksyn, Durabond, Permaleather, and Skivertex.

Vinyl. This is a synthetic petrochemical material that is very durable, weatherproof, and flexible and can also be grained like leather.

Leather Bindings (in approximate order of quality):

(A note on grains of leather: "grain" refers to the texture of the leather. The natural grains of leather are brought out by hand treatment. These are found on the finest bindings and include hand grain, natural grain, and pin-seal grain. "Embossed" grains are pressed onto leathers with plates to produce many distinctive patterns, such as antique, buffalo, legostre, levant, oasis, ostraleg, and seal grains.)

Bonded leather. This popular and relatively inexpensive binding is made from leather fibers bound by latex and grained to look like leather. It is durable and flexible, especially as the bonding agents have been improved, and in some cases is indistinguishable from genuine leather. Genuine leather, however, will wear longer.

French Morocco. This is genuine leather, usually sheepskin, embossed with various grains and is the least durable of the leather bindings. This is also known as Skiver.

Persian Morocco. Made from the hides of hair sheep and embossed with various grains, it is superior in quality and durability to French Morocco.

(Top grain) cowhide. This is a supple and durable leather that can be embossed with any grain. Cowhide is the top grade of binding in many study Bibles.

Pigskin or Croupon. Durable, soft, and flexible, pigskin is usually polished to a high gloss.

Calfskin. This is a very fine leather made from the hides of young calves.

Buffalo, East India, and India calfskin. These tough leathers are all made from the hide of water buffalo and differ basically in the way they are grained.

Morocco. Perhaps the best known of all leather bindings, this is an extremely durable goatskin; it may have an embossed or natural grain.

Hand-grained and natural-grained Morocco. This has a natural grain worked up by hand. Many people feel that this soft, luxurious leather is the finest available.

Polished Morocco. This is goatskin that has been finished to produce a smooth surface with just a trace of the original grain.

Few Bibles other than the KJV have more than three or four grades of bindings for any one style. But as people compare and evaluate versions and editions, they may encounter most of these lovely leathers.

Binding Styles

Flush cut. This cover style is usually used with paper and kivar bindings, where the cover is exactly the same size as (flush with) the pages.

Limp. In this style, the cover extends only 1/8" to 1/4" beyond the edges of the leaves. Although usually applied to flexible (inexpensive) covers, this term can refer to a rigid binding.

Over-boards. Here the cover material, cloth or leather, is placed over stiff cardboard. It is used most often for cloth bindings and large pulpit Bibles, which need reinforcement.

Padded over-boards. This Bible cover sandwiches a layer of foam between the boards and the cover material. It is often used for family Bibles and other large gift Bibles.

Snap-flap or button-flap. This binding features a lengthened back cover that is folded over the front as a flap and is snapped down to hold the Bible shut. It protects the pages and edging when the Bible is not in use.

Zipper. A popular feature of children's Bibles, this is a binding like that of the divinity circuit (below), which overlaps and can be zipped completely shut to protect the pages and edging.

Divinity circuit. In this older style of binding, the covers overlap enough to touch when the book is closed. It is rarely used today, because the edge tends to crack along the crease of the overlap.

Half-circuit. In this modified version of the divinity circuit, the covers overlap the pages of the book but do not touch.

Binding Details

Cover lining. This material lines the inside front and back covers of the Bible and is stronger, more flexible, and more durable than regular paper linings. Linings can be made of synthetics or of bonded or genuine leather. Better leather bindings should also be leather-lined.

Gold or silver fillet. This refers to a gold or silver design or line that frames the inside cover of higher-quality Bibles. It is decorative rather than useful.

Stained edges. Less expensive Bibles, especially children's Bibles, have pages with tinted edges to complement or match the cover color and protect the pages from showing dirt.

Gold or silver edges. Genuine gold or silver leaf (or a metallic facsimile) is bonded under heat to the page edges of the Bible after they have been sanded and burnished to create a smoothe surface. Newer, less expensive processes spray-paint the edges. Both methods protect and add durability to the pages.

Ribbon markers. One or two ribbons may be bound into the top of the Bible spine for use as bookmarks.

Thumb-indexing. Thumb-sized grooves are cut in the edges of some Bibles. These grooves are cut to end at the beginning page of each book of the Bible to facilitate location. A reinforced tab on that page lists the book abbreviation and helps protect the page from wear. Although it is useful for those who do not know their way around the Bible, this feature contributes to the wear and dog-earing of the page edges, and the tabs often tear.

A FINAL WORD ON FORMAT

The information on these last few pages may have been more than one needs to know for a personal selection process, but it will help those who are in a position to advise others.

Even with all these options, some versions and editions are limited to one or two kinds of binding or they may not be assembled quite the way one likes. Although layout, type size, and trim size cannot be changed, one can change the binding and certain other features by going to a custom jobber.

When I worked in a used-book store, I became involved with bookbinders, artisans who create custom bindings and restore aged tomes. Many seminary students went to bookbinders to have Greek and Hebrew Testaments bound together or to have a favorite study Bible rebound with several dozen pages of blank or ruled writing paper.

I regularly encountered students and pastors who would buy used or paperback Bibles, have them customized with stained edges, extra study features from other books, several ribbon markers, and a handmade binding. This is an expensive way to go, and one will certainly want to check out the handiwork of the local binders before giving them a commission. But their work can result in a more satisfying lifetime study Bible than any publisher has yet produced.

HOW TO CHOOSE THE FORM OF THE TEXT BIBLE OR STUDY BIBLE

Determine the layout (pp. 176-81)

A text Bible offers more choices than a study Bible does. If you are choosing a study Bible, go on to section B. The KJV, of course, has the most options. The NIV comes in single- and double-column and in study editions. There are also varieties in RSV, NASB, TEV, LB, and NKJV; other versions are much more limited.

A. Most versions do not have a choice of verse vs. paragraph format.

B. Determine the type size you prefer.
   1. Remember to take time to read your potential Bible for more than a minute or two and under different lighting conditions (if you can find them).
   2. Remember, too, that large print is not only for sight-impaired readers.

C. Determine the trim size best suited to your needs.
   1. If the Bible must be portable, be sure it is of manageable size and weight.
   2. If the Bible is for home study, size is no object.

Determine the quality of the binding (pp. 181–84)

A. Paperback and kivar
   1. For awards and other giveaways
   2. For collecting translations for comparative study
   3. For economic necessity

B. Cloth
   1. Long lasting
   2. Sturdy
   3. Economical

C. Imitation leather and bonded leather
   1. Long lasting
   2. Flexible
   3. Economical (vs. genuine leather)

D. Leather
   1. Long lasting (and more expensive)
   2. Beauty

ON THE CARE AND FEEDING OF YOUR NEW BIBLE

A new Bible, like a new car, will wear longer if it is broken in and kept up properly. Following these few tips may add years to the life of your Bible's binding.

When you get your Bible home, take the time to prepare it for use. If it is leather-bound or flexible, hold the spine in your left hand and gently flex the Bible from side to side with your right. Slowly fan the pages with your right thumb once or twice to begin to separate the pages. Repeat the process with the spine in your right hand. If the Bible has a hard cover, you can flex and fan through it by placing the spine on a flat surface, opening the covers, and working with the body of the book only.

To break in your Bible, start by placing its spine on a flat surface. Open the covers and gently press down a few pages at a time, first on one side and then the other, working to the center of the volume. This will loosen the binding properly so that it will have a long life of good service. It may be helpful to repeat this process at least once. Never open your Bible carelessly, since this may cause the first and last signatures to break loose.

Do not store your Bible where there is excessive dry heat or too much humidity. Dry heat will dry out and crack the leather and the binding glue. Humidity may cause mold to grow on the leather; it can also warp the pages, soften the glue, and cause the gold edges and lettering to deteriorate. Humidity can have the same effect on plastic and other synthetic Bible covers. If your Bible came in a box, keep the box for storage.

Take care of the leather binding. Use a leather preservative, such as lexol or saddle soap once every six months. Also handle it regularly, gently rubbing the entire cover with clean hands. Natural oils from your hands help restore oils the leather loses. If you have a white binding, clean it carefully, using white leather dressing or a clean cloth that has been dipped in mild soapsuds and wrung out.

Chapter 7

A CORE LIBRARY:
BASIC BOOKS FOR
BETTER BIBLE READING AND STUDY

The most important thing one can do with the Bible is to *read it.* No amount of study, research, or course-taking can substitute for personal time spent in thoughtful reading of the Word of God.

And in reading, one should never forget that the Bible is not only a word from God but also a word about God. Problem texts and doctrinal debate should not get in the way of one's seeing the Lord and learning to worship him. The Old Testament should not be neglected, for there also, much of the character and purpose of God are revealed. The New Testament writers expected people of New Testament times to know the Hebrew Scriptures, so they did not bother to repeat what was written there.

This volume was written to help one choose and begin to use the English Bible best for him or her. As one reads and studies the Bible, questions will no doubt arise. With time, even the many features of a thorough study Bible will run dry. That is where the companion volume, *Books About the Book,* comes in. In that "Guide to Biblical Reference Works," I work the reader through the process of supplementing a study Bible with the most useful of the many outstanding reference books currently available.

Although I am certain that readers of *Words About the Word* will want to work through the details and resources of *Books About the Book,* I will here give a brief overview of its approach and some key titles that can answer some of the questions not anwered by a study Bible.

UNDERSTANDING WHAT ONE READS

All of us at one time or another have identified with the Ethiopian eunuch. When Philip asked him if he understood what Isaiah had written, he replied, "How can I unless someone explains it to me?" (Acts 8:31). In the absence of Philip, two kinds of skills can greatly aid us in our understanding: knowing how to read the Bible as literature and knowing how to use the correct biblical reference books to answer the questions that come up in our reading.

Gordon D. Fee and Douglas Stuart produced a guide to understanding the Bible, entitled *How to Read the Bible for All Its Worth* (Zondervan, 1981). In thirteen chapters, these Bible scholars give valuable and practical insights on reading the *literatures* of the Bible—for one does not read Revelation the same way one reads Ruth, or poetry as one reads Peter! In a six-page appendix they also give guidance in choosing and using Bible commentaries.

Fee and Stuart explain how to read carefully and with better understanding. In addition, for those who want to study any book of the Bible in detail, I recommend Robert A. Traina's *Methodical Bible Study* (Zondervan, 1985 [1st ed. 1952]). This classic of English Bible study outlines the process of following the steps of observation, interpretation, evaluation and application, and correlation, and it details the processes involved in each step.

Two smaller books summarize Traina's approach in a more concise and basic form. David L. Thompson's *Bible Study That Works* (Zondervan, 1982) and Oletta Wald's *Joy of Discovery in Bible Study* (Concordia, 1975) are both excellent primers for individuals and groups alike.

Chapter 16 of *Books About the Book* lists additional resources for Bible reading and interpretive skills.

ANSWERING QUESTIONS

Books on reading and interpretive skills prepare one to read and study the Bible more carefully and conscientiously. But even the most skilled student needs additional resources for answering questions about word meanings; historical, geographical, and cultural backgrounds, theological ramifications, and the like. Like the Ethiopian eunuch, we have reference *people* also, but we do not have access to them twenty-four hours a day!

THE BIBLE HANDBOOK

The reference book easiest to use is the Bible handbook. Because it is arranged in biblical order, you do not need special skills to use it. For each Bible book it provides introductions, outlines, maps, illustrations, and commentary and helps you anticipate major questions. Those who already have a study Bible with handbook features built in, such as the *Ryrie Study Bible* or *NIV Study Bible*, will not need a separate Bible handbook, but for those who do not, a handbook will be an immense help.

Halley's Bible Handbook (Zondervan, 1965 [1st ed. 1924]) is strong on spiritual insights and is the best-selling book of its kind. *Unger's Bible Handbook* (Moody, 1966) is more up-to-date, with more commentary, and is also available in a full color edition, enlarged by Gary N. Larson (Moody, 1984). *Eerdmans' Handbook to the Bible* (Eerdmans, 1983 [1st ed. 1973]), by David and Pat Alexander, is another outstanding option and an international best-seller.

Chapter 3 of *Books About the Book* lists other Bible handbooks and explains how to choose and use the one best for each person's needs or preference.

THE BIBLE DICTIONARY AND ENCYCLOPEDIA

A Bible dictionary and a multivolumed Bible encyclopedia make available a rich resource of information in a different arrangement from that of the Bible handbook. Arranged in alphabetical order, they contain biblical and historical information about Bible people, places, books, events, and customs. Many also provide a bibliography of resources for additional study.

The New Compact Bible Dictionary (Zondervan, 1967) is a concise, illustrated dictionary, available in paper and cloth. *The Zondervan Pictorial Bible Dictionary* (Zondervan, 1967 [1st ed. 1963]), *Unger's Bible Dictionary* (Moody, 1966 [1st ed. 1957]), and *Nelson's Illustrated Bible Dictionary* (Nelson, 1986) are larger works from a conservative perspective intended for general readers.

Two dictionaries more academic and up-to-date will meet the needs of most students, pastors, and teachers. *The New Bible Dictionary* (Tyndale, 1982 [1st ed. 1962]) is an outstanding evangelical volume and *Harper's Bible Dictionary* (Harper, 1985) represents the cutting edge of critical scholarship.

Bible encyclopedias address more subjects in more detail because of their multivolume format. At the top of the list for the evangelical are Eerdmans' four-volume revision of the classic *International Standard Bible Encyclopedia* (Eerdmans, 1979—), with volume 4 still to be released, and the *Zondervan Pictorial Bible Encyclopedia* (Zondervan, 1975). You may also wish to purchase the *Interpreter's Dictionary of the Bible* (Abingdon, 1962; Supplement, 1976); this is the standard academic set, produced by Protestant, Catholic, and Jewish scholars.

A Bible dictionary or encyclopedia is an excellent companion to any study Bible—even those that include a concise dictionary, such as *The Master Study Bible*. Chapter 4 of *Books About the Book* explains how to choose and use the Bible dictionaries and encyclopedias best suited for a person's needs.

DICTIONARIES OF ENGLISH, GREEK, AND HEBREW

In addition to Bible dictionaries, a student of the Bible will need one or more language dictionaries. A good English dictionary is an indispensable tool for quick definitions of unfamiliar terms. I have found that my Funk & Wagnalls *Standard Desk Dictionary* more times than not will give me a good definition of an unfamiliar or technical term in one of my reference books. It also regularly gives a theological definition to a biblical or doctrinal term. Of course, there are many good English dictionaries, and most people have one. I am not recommending one title over another; I am simply suggesting that you put the dictionary to good use in your study of the Bible.

For insights into biblical languages, the best all-around resource is Richard's *Expository Dictionary of Bible Words* (Zondervan, 1985). Vine's *Expository Dictionary of the New Testament* (Revell, 1940; reprinted by Zondervan et al.), is still useful after five decades. It is also available in an "Expanded Edition" (Bethany, 1984), which James A. Swanson and I have keyed to more modern and more thorough resources.

Chapter 13 of *Books About the Book* lists other more thorough and technical books on biblical languages and explains how to learn to use them to supplement one's English Bible study.

THE TOPICAL BIBLE AND BIBLE CONCORDANCE

Two kinds of reference books serve as indexes to biblical content. The Bible concordance is a word index, designed to be used with a specific translation of the Bible, while the topical Bible is a conceptual index that can be used with any translation of the Bible. We will look at this more flexible tool first.

Best known is *Nave's Topical Bible*, originally published in 1897 and available in reprint from a variety of publishers, including Baker, Holman, Nelson, and Riverside. Tyndale publishes *Nave's Topical Living Bible* (1982), Zondervan has *The New Nave's Topical Bible* (1969), and Moody has an "Expanded Edition" (1974).

All of these editions give biblical references that relate to various topics and their subtopics *and* print out the text of the KJV (or LB) for many of the references. This saves some page flipping to look up these references but does not really give you enough text to study the verses in their context. *Nave's Compact Topical Bible* (Zondervan, 1972) gives you more topics and more verses in a smaller book by summarizing instead of reproducing the biblical text, and is thus the best buy in a topical Bible.

Most study Bibles come with a concise concordance, which is handy as a verse finder and for limited word studies. But more thorough research requires a more thorough concordance. A "complete" concordance is a list of all or most appearances of the key words of a Bible translation. "Exhaustive" and "analytical" concordances also let you know the Greek, Hebrew, and Aramaic words that underlie the English.

Because it is a word index, your concordance must match your version. The following are the standard concordances currently available:

KJV CONCORDANCES

Cruden, Alexander. *Cruden's Unabridged Concordance.* 3rd ed. Baker, 1769/1953 (1st ed. 1737).

Cruden, Alexander et al., eds. *Cruden's Complete Concordance.* Reprint ed. Zondervan, 1968 (1st ed. 1930).

Cruden, Alexander and John Eadie. *Cruden's Concordance: Handy Reference Edition / Cruden's Compact Concordance.* Reprint ed. (1st ed. nd). Zondervan (1968), Word (1977), Baker (1982).

Strong, James et al., eds. *Strong's Exhaustive Concordance of the Bible.* Reprint ed. Abingdon et al., 1980 (1st ed. 1890). "Corrected edition." Nelson, 1984.

Young, Robert. *Young's Analytical Concordance to the Bible.* 22nd [1922] ed. Revised by William B. Stevenson. Eerdmans, 1964 (1st ed. 1872). "Newly Revised and Corrected edition." Nelson, 1982.

RSV CONCORDANCES

Abbey of Maredsous. *A Concordance to the Apocrypha/Deuterocanonical Books of the Revised Standard Version.* Eerdmans, 1983.

Ellison, John W. *Nelson's Complete Concordance of the Revised Standard Version Bible.* 2nd ed. Nelson, 1972 (1st ed. 1957).

Morrison, Clinton. *Analytical Concordance to the Revised Standard Version of the New Testament.* Westminster, 1979.

Whitaker, Richard E. *Eerdmans' Analytical Concordance to the RSV.* Eerdmans, 1986.

NASB CONCORDANCE

Thomas, Robert L. et al., eds. *New American Standard Exhaustive Concordance of the Bible.* Holman, 1981.

NAB CONCORDANCE

Hartdegen, Stephen J. *Nelson's Complete Concordance of the New American Bible.* Nelson/Liturgical Press, 1977.

NIV CONCORDANCES

Goodrick, Edward W., and John R. Kohlenberger, III. *The NIV Complete Concordance.* Zondervan, 1981.
———. *The NIV Handy Concordance.* Zondervan, 1982.

NKJV CONCORDANCE

Complete Concordance to the Bible: New King James Version. Nelson, 1983.

GNB/TEV CONCORDANCE

Robinson, David, and L. Jane Rowley. *Concordance to the Good News Bible*. Nelson/British and Foreign Bible Society, 1983.

SEVERAL-VERSION NEW TESTAMENT CONCORDANCE

Darton, Michael. *Modern Concordance to the New Testament*. Doubleday, 1976.

Chapters 5–6 of *Books About the Book* explain the features and functions of topical Bibles and Bible concordances and show you how to use them for comprehensive biblical research.

The Bible Commentary

The four types of reference books listed above guide you in firsthand Bible study. A Bible commentary presents you with the end result of biblical study and is useful for help in understanding verses that are difficult or controversial, and for checking and comparing with your own conclusions.

Chapter 11 of *Books About the Book* lists hundreds of one-volume commentaries and multivolume sets, and also explains how to use commentaries for research and comparative study. Here we will list only a few major one-volume commentaries from various perspectives. I recommend that you obtain three or four to use at the same time—much as you would use more than one translation of the Bible for comparison and contrast.

Standard conservative works include the *Wycliffe Bible Commentary* (Moody, 1962) and the *New Bible Commentary* (Eerdmans, 3rd ed., 1970 [1st ed. 1953]). More recent are the *Concordia Self-Study Commentary* (Concordia, 1971, 1979) and the *Bible Knowledge Commentary* (2 vols., Victor, 1983–1985). Zondervan's *International Bible Commentary* (1986) is an updated edition of their *New Layman's Bible Commentary* (1979). The classic commentaries of Matthew Henry; Adam Clarke; and Jamieson, Fausett, and Brown are set in parallel columns in two-volume *Bethany Bible Commentary* (Bethany, 1983–1985).

Peake's Commentary on the Bible (Nelson, 1962) is the standard work from an academic, liberal Protestant perspective. Outstanding for its general articles as well as its detailed comments, the *Jerome Biblical Commentary* (Prentice-Hall, 1968) represents modern Catholic scholarship.

BUILDING YOUR LIBRARY FROM THE BIBLE OUT

The first six chapters of *Words About the Word* are a guide to choosing and using your Bible. This final chapter is a summary of *Books About the Book,* which is a guide to biblical reference books. Once you have taken the time to choose a few translations for comparative reading and research and a study Bible based on your primary version, you are ready to build a core of key resources to facilitate your reading and research.

Your first priority is a good English dictionary. Second, if your study Bible does not have adequate introductions and notes (or if you want the illustrations of the color editions), you should get a Bible handbook. Third, a Bible dictionary or encyclopedia will go beyond the basic definitions to give you biblical, historical, and theological information on people, places, events, and objects of the Bible. Fourth and fifth, a topical Bible and a concordance will supplement the reference system and the concise concordance of your study Bible.

Aside from the English dictionary, these other books—which I call a core library—can be purchased for as little as $30 in paperback, $100 in cloth, or $200 if you buy a multivolume encyclopedia. You can add a commentary or two to your handbook or study Bible notes and a dictionary of biblical language as you feel the need to add detail and depth to your study.

You can decide the level at which you want to enter and the level you want to work toward. You are limited only by your desire, stamina, and, of course, monetary resources. But knowing how to choose the right book for the right insights will make every cent you invest in your library pay off. And again, that is what *Books About the Book* is all about.

I wish you God's very best as you continue to seek His will in His Word!

APPENDIX A

A SUMMARY OF THE PROCESS OF SELECTING ONE'S BIBLE
(and Key to the Concepts of this Book)

A. **Determine the textual content ("canon") (ch. 1; ch. 4, pp. 108–9)**
   1. Old and New Testaments (most Protestants)
   2. Old Testament and New Testament with Apocrypha (most Catholics) (for Apocrypha, see ch. 1, pp. 25–27)
   3. Old Testament only (most Jewish) (for Jewish canon, see ch. 1, pp. 23–25)
   4. New Testament only

B. **Determine the needs (chapters 3 and 4)**
   1. Determine reading level (ch. 3, pp. 59–62, see chart on p. 61; ch. 4, pp. 110–11)
      a. Age
      b. Education: secular and ecclesiastical
      c. Literacy or literary appreciation
      d. Familiarity with ecclesiastical vocabulary
   2. Purpose (ch. 4, pp. 110–11)
      a. Reading
         1) General study
         2) Devotional
         3) Public reading
      b. Detailed analysis: word study and diagramming
      c. Comparison: in general or within a congregation
      d. Communication: preaching, teaching, writing
      e. Gift (See C. and F. below)
      f. Conformity within a congregation

C. **Determine the options (chapter 4: survey of versions pp. 82–107; top-ten versions chart, p. 81; outline of evaluation procedure, pp. 118–19)**
   1. For children (through junior high)
   2. For those with limited reading ability and little or no church background
   3. For youth and adults with no reading difficulty but little or no church background

4. For youth and adults from a conservative church background
5. For youth and adults from a mainline or liberal church background
6. For youth and adults from a Catholic background
7. For youth and adults from a Jewish background
8. For those with an appreciation of literature and literary English
9. For those who want to do word and sentence analysis

D. Determine study features, if desired (ch. 5, see chart on pp. 169–72):
1. Introductions and outlines
2. Cross references
3. Textual notes:
   a. Simple explanations
   b. Topical synthesis
   c. Interpretive: note theological and/or critical preference
4. Concordance
5. Topical index
6. Dictionary
7. Maps
8. Illustrations and charts
9. Essays, articles, and other helps
10. Historical and harmony charts and outlines

E. Determine the layout (if there are options in the version) (ch. 6, pp. 176–81)
1. Verse format or paragraph format
2. One-column or two-column
3. Type size and color (red-letter)
4. Trim size (book dimensions)

F. Determine the binding quality (ch. 6, pp. 181–84)
1. Paperback and kivar (low cost)
   a. For awards and other giveaways
   b. For collecting translations for comparative study
   c. For economic necessity
2. Cloth (economy and durability)
   a. A permanent version
   b. Can stand on a shelf
3. Imitation and bonded leather (economy)
   a. A permanent version
   b. Flexible
   c. For economic necessity (vs. genuine leather)
4. Leather (durability and beauty)
   a. A permanent version
   b. Genuine leathers are most durable, but also most expensive

APPENDIX B

A LIST OF NAMES AND ADDRESSES OF PUBLISHERS AND DISTRIBUTORS

Most of the people who read this book have access to a local Christian bookstore that already stocks or can order any of the Bibles and reference books I mentioned in the text and bibliographies. But many live in smaller towns or rural settings with no bookstore at all. They depend on the occasional trip to the "big city" or on mail order services to add to their libraries.

Thus for the benefit of booksellers and the book-buying public I have included this list of names and addresses. First I list the publishers, from whom booksellers can order and anyone can request information. Second are the distributors, for booksellers only. Third is a brief listing of mail-order services, including a couple of used book stores for finding unusual and out-of-print Bibles.

PUBLISHERS

AMG Publishers, Dept. BSD5, 6815 Shallowford Road, Chattanooga, TN 37422

Abingdon Press, 201 Eighth Avenue South, Box 801, Nashville, TN 37202

American Bible Society, P.O. Box 5656, Grand Central Station, New York, NY 10163

Baker Book House, Box 6287, Grand Rapids, MI 49506

Bethany House, 6820 Auto Club Road, Minneapolis, MN 55438

Bible for Today, The, 900 Park Avenue, Collingswood, NJ 08108

Brill; see American Bible Society

Cambridge University Press, 32 East 57th Street, New York, NY 10022

Catholic Book Publishing Co., 257 West 17th Street, New York, NY 10011

Christian Booksellers Association, 2620 Venetucci Blvd., P.O. Box 200, Colorado Springs, CO 80901

Christian Literature International, Box 777, Canby, OR 97013

Concordant Publishing Concern, 15570 West Knochaven Road, Canyon Country, CA 91351

Concordia Publishing House, 3558 South Jefferson Avenue, St. Louis, MO 63118

Dake Bible Sales, P.O. Box 1050, Lawrenceville, GA 30246

Deutsche Bibelstiftung Stuttgart; see American Bible Society

Doubleday & Co., Inc., 245 Park Avenue, New York, NY 10167

Fleming H. Revell Company, Old Tappan, NJ 07675

Fortress Press, 2900 Queen Lane, Philadelphia, PA 19129

Foundation Press, 1121 North Kraemer Place, P.O. Box 6439, Anaheim, CA 92806

Gospel Publishing House, 1445 Boonville Avenue, Springfield, MO 65802

Harper & Row, 1700 Montgomery St., San Francisco, CA 94111

Harvard University Press, 79 Garden Street, Cambridge, MA 02138

Harvest House, 1075 Arrowsmith, Eugene, OR 97402

Hendrickson Publishers, P.O. Box 3473, Peabody, MA 01961

Here's Life Publishers, P.O. Box 1576, San Bernardino, CA 92402

Holman Bible Publishers, 127 Ninth Avenue, North, Nashville, TN 37234

International Bible Publishing Co., Inc., One World Trade Center, Suite 7967, New York, NY 10048

International Bible Society, 144 Tices Lane, East Brunswick, NJ 00816

InterVarsity Press, P.O. Box 1400, Downers Grove, IL 60515

Jewish Publication Society, 1930 Chestnut Street, Philadelphia, PA 19103

John Knox Press, 341 Ponce de Leon Avenue, N.E., Atlanta, GA 30365

Judson Press, P.O. Box 851, Valley Forge, PA 19482

Julian G. Anderson, P.O. Box 1751, Naples, FL 33939

Keter Publishing House Jerusalem, P.O. Box 7145, Jerusalem, Israel

Kirkbride Bible Co., Inc., P.O. Box 606, Indianapolis, IN 46206

Kregel Publications, P.O. Box 2607, Grand Rapids, MI 49501

KTAV Publishing House, Inc., 75 Varick Street, New York, NY 10013

Macmillan Publishing Company, 866 Third Avenue, New York, NY 10022

Moody Press, 820 North LaSalle Drive, Chicago, IL 60610

New Leaf Press, P.O. Box 311, Green Forest, AR 72638

Our Sunday Visitor, Inc., 200 Noll Plaza, Huntington, IN 46750

Oxford University Press, 200 Madison Avenue, New York, NY 10016

Paulist Press, 997 Macarthur Blvd., Mahwah, NJ 07430

Penguin Books, 625 Madison Avenue, New York, NY 10022

Philipp Feldheim, Inc., 200 Airport Executive Park, Spring Valley, NY 10977

Prentice-Hall, Inc., General Book Marketing, Box 500, Englewood Cliffs, NJ 07632

Princeton University Press, 41 William Street, Princeton, NJ 08540

Random House, 201 East 50th Street, New York, NY 10022

Reader's Digest Association, Inc., Pleasantville, NY 10570

Schmul Publishing Co., Inc., P.O. Box 4068, Salem, OH 44460

Standard Publishing, 8121 Hamilton Avenue, Cincinnati, OH 45231

Sweet Publishing Company, 3934 Sandshell, Fort Worth, TX 76137

TAN Books and Publishers, P.O. Box 424, Rockford, IL 61105

Thomas Nelson Publishers, Nelson Place at Elm Hill Pike, P.O. Box 141000, Nashville, TN 37214

Trinitarian Bible Society, 217 Kingston Road, London, SW19 3NN, England

Trinitarian Bible Society (Canada), 39 Caldwell Crescent, Brampton, Ontario, Canada, L6W 1A2

Tyndale House Publishers, Inc., 336 Gundersen Drive, P.O. Box 80, Wheaton, IL 60189

United Bible Societies; see American Bible Society

University of Chicago Press, 5801 Ellis Avenue, Fourth Floor, S., Chicago, IL 60637

Westminster Press, 925 Chestnut Street, Philadelphia, PA 19107

William B. Eerdmans Publishing Co., 255 Jefferson Avenue, SE, Grand Rapids, MI 49503

William Carey Library, 533 Hermosa Street, South Pasadena, CA 91030

Word Books, P.O. Box 1790, Waco, TX 76796

World Bible Publishers, Inc., Box 2008, Iowa Falls, IA 50126

Zondervan Bible Publishers, 1415 Lake Drive, SE, Grand Rapids, MI 49506

DISTRIBUTORS

Riverside Book & Bible, Box 370, Iowa Falls, IA 50126

Spring Arbor, 10885 Textile Road, Belleville, MI 48111

5614 N.E. Hassalo, Portland, OR 97213

909 Avenue 'S', Grand Prairie, TX 75050

2934 E. Las Hermanas St., Compton, CA 90221

MAIL ORDER RESOURCES

The Archives Bookshop, 1387 E. Washington, Pasadena, CA 91104

Baker Book House, Mail Bookstore, P.O. Box 6287, Grand Rapids, MI 49506

Christian Book Distributors, P.O. Box 3687, Peabody, MA 01961

Eisenbraun's, P.O. Box 275, Winona Lake, IN 46590

Puritan Reformed Discount Book Service, 1319 Newport Gap Pike, Wilmington, DE 19804

USED BOOK RESOURCES

The Archives Bookshop, 1387 E. Washington, Pasadena, CA 91104

Baker Book House, Used Book Division, P.O. Box 6287, Grand Rapids, MI 49506

B. H. Blackwell, Ltd., 50 Broad Street, Oxford, England OX1 3BQ

Kregel Publications, Used Book Division, 525 Eastern Avenue, S.E., Grand Rapids, MI 49501

Nelson's Bookroom, Lydbury North, Salop, England, SY7 8AS

Noah's Ark Book Attic, Stony Point, Route 2, Greenwood, SC 29646

Richard Owen Roberts, 205 E. Kehoe Blvd., Wheaton, IL 60187

NOTES

CHAPTER 1

[1] Most modern English versions use the same names and spellings for the books of the Bible. Some older versions and reference books, however, use names and spellings that reflect different language or manuscript traditions. This is especially true of older Catholic versions whose Old Testament spellings more closely follow the Greek and Latin than the Hebrew. The following list shows most variations:

Common Title	Variations
Joshua	Josue
1 and 2 Samuel	1 and 2 Kings
1 and 2 Kings	3 and 4 Kings
Chronicles	Paralipomenon
Ezra	Esdras or 1 Esdras
Nehemiah	Nehemias or 2 Esdras
Ecclesiastes	Qoheleth
Song of Songs	Song of Solomon (or Canticle of Canticles)
Isaiah	Isaias
Jeremiah	Jeremias
Ezekiel	Ezechiel
Hosea	Osee
Obadiah	Abdias
Jonah	Jonas
Micah	Micheas
Habakkuk	Habacuc
Zephaniah	Sophonias
Haggai	Aggeus
Zechariah	Zacharias
Malachi	Malachias
Revelation	Apocalypse (of John)
Tobit	Tobias
Maccabees	Machabees
Ecclesiastes	Sirach or The Wisdom of Jesus Son of Sirach or Ben Sira

[2] The traditional Apocrypha does not include 3 and 4 Maccabees and Psalm 151.

[3]The numbering of the Esdras books is problematic. In many ancient versions, 1 Esdras refers to Ezra-Nehemiah. In others, 1 and 2 Esdras refer to Ezra and Nehemiah, respectively. Thus, what are 1 and 2 Esdras in this list are often 3 and 4 Esdras in other lists and reference books.

[4]The NOAB is not just a Catholic Bible, it is a "Common Bible," for use by Catholics, Protestants, and Orthodox.

[5]Here and for the rest of this chapter, "Orthodox" refers not to traditional or conservative theology, but to the Eastern branch of the Christian church that broke from Roman Catholicism in the eleventh century. It is sometimes referred to as the Greek or Russian Orthodox church, though these are just two of its many branches.

[6]This 22/24-book listing is in the same order as the 39-book list from the Tanakh in chart 1. The Tanakh retained the traditional Hebrew order, but followed the practice of separating Samuel, Kings, Chronicles, and Ezra-Nehemiah into eight separate books and the "Minor Prophets" into twelve, thus creating 39 from 24.

[7]Ruth and Lamentations are taken from the "Megilloth" and added here to make the 22-book arrangement.

[8]Of the three subdivisions of the "Kethubim," only the "Megilloth" is universally acknowledged as a titled grouping.

[9]No doubt some have noticed that the Book of Daniel is not among the prophets, and others may wonder why the Psalms of David are also not considered part of prophecy. The reason is that although Daniel and David both prophesied, neither was formally a prophet. David was a king and Daniel was a wise man in the court of a pagan ruler. And again, these canonical categories are general, not exact. For a thorough discussion on the groupings of the Hebrew canon, see Beckwith, *The Old Testament Canon of the New Testament Church*, pp. 181–234.

[10]The Book of Jude (14–15) apparently quotes from the pseudepigraphal Book of 1 Enoch. But it does not necessarily follow that he thought it was inspired or canonical. Paul quotes pagan Greek philosophers (Acts 17:28; Titus 1:12) but certainly did not believe them to be inspired.

CHAPTER 2

[1]Metzger, *The Text of the New Testament* (Oxford, 1968), p. 194.

[2]*Selected Shorter Writings of Benjamin B. Warfield—II* (Presbyterian and Reformed, 1973), p. 5.

*s3*The New Testament: An Introduction to Its Literature and History* (Banner of Truth, 1976), p. 167.

CHAPTER 3

[1]Quoted by Bruce in *History of the Bible in English* (Oxford, 1978), p. 29.

[2]Quoted in ibid., p. 96.

[3]Ibid., pp. 99–100.

[4]The results of these studies, "A Readability Report on the New International Version," is available on request from Zondervan Bible Publishers, 1415 Lake Drive S.E., Grand Rapids, MI 49506.

[5]This information was provided to me by Sweet Publishing, who publish the International Children's Version, though I personally worked through the evaluation of the NKJV, which their study had not included.

[6]Later editions of the KJV put "but" into italics to indicate that this conjunction was not in the Greek.

[7]For example, rather than attempting to explain the difficult concept represented by the Hebrew word חֵרֶם in an expansive translation, the NIV explains the word in footnotes (e.g., Lev. 27:28–29) and in the notes of the NIV Study Bible (Lev. 27:28; p. 183): "The Hebrew term refers to the irrevocable giving over of things or persons to the LORD, often by totally destroying them."

[8] *Trials of a Translator* (Sheed and Ward, 1949), pp. 4–5.

[9] Ibid., pp. 7–8.

[10] *Toward a Science of Translating* (Brill, 1964), p. 192.

[11] The one exception, John 20:28, is Thomas's statement "My Lord and my God," which one could possibly explain away as Thomas's own emotional response rather than as a teaching of the Bible, though Jesus apparently accepted the words as valid.

[12] See Jack P. Lewis, *The English Bible From KJV to NIV* (Baker, 1981), chapter 3, "Doctrinal Problems in the King James Version."

[13] Adapted and expanded from Carson, *The King James Version Debate* (Baker, 1979), p. 64.

CHAPTER 4

[1] This chart is based on the sales statistics from Spring Arbor Distributors, the largest wholesaler of Christian books and Bibles in the United States. Their report is probably the best single gauge of Bible sales in the country.

[2] The first English version to translate the personal name of God as Yahweh was the Emphasized Bible, translated by Joseph Bryant Rotherham in 1872–1902. The ASV (1901) had consistently translated the divine name by the hybrid English form "Jehovah," as does the New World Translation of the Jehovah's Witnesses.

AUTHOR INDEX

TITLE INDEX

SUBJECT INDEX

SCRIPTURE INDEX

OLD TESTAMENT INDEX

NEW TESTAMENT INDEX